THE FATE OF *KNOWLEDGE*

Helen E. Longino

PRINCETON UNIVERSITY PRESS   PRINCETON AND OXFORD

Copyright © 2002 by Princeton University Press
Published by Princeton University Press, 41 William Street, Princeton,
New Jersey 08540
In the United Kingdom: Princeton University Press, 3 Market Place,
Woodstock, Oxfordshire OX20 1SY
All Rights Reserved

Library of Congress Cataloging-in-Publication Data

Longino, Helen E.
  The fate of knowledge / Helen E. Longino.
    p. cm.
  Includes bibliographical references and index.
  ISBN 0-691-08875-6 (alk. paper) — ISBN 0-691-08876-4 (pbk. :
alk. paper)
    1. Knowledge, Sociology of.   I. Title.

BD175 .L665 2001
121—dc21

2001036267

British Library Cataloging-in-Publication Data is available

This book has been composed in Janson

Printed on acid-free paper. ∞

www.pup.princeton.edu

Printed in the United States of America

1   3   5   7   9   10   8   6   4   2

1   3   5   7   9   10   8   6   4   2
(Pbk.)

_____ To my teachers in philosophy, especially _____

SUE LARSON

AARON SLOMAN

STEPHEN BARKER

PETER ACHINSTEIN

MARJORIE GRENE

Contents

THIS BOOK owes its existence to many intellectual interactions and opportunities. It began life as a much more ambitious project, a rearticulation of the thesis of the sociality of knowledge and its defense against critics, and then an application of the thesis to new case studies, including a discussion of the relation between oppositional or partisan science in the West and approaches to science in newly industrializing postcolonial societies. Eventually it became clear that the philosophical thesis required more elaboration and that the other two parts of the project needed and deserved lengthier and independent treatments. This book, then, is the first installment: a reaffirmation of the thesis of the sociality of knowledge, tempered by the very helpful and stimulating criticism I have encountered, and developed in relation to other recent work, both empirical and philosophical, in social theory of science.

I am grateful both to individuals and to institutions for stimulus and opportunity. Ken Waters read and commented on each chapter, sometimes in several drafts, as they took shape. The influence of our conversations on philosophy and biology permeates this book. Elizabeth Anderson and Richard Grandy each read a draft of the entire manuscript and made numerous helpful suggestions for its revision. I owe all three of these friends and colleagues a deep debt of gratitude for the generosity and critical spirit with which they responded to this work. While these readers cannot be blamed for the book's remaining flaws, they are certainly responsible for much that is good about it. In addition, participants in my graduate seminar, Philosophy 8660, in spring 1999, read an early draft of most of the present chapters. Their individual interventions are noted in the text, but the seminar as a whole provided an invaluable opportunity to try these ideas out with a sophisticated group of readers.

Many ideas in the text are the consequence of conversation or correspondence with, among others, Paul Boghossian, Robert Brandon, Nancy Cartwright, Amita Chatterjee, J. Richard Creath, John Dupré, Catherine Elgin, Miranda Fricker, James Griesemer, Jennifer Hornsby, Don Howard, Irfan Habib, Evelyn Fox Keller, Philip Kitcher, Bruno Latour, Kathleen Lennon, Elisabeth Lloyd, Jane Maienschein, Valerie Miner, Shefali Moitra, Lynn H. Nelson, Dhruv Raina, Alan Richardson, Robert Richardson, Steven Schiffer, Frederick Schmitt, Miriam Solomon, Elizabeth Spelman, Sharon Traweek, Vivian Weil, William Wimsatt, Alison Wylie, and my colleagues in Minneapolis, John Beatty, Ron Giere, Geoffrey Hellman, Steven Kellert, David MacCallum,

Michael Root, Patti Ross, Wade Savage, and Naomi Scheman. I have undoubtedly forgotten many other exchanges that clarified my thinking. I apologize for not listing the many others from whom I have learned.

I am grateful to Rice University and to the University of Minnesota for research and sabbatical leaves that enabled me to begin and then substantially advance the project. The Michael and Penny Winton Visiting Scholars Program at the University of Minnesota afforded me a reduced teaching load and respite from administrative responsibilities in 1993–94 and 1994–95. A month's stay at the Rockefeller Foundation's Villa Serbelloni in Bellagio in the summer of 1994 became a critical turning point. The Centre for the Philosophy of Natural and Social Sciences at the London School of Economics offered hospitality and collegiality in winter and spring of 1998. The National Science Foundation (in grant SBR 9731088) supported me in research that was to have been included in this volume, but is and will be reported in different venues. A McKnight Foundation Award for Research in the Humanities helped fund research assistants in 1998, 1999, and 2000. Steve Lelchuk of the Minnesota Center for Philosophy of Science provided technical assistance at crucial moments. Sara Hottinger and Elizabeth Lunstrum, in their roles as research assistants, provided invaluable assistance in the final collection of references and compilation of the bibliography. Finally, I am grateful to the editors at Princeton University Press for their consistent encouragement of this project, Ann Wald before she left for other shores and Ian Malcolm, who has exercised just the right blend of pressure and patience in the final stages.

My mother and sisters, Helen O'Brien Longino, Michele Longino, and Virginia Jordan, have been unfailingly supportive; Bill W. and his friends continue to provide good counsel; and my companion, Valerie Miner, makes all of life an adventure.

Portions of previously published work are redistributed in some of the following chapters. I am grateful to the publishers of "The Fate of Knowledge in Social Theories of Science," in *Socializing Epistemology: The Social Dimensions of Knowledge*, edited by Frederick Schmitt (Totowa, N.J.: Rowman and Littlefield, 1994), and "Epistemology for Biological Pluralism," in *Epistemology and Biology*, edited by Richard Creath and Jane Maienschein (Cambridge: Cambridge University Press, 2000), for permission to use revised sections of those papers here. I am also grateful to the National Museum of Women in the Arts for permission to use the painting, *The Town*, by Maria Elena Vieira da Silva on the cover of the book.

THE FATE OF *KNOWLEDGE*

CHAPTER ONE

Introduction: The Rational-Social Dichotomy

THE FATE OF KNOWLEDGE explores the epistemological consequences of two shifts in current philosophy of science: the growing recognition of the social character of scientific inquiry and the increasing acknowledgment of explanatory plurality in various scientific fields. Although not universally embraced, sociality and plurality have both been advanced by philosophers concerned to elucidate current practices in the sciences. These themes have important, if subtle, bearing on one another, given the interconnections between epistemological and metaphysical thought. This book focuses on epistemological concerns related to the sociality of inquiry, but takes up, as one direction of application, the implications for scientific pluralism of a social approach to scientific knowledge.

My aim in this book is the development of an account of scientific knowledge that is responsive to the normative uses of the term "knowledge" *and* to the social conditions in which scientific knowledge is produced. Recent work in history, philosophy, and social and cultural studies of science has emphasized one or the other. As a consequence accounts intended to explicate the normative dimensions of our concept—that is, elaborating the relation of knowledge to concepts such as truth and falsity, opinion, reason, and justification—have failed to get a purchase on actual science, whereas accounts detailing actual episodes of scientific inquiry have suggested that either our ordinary normative concepts have no relevance to science or that science fails the tests of good epistemic practice. This can't be right. The chapters that follow offer a diagnosis of this stalemate and an alternative account. I argue that the stalemate is produced by an acceptance by both parties to the debate of a dichotomous understanding of the rational and the social.

The dichotomy between the rational (or cognitive) on the one hand and the social on the other structures both (1) the disagreements between the practitioners of the social and cultural studies of science and the philosophers and (2) the constructive (or deconstructive) accounts they all offer of scientific knowledge. Cognitive rationality and sociality are dichotomized when they are treated as definitionally excluding one another. According to the dichotomous understanding of these notions, if an epistemic practice is cognitively rational, then it cannot be social. Conversely, if an epistemic practice is social, then it cannot be cognitively rational.[1] What further is meant by "rational" or "cognitive" and by "social" varies from scholar to scholar. Roughly, rational or cognitive approaches are those that focus on evidential or justifying reasons in accounting for scientific judgment. Social (or sociological) approaches, by contrast, focus either on the role of nonevidential (ideological, professional) considerations or on social interactions among the members of a community rather than on evidential reasons in accounting for scientific judgment. Part of my task is to bring out the assumptions regarding cognitive rationality and sociality that make the dichotomy so compelling to a wide range of thinkers about the sciences. Rejecting these assumptions will open a way for the social account that I claim to be necessary for an epistemology of science inclusive of the full range of cognitive processes in the sciences.[2]

The argument of this book is directed explicitly at scientific knowledge. There are, however, reasons to see it as encompassing knowledge in general, or at least empirical knowledge in general. First, elements of scientific cognition on which the argument rests—observation and reasoning—are elements of empirical cognition in general. And, although important differences exist between scientific cognition and general empirical cognition, these do not bear on the normative issues involved in the ascription of knowledge. Second, the interdependence of scientists that sociological researchers have demonstrated is arguably a characteristic of all cognitive agents. A number of philosophers have argued recently that reliance on testimony is pervasive throughout our ordinary cognitive lives.[3] We rely on what automobile mechanics, computer consultants, plumbers, physicians, historians, designated experts of all sorts, tell us, and weave that into the fabric of our beliefs. And, as cognizers, we are inducted from infancy into a complex set of assumptions that undergird our most mundane beliefs, so much that they come to be almost constitutive of our inferential capacities.[4] Everyday knowledge is a matter

---

[1] I use "cognitively rational" and "cognitive rationality" to distinguish the kind of rationality in question here from pragmatic rationality, which is not understood as excluding the social in the same way.

[2] Hilary Kornblith (1994) has recognized part of this dichotomizing tendency. He notices a tendency on the part of sociologists to ignore or even deride the role of the truth of p in explaining belief that p. He diagnoses this tendency as a function of their assumption that truth-linked explanations are automatically undermined by successful social explanation. Kornblith argues that there is no necessary incompatibility between these two kinds of explanation. He does not, however, comment on the converse assumption nor the hold of both on philosophers as well as on sociologists. If my analysis is correct, there is a shared deep structure to the views of the philosophers and the sociologists that must be rejected if there is to be a genuine integration of truth-linked and social explanation.

[3] See Coady 1992; Hardwig 1985, 1991; Kornblith 1987, 1994; Schmitt 1988.

[4] Amanda Vizedom (2000) briefly discusses an artificial intelligence (AI) project whose

of using our common sense in making judgments and inferences concerning aspects of experience that matter to us. Scientific investigation is a matter of extending the knowledge we have, of testing new proposals, of sometimes overturning common sense. The assumptions of common sense and the institutions that certify certain sorts of experts are of such long standing as to be past the kind of critical scrutiny that is required for assumptions that support inferences in the sciences. Nevertheless, the logical structure is parallel and, if those who emphasize the role of mundane background assumptions in our ordinary cognitive lives are correct, arguments about the nature of scientific knowledge are relevant to understanding the character and possibility of ordinary empirical knowledge.

PREDECESSORS

Contemporary philosophers who are exploring social dimensions of science or of knowledge are not the first to affirm the sociality of knowledge. Both John Stuart Mill and Charles Sanders Peirce in the nineteenth century and Karl Popper in the twentieth emphasized social aspects of knowledge or science that form part of the account developed in this book. Mill and Peirce wrote extensively on science, logic, and method, but they were also concerned to write of knowledge and truth in ways reflective of the actual situation of those who seek knowledge. The fundamental premise of Mill's discussion in the chapter "Liberty of Thought and Discussion" in *On Liberty* is based on the fallibility of human knowers.[5] Peirce emphasizes the fallibility of individual knowers and offers a definition of truth that emphasizes the community of inquirers.[6] Popper's embrace of criticism follows from more abstract considerations: his views about induction and consequent emphasis on falsification as the method of science.[7]

Mill's arguments occur in the context of his essay on the social and political topic of freedom rather than in the context of his logical and methodological writings, and his examples concern primarily religious belief and social and political beliefs. But a passing reference to earlier

---

aim is to model everyday inferences. Cyc® proposes that previous AI projects have failed because they have not taken into account "the store of 'commonsense assumptions' on which the everyday inferences depend" (Vizedom, 187). Part of the Cyc® project involves identifying those assumptions and entering them into the Cyc® Knowledge Base. For more information one can go to the Cycorp website: <www.cyc.com>.

[5] Mill 1859.

[6] Peirce 1877, 1878. All quotations are taken from the volume of selected writings by Peirce (1958) edited by Philip Weiner.

[7] Popper 1968.

controversies in astronomy and in chemistry and the very general character of his arguments suggest he intended his remarks to apply to any kind
of knowledge or truth claim. His four reasons for recommending complete freedom of thought and unrestricted freedom of expression all rest
on the assumed fact of individual human cognitive frailty: those who
would restrict thought and its expression might be wrong and the truth
lie with those whose thought is condemned; even if those who would
restrict thought are in possession of the truth, (1) it is not likely to be the
whole truth, and no one is, in any case, justified in claiming certainty,
and (2) the reasons for and meaning of even true doctrines will be lost in
the absence of contrary opinion. Mill, that is, is arguing that untram-
meled opportunity for and practice of critical discussion of ideas is necessary for assuring us of the justifiability of the (true) beliefs we do have
and for overcoming falsity or the incompleteness of belief or opinion
framed in the context of just one point of view.[8] At numerous other
points, for example, the form of empiricism we each embrace, our views
differ. Nevertheless, on the necessity of critical interaction for the integrity of knowledge Mill's view and the one I defend do coincide.

Charles Sanders Peirce's arguments concerning the social dimension of
knowledge have a somewhat different basis than Mill's. While he too
believes in the frailty of individual human knowers, his pragmaticist theory of meaning also lies behind the apparently consensual theory of truth
and reality that he offers. I say "apparently" because his precise view
seems to me subject to different interpretations depending on which
other of his remarks are juxtaposed to those on truth. In his essay, "How
to Make Our Ideas Clear," he famously said that: "The opinion which is
fated to be ultimately agreed to by all who investigate is what we mean
by truth, and the object represented is the real."[9] This definition is
offered as exemplifying the pragmaticist principle of defining a concept
by reference to those "effects, which might conceivably have a practical
bearing, we conceive the object of our conceptions to have."[10] Whatever
opinion succeeds in the long run in obtaining the consent of all who
consider it has had the effect of so succeeding. Should we read Peirce as
stating that truth (and the real) depends on our agreement, that it is, as
some might say, manufactured by that agreement? Or should we read
him as stating that it is the inevitable effect of that which exists independently of us that it will in the end produce agreement? A clarificatory
passage that follows suggests the first interpretation. "[R]eality is inde-

---

[8] Mill's arguments illustrate the moral complexion of much writing on objectivity discussed by Lorraine Daston (1992).

[9] Peirce 1878; 1958, 133. All quotations are from the Wiener edition of selected writings
of Peirce (1958).

[10] Pierce 1958, 124.

pendent not of thought in general, but only of what you or I or any finite number of men may think about it."[11] This does seem to make reality thought-dependent. On the other hand, in the very next paragraph, he states that "it is unphilosophical to suppose that, with regard to any given question (which has any clear meaning), investigation would not bring forth a solution of it, if it were carried far enough."[12] And in "The Fixation of Belief," he affirms the following as the "fundamental hypothesis" of science. "There are real things, whose characters are entirely independent of our opinions, . . . [that] affect our senses according to regular laws, and by taking advantage of the laws of perception we can ascertain by reasoning how things really are."[13] Here, reality seems independent of all thought, general or individual.

These apparent conflicts may be reconciled in a single coherent interpretation of Peirce. But closer readers of Peirce than I have differed on just how to interpret his theory of truth and reality.[14] Certainly, it is clear that whatever truth is, Peirce thinks it both attainable and beyond the cognitive reach of any single individual. In another essay, a critique of Cartesianism, recommending what he takes to be the practice in the empirical sciences, he states, "We individually cannot hope to attain the ultimate philosophy which we pursue; we can only seek it for the community of philosophers."[15] Inquiry is a community, a social, activity, and its success is achieved by community practices, not by solitary ones. In an echo of Mill's discussion, he says of the "Critical Common-sensist" that he "attaches great value to doubt. . . . he invents a plan for attaining to doubt . . . and then puts it into practice."[16] Doubt is inculcated by the contrary opinions of others. So critical interaction is necessary for the improvement of individual opinion and also for the attainment of the (ultimate) truth by the community (consisting of all investigators who have ever lived). There are enough tantalizing remarks scattered throughout these essays to make the prospect of interpreting Peirce an attractive and rewarding, as well as challenging, one. But what follows is not in any way an interpretation of what he might, could, or should have meant. I do, however, join Peirce in emphasizing the role of the community in the production or attainment of knowledge.

The challenge to philosophy of reconciling the cognitive rationality of the sciences with the conditions of their practice is vividly illustrated in the work of Sir Karl Popper, often considered to have originated social

[11] Ibid., 133.
[12] Ibid., 134.
[13] Peirce 1877; 1958, 107–8.
[14] Cf. Rorty 1982; Haack 1993.
[15] Peirce 1868; 1958, 40.
[16] Peirce 1905; 1958, 214.

epistemology with his emphasis on the importance of criticism in the development of scientific knowledge. But Popper vacillated in his conception of criticism.[17] At times he wrote as though criticism is wholly a matter of logical relations in what he came to call World Three, a world of propositional content, which is the objective world of knowledge. What sets this world apart from World Two—the subjective world of human belief states and human interactions—is its determinate character. That a theory is or is not a solution to a problem situation, that it does or does not contradict another theory, that it does or does not have a particular empirical consequence, are all matters of determinate logical relations, independently of their being thought. Criticism is just correctly identifying the consequences of a theory and comparing them to the empirical basis of science. This kind of criticism, hypothesis testing that can be accomplished by any individual with the power of correct ratiocination, is at the heart of his falsificationist methodology for science.

At other times, he writes as though criticism is a social matter—an affair of competing scientists trying to demonstrate the inadequacies of one another's theories by means of alleged observational discrepancies or conceptual and metaphysical shortcomings. This social activity is necessary for Popper's picture, at least as an engine of the hypothesis-testing criticism that identifies the logical relations that are the substance of critical interaction, but it is also its undoing. It is necessary because Popper's Third, objective, World is static. Something must generate the confrontation of theory with theory or of theory with experience that animates criticism, and the only candidate is the attitudes and actions of persons—scientists—who, for whatever reason, subject theories to criticism. It is the undoing of Popper's picture because, while he treats the logical relations of World Three as determinate, he minimizes the fact that there may be many logical trajectories between any given hypothesis or theory and a set of data. Given the gap between theory and data, there are many different assumptions that can fill it, and hence many possible trajectories between the elements of any given problem situation and theory pair. Back in the real world of real scientists, Popper's World Two, there are many constraints operating to limit the range of assumptions that will mediate perceived relations between theory and data. Which of the myriad sets of logical trajectories that can be followed from theory to the empirical basis that is the concern of any particular scientist or of any given scientific community at any given time is a matter not only of logic but also of contingent factors operating in the world of human affairs.

---

[17] I draw here on Popper 1972 and freely admit to glossing over many of the intricacies of his argument in the interest of the particular observation I wish to make.

The objective world is a world of multiple possibilities. Selection among, or activation of, one or more of those possibilities lies outside the scope of Popper's epistemology. Unlike the discussions by Mill and Peirce, Popper's theory of scientific knowledge deliberately bypasses the connection to science and inquiry as practiced and remains an epistemology of the ideal. By treating the rational and the social as so exclusive of each other as to occupy different worlds, Popper falls victim to the dichotomy in spite of having had some of the tools to escape it.

PREVIEW

The first section of *The Fate of* Knowledge examines the operation of the dichotomy between the rational and the social in the work of contemporary scholars in science studies. Chapter 2 engages with work in social and cultural studies of science, which can be roughly divided into two main streams. One has focused on the relationship between scientific knowledge and relatively large-scale professional and ideological social formations. Members of the so-called Edinburgh school or Strong Programme have been at the forefront of this line of analysis, producing books like Andrew Pickering's *Constructing Quarks* and Steven Shapin and Simon Schaffer's *Leviathan and the Air Pump*.[18] This tradition has focused on scientific controversy, demonstrating the professional and political interests bound up with different sides in a controversy, and arguing that the resolution of the scientific face of controversy is determined by a resolution of the political or professional face—that is, that knowledge or what counts as knowledge is determined by social interests.

The other stream, often identified as laboratory studies or microsociology, has focused on the interactions within and between laboratories and research programs and on the efforts required to export laboratory work into the nonlaboratory world. Here, the explanatory weight falls on the multiple small decisions taken in the course of research. These decisions, according to practitioners like Karin Knorr-Cetina or Bruno Latour, are diverse in nature and have multiple dimensions. The overall aim for any researcher is being able to continue her or his research, and any considerations related to that goal—funding, connection to other research programs or to industrial applications, ease of representation, as well as empirical considerations—are legitimate constituents of research decisions. Knowledge is produced by an amalgam of heterogeneous acts and not by a particular kind of truth-producing activity guided by logic. Knorr-Cetina and others emphasize the contin-

---

[18] Pickering 1984; Shapin and Schaffer 1985.

gency of scientific decisions, implying that contingent relations escape the purview of the normative philosopher. Both kinds of scholarship in social studies of science have produced brilliant and provocative historical and sociological analysis. What concerns me is the claim that these analyses show the irrelevance of normative philosophical concerns to real science. I will show how this claim is the product of the rational-social dichotomy.

The work in social and cultural studies has stimulated a range of responses from philosophers. Some, like Larry Laudan, have simply rejected the relevance of this work to philosophical concerns, or, like Alvin Goldman, have seen it as empirically and conceptually misguided. Some, like Philip Kitcher or James Brown, have tried to take the sting out by sifting through the claims of sociologists and sociologically oriented historians, attempting refutation of those they deem extremist, and then incorporating a sensitivity to history or sociological analysis into their constructive accounts of inquiry. In chapter 3, I argue that these efforts, too, are vitiated by a commitment to the dichotomy of the rational and the social.

In the central chapters of the book, I offer an account of scientific knowledge that not only avoids the dichotomy but integrates the conceptual and normative concerns of philosophers with the descriptive work of the sociologists and historians. This involves first disambiguating three senses of knowledge (as content, as practices or procedures, and as state), analyzing the constituents of the dichotomy in order to remove the aura of self evidence that attends it, and finally offering nondichotomizing accounts of each sense. Knowledge as content is the product of the exercise of basic cognitive capacities that conforms to its intended object. So far, the account is within the mainstream of philosophy. But I argue that these cognitive capacities are, in science, exercised socially, that is, interactively. I also argue that "conforms" encompasses a family of semantic success terms and that such a latitudinarian view is required by the varied character of scientific content.

Two features of scientific inquiry make its epistemology more complicated than traditional philosophy of science has appreciated. One is this social character of its cognitive, or knowledge-productive, capacities. The second is the gap between its explanatory resources (data) and its explanatory aspirations (theories).[19] I reiterate and expand the argument developed in my first book, *Science as Social Knowledge*,[20] that individual observation and reason must be supplemented by social processes such as

---

[19] Of course, there's more to knowledge than data and theories, but this oversimplification serves for the point.
[20] Longino 1990.

critical discursive interaction and that a more complete epistemology for science must include norms that apply to practices of communities in addition to norms conceived of as applying to practices of individuals. I incorporate these norms into an account of epistemic acceptability, and use the normative concepts of epistemic acceptability and conformation to provide nondichotomous accounts of knowledge in the three senses distinguished previously. Following through on the consequences of the analysis means breaking with conventional views of scientific knowledge as permanent, as ideally complete, and as unified or unifiable. This break, in turn, means accepting the provisionality, partiality, and plurality of scientific knowledge. Many philosophers would be content to accept this as a characterization of science today, but not of science in the future, or of ideal science. Epistemology ought to be for that ideal science. I insist instead on an epistemology for living science, produced by real, empirical subjects. This is an epistemology that accepts that scientific knowledge cannot be fully understood apart from its deployments in particular material, intellectual, and social contexts.

Contemporary philosophers have both resisted the strong form of sociality in knowledge defended here and developed different articulations and interpretations of a strong social approach. In chapter 7, I take up a series of objections to the view. I use the distinction between the modalities of knowledge to solve some of the puzzles that philosophers have posed regarding the nature of individual epistemic agency in a social approach to knowledge. I show how the account, while flexible enough to accommodate pluralism, also has the resources to identify both wrongheaded content and wrongheaded practices. Finally I explore differences between my views and those proposed by other strongly social philosophers of science, such as Miriam Solomon, Steve Fuller, and Joseph Rouse.

In the eighth and final substantive chapter of the book, I apply the socialized conception of knowledge to the new pluralism in philosophy of science. I review a number of different instances of theoretical plurality in recent and contemporary biology. These instances exhibit differences in approach—that is, in methods and questions addressed to a phenomenon or different initial characterizations of a common domain or both. While some of the examples are subjects of ongoing controversy, I appeal to some recent historical and philosophical scholarship to show how even apparently settled issues like the synthetic theory of evolution and the structure of genes are better understood in the pluralist framework of the social account. In a brief concluding chapter, I indicate some of the other directions in which the argument of the book can be pursued.

SOME PHILOSOPHICAL PRELIMINARIES

The approach to knowledge I take in this book is naturalist in the sense that it treats the conditions of knowledge production by human cognitive agents, empirical rather than transcendental subjects, as the starting point for any philosophical theory of knowledge, scientific or otherwise. It is not naturalist in the sense of treating knowledge as a natural kind whose nature or essence can be discovered (by scientific or philosophical methods). Belief, as a psychological state, is a kind of some sort, but knowledge is not a separate kind to be distinguished from belief as the psychological state of doubt can be distinguished from the psychological state of certainty. If knowledge is a kind at all, it is an unnatural kind, a product of human activities. As a product of human activities, it belongs in the category of other such things, like tables and chairs, but it is not a substantial kind as these, however artifactual, are. It is, rather, a status certain kinds may have. "Knowledge" is what Gilbert Ryle called a "success term," ascribed to exemplars of certain kinds—in this case: beliefs, claims, theories—when they satisfy certain conditions. "Knowledge" and its cognates, then, are normative concepts.

A philosophical theory of knowledge spells out the conditions that our use of the term "knowledge" indicates must be satisfied for correct ascription. On this understanding, a philosophical theory of knowledge is neither purely descriptive nor purely prescriptive. It requires a characterization of empirical subjects and of the situations in which they seek to produce (things that have the status of) knowledge. This is descriptive. It also involves a characterization of the conditions satisfaction of which they take the status to imply. This constitutes a spelling out of the prescriptions implicit in the ascription and withholding of that status. Filling in the details between the empirical conditions of knowledge production and the ideal conditions of success is the job of philosophical theory. The fate of *knowledge* lies in the consequences of those details.

CHAPTER TWO

Taking Social Studies of Science Seriously

SOCIOLOGISTS AND anthropologists of science have posed a significant challenge to philosophy. Through a number of different case studies, they have argued that scientific knowledge is not developed by the application of procedures ratified by epistemological norms of the sort recognized by philosophers. Instead, scientists use any means necessary—negotiate, borrow, barter, and steal—to get their interpretations accepted, their aim being to win or at least survive in the game of science. "Science is socially constructed" has become both a rallying cry and a banal comment, but this motto does not mean the same thing to all who use it. And the difference makes a difference.

According to the so-called Strong Programme in the sociology of scientific knowledge (SSK), good and bad, successful and unsuccessful science must be explained in the same way.[1] One can not explain good science by appealing to rationality and bad science by appealing to distorting social factors. In both kinds of case what does the explanatory work is interests: ideological-political interests, professional interests, individual career interests. In the Strong Programme, to say that science is socially constructed is to say that it is (primarily) the congruence of a hypothesis or theory with social interests of members of a scientific community that determines its acceptance by that community (rather than a congruence of theory or hypothesis with the world). Whether that theory or hypothesis then gains general acceptance is a function of social interactions of the community endorsing or advocating it with other communities constituting the larger scientific community.

The empirical laboratory studies done by Karin Knorr-Cetina, Bruno Latour, and others understand social construction differently.[2] For them, the procedures of science are social in the sense of involving social interactions, rather than in the sense of writing social relations into (our conceptions of) nature. They focus on the procedures of the laboratory,

---

[1] Philosophers have engaged most with the Strong Programme in the sociology of science associated with the University of Edinburgh and as represented in the work of Barry Barnes and David Bloor. See Barnes 1977; Bloor 1991; Barnes and Bloor 1982. This program has attracted the attention of a number of philosophers; see for example, a sympathetic if critical reading by Mary Hesse (1980), and much less temperate responses from Larry Laudan (1984a), among others.

[2] Knorr-Cetina 1983; Latour 1983.

rather than on the rhetoric of advocacy. Their "slice of life" documentation of those interactions shows (in the cases studied) that the procedures by which scientists certify results and validate hypotheses involve a hodgepodge of "internal" and "external" considerations. From this they conclude that distinguishing between the purely cognitive and the social—or interest-laden—bases of hypotheses is impossible. In the grip of the rational-social dichotomy, they conclude further that the normative concerns of philosophers are, as a consequence, idle: the wheels of prescription may spin in philosophy but they fail to engage the gears in actual epistemic communities.

In both of these programs, social construction is used in an epistemological sense—namely, it is a characterization of what goes into persuading a scientist or community of scientists of the plausibility, worth, or truth of an idea. Another use of this rubric is metaphysical or ontological: social construction can be contrasted with "natural construction or production." In this sense both collectively constructed artifacts and deliberately created political entities like constitutional democracies are social constructions. But social construction is also contrasted with "real." In this sense the subject of an urban myth or a hysterical epidemic might be a social construction. Many philosophers and scientists who are offended by the claim that science is socially constructed are reading "social construction" primarily in this last sense, which suggests that the natural world is a product of human effort. Both advocates and opponents of social construction often fail to distinguish the epistemological and the ontological senses, so that the opprobrium showered on perceived misapplications of the ontological is automatically extended to the epistemological sense.

In addition to the work produced by historians and sociologists, a new form of analysis has recently entered science studies, namely cultural studies of science. Like cultural studies in the academy, cultural studies of sciences is a multidisciplinary inquiry, combining aspects of literary and art theory and criticism, history, sociology and anthropology, rhetorical theory and analysis, and cultural theory drawn primarily from philosophers in the continental tradition. Some work in cultural studies of science analyzes metaphors and other literary aspects of science,[3] other work in attempts to understand the practices of science, including the making of meaning, in their cultural settings.[4] To the extent these studies are thought to have implications for our epistemological understanding of the sciences, they presume one or another of the kinds of sociological and historical analyses I have just described. In this chapter, my intention

[3] See, for example, Beer 1983, 1986, 1996; Hayles 1990; Squier 1994.
[4] See, for example, Biagioli 1993; Traweek 1988, 1992.

is to evaluate the epistemological claims made in both the Strong Programme in the sociology of scientific knowledge and the microsociological work of Knorr-Cetina and Latour—to show how their conclusions are shaped by an implicit commitment to the rational-social dichotomy and, how, after deleting the dichotomy, the sociological work has something of great interest to offer the philosopher.

THE STRONG PROGRAMME IN SOCIOLOGY
OF SCIENTIFIC KNOWLEDGE

A good place to start is with Steven Shapin's "History of Science and Its Sociological Reconstruction."[5] Shapin differentiates, categorizes, and summarizes a number of historical case studies as support for the rather modest claim that sociological reconstruction—that is, the analysis of the role social interests play in the production of scientific knowledge—has a place in the history of science. These case studies are designed to display the actual processes, deliberations, and arguments that constitute particular debates and their resolution. Among them, Shapin distinguishes scientific debates shaped by professional interests internal to the sciences, debates shaped by struggles for authority and credibility, cases showing the relation of the content of scientific knowledge to concerns in the wider social context. These latter include both scientific use of cultural resources and social use of natural science resources (i.e., of scientific representations of nature and the natural). Shapin's argument is that, because there are so many studies already fruitfully illuminating a variety of (kinds of) scientific decision points, there is no question but that the sociological approach is useful to the historical understanding of the sciences. The philosophical position he is rejecting is, thus, a historiographical view about the proper ingredients to include in a historical account of any episode in the sciences.

The kind of history Shapin rejects is both internalist and "Whig" history: an approach to the history of science that takes scientific change (1) to be propelled only by issues arising within the practice of science narrowly construed, that is, as purely cognitive activity, constituted as such by the goal of obtaining truth; and (2) to be progressive, that is, read as leading to the present state of scientific knowledge, which is itself a stage on the way to complete knowledge of the natural world. Against such a position all he need establish is methodological space for the sociologically informed history he advocates. Nevertheless, in his summary of the methodological precepts of such history, he goes beyond this require-

[5] Shapin 1982.

ment. Two of the precepts are relatively conservative. The first recommends a practice attributed to the history of ideas: the historian should treat culture as mutable and transmitted by specific institutions that leave their mark on it. The second recommends regarding scientists as producing knowledge against the background of their culture's inherited knowledge, their collectively situated purposes, and the information they receive from natural reality. While both of these constitute rejections of internalism, as long as "knowledge" is read as "what counts as knowledge" there is nothing out of the ordinary here, either. The third precept, however, forces a different reading. The sociologically inclined historian should treat the generation *and* evaluation of knowledge as goal-directed.

In the conventional (since Reichenbach) distinction between discovery and justification, philosophers have accepted that the processes of discovery (or generation) are properly understood as causal and as influenced by many factors, including goals and purposes. Justification (or evaluation), on the other hand, is a cognitive activity or logical relation. In the standard view, it is governed by the goal of only accepting as true what is true. In Reichenbach's view, it is a relation only and so not governed by any goals whatsoever. There are multiple senses in which evaluation could be thought of as goal-directed. One could, for example, see pragmatic goals involved in selecting what kinds of claims to evaluate or which of equally justifiable claims to act on. Shapin seems to have in mind a fairly direct connection between taking and having others take a claim to be true and the satisfaction of some aim—for example, between taking as true claims about relative cranial capacity and legitimizing racial subordination. If justification (or evaluation) can be directed by any goal whatsoever, as Shapin's examples suggest, then no distinction can be made between "knowledge" and "what passes for knowledge in context C." This kind of claim, implicit or explicit, draws the attention of philosophers. The first two principles Shapin has articulated are sufficient to accommodate the cases cited in this early paper and to make space for the sociologically informed history that he advocates. Thus, Shapin has no need to make such a strong claim as is represented by the third precept. It is, however, central to the Strong Programme's conception of science and science studies, and it foreshadows the claims about the seventeenth-century acceptance of the experimental method that Shapin will make with Simon Schaffer.[6] While Shapin offers no argument for it, it comes for free from the first two precepts if one assumes the dichotomy between the rational and the social discussed in the previous chapter. Thus the dichotomy is what licenses the move from historical to concep-

[6] Shapin and Schaffer 1985.

tual claims. The approach signaled by Shapin's third principle is defended more directly in joint and independent work by Barry Barnes and David Bloor.

The essay by Barnes and Bloor, "Relativism, Rationalism, and the Sociology of Knowledge," is one of the foundational works of the Edinburgh School Strong Programme.[7] It purports not only to sweep away any philosophical objections to the Strong Programme's approach to history, but also to advance and defend a thoroughgoing relativism with respect to science and any other form of belief. Barnes and Bloor articulate a tripartite thesis:

1. Beliefs on a certain topic vary.
2. Which of these varying beliefs will be found in a given context depends on, or is relative to, the circumstances of the users. . . .
3. The credibility of all beliefs is equally problematic, regardless of their truth and falsity.[8]

This last is the so-called symmetry thesis, and Barnes and Bloor gloss it as meaning that a sociologist, whether or not she or he evaluates a belief as true or false, must search for the causes of its credibility (presumably, to those who believe it).

There are more and less contentious ways of interpreting these theses. I give just two alternative readings for each of them:

SSK1A: Beliefs held by individuals about the same topic vary in content, emphasis, and the like.

SSK1B: Beliefs held by individuals about the same topic are contradictory.

SSK2A: Which of a set of varying beliefs will be held by individuals in a particular context depends on circumstances such as the reasons or evidence available to those individuals.

SSK2B: Which of a set of varying beliefs will be held by individuals in a particular context depends on circumstances other than reasons or evidence available to those individuals.[9]

SSK3A: For any given belief, regardless of whether it is true or false, rational or irrational, its being taken to be true or reasonable in a context requires causal explanation.

SSK3B: For any given belief, regardless of whether it is true or false, rational or irrational, its being taken to be true or reasonable in a context requires a causal explanation that makes no reference to the truth of or reasons for the belief.

[7] Barnes and Bloor 1982.

[8] Ibid., 22–23. I have slightly rewritten the third thesis for syntactical purposes.

[9] The alternative interpretations of the first thesis, when substituted in the interpretations of the second, generate four possible interpretations.

Further variations are possible, but this set is sufficient to show the ambiguity of the principles. If we take the A reading, their three theses could mean just that which of the range of possible (true) beliefs one will come to hold about a subject will depend on additional features of the believer's context, and that all beliefs are equally problematic (i.e., in need of explanation) as regards their being taken as true or false in the contexts in which they are so taken. Given that scientific inquiry is practiced by human beings situated in particular historical and geographical settings, the weaker interpretations are all that is required to support sociologically informed history (of the kind recommended by Shapin). The tenor of Barnes and Bloor's rhetoric, however, and their characterizations of the thesis to which they are opposed make it clear that they intend stronger meanings, more like B than like A.

The "rationalist" thesis they oppose includes two claims:

1. Rational or true beliefs are explained by the fact that they are true or rational.

2. Irrational (or false) beliefs alone call for a sociological, or causal, explanation.

Explicitly stated, these claims are so implausible, if not confused, as to make it seem that Barnes and Bloor are stacking the deck by treating them as the opposition. The point, however, is not that these principles have been explicitly endorsed, but that their implicit acceptance has driven much history and philosophy of science. There are at least two ideas that the sociologist might find offensive or problematic. One is the detachment of belief from believer and consequent idealization of cognitive agency. The other is that one can make sense of the claim that a belief is rational apart from some characterization of the context (historical, social, pragmatic) in which it is assessed. Both of these ideas are inherent in the supposition discussed earlier as Popper's view that there is an autonomous realm of logical relations that, given some premise, in and of itself determines the rationally correct conclusion, and that this serves as an ideal against which human cognitive agency is to be assessed. Although one might expect a sociologist to focus on the characterization of cognitive agency, Barnes and Bloor instead go after the other central idea, namely that of the intrinsic truth, plausibility, or reasonableness of the proposition believed.

In staking their argumentative ground on truth and rationality, rather than on the more empirically tractable and amenable notion of cognitive agency, Barnes and Bloor take on not just historiography but philosophy of science, logic, and epistemology. They address two kinds of argument that might be offered against their symmetry thesis and in support of the "rationalist" anti-symmetry thesis. These arguments concern not the characterization of spatiotemporally located cognitive agents but the status of certain kinds of propositions, those traditionally taken as foundational in foundationalist theories of knowledge. Regarding the possibility of a set of basic beliefs they address two considerations. One is that there is a class of beliefs "visible by their own light." Such are often said to be experiential or observational beliefs. But, say Barnes and Bloor, making sensory discriminations in our environment is a matter of exercising the capacities and skills of animal organisms. Representation (sententially or otherwise) of the items and elements discriminated is a matter of employing collectively meaningful patterns of representation, which patterns will vary from culture to culture. Experiential beliefs, then, are not self-evident. Another consideration they dismiss is one they attribute to Martin Hollis and Steven Lukes: that a common core of true beliefs and rationally justified patterns of inference must exist in order that communication (i.e., translation) across different languages can take place. But, Barnes and Bloor argue, because initial language learning does not involve translation, there must be another way to learn another's language than by translation of those sentences expressing the alleged common core. There is, thus, no need to postulate such a common core. As for rationally justified inference patterns, they cite well-known problems in philosophy of logic—for example, the circularity demonstrated to Achilles by the Tortoise in Lewis Carroll's fable and A. N. Prior's work on logical connectives. This work suggests that attempts at explicit justification or proof of the validity of valid inference patterns issue in circularity or infinite regresses. A priori argument cannot generate a set of universally held empirical beliefs, nor can it fix a set of inference patterns as definitive of valid reasoning across all human communities.

Having thus laid waste to "rationalist" prejudices, Barnes and Bloor claim there is no alternative to relativism—that is, to the view that identifies truth with truth for S, for any S. This argument for relativism is offered as a manifesto for the Strong Programme, also known as "the interest thesis," for the view that controversies in science are (1) characterized by the social interests attached to the contending positions; (2) settled or "closed" as a consequence of or in the course of settling the conflict of those interests, usually by one set having the political resources to attain or retain dominance; and (3) not decidable by an independent set of facts (or by independent reality).[10] But what makes these arguments against the self-ratifying character of observation or of valid inference patterns arguments for relativism and the interest thesis is the hidden premise dichotomizing the rational-cognitive and the social.

---

[10] There have been various articulations of the interest thesis. Some clear examples are to be found in Barnes 1983 and in Pickering 1984.

Absent this premise, the arguments of Barnes and Bloor show merely that the claims of the rationalist thesis cannot be held a priori. Of course, just because a priori argument cannot demonstrate the universality of a set of beliefs or universal acceptance of a set of inference patterns, this does not show that there is no such set of empirical beliefs, or of inference patterns. But it becomes an empirical matter whether there is such universality. The same holds for the strong "anything goes" relativism and for the interest thesis. These, too, are empirical, rather than a priori demonstrable.

Barnes and Bloor elsewhere seem to recognize this. They stress that their relativism does not claim that truth and falsity, rationality and irrationality, are meaningless, but that they are always and only locally meaningful, rather than transcendentally universal, distinctions. Bloor, in particular, argues that it is not only social interests and political maneuvering that are involved in the explanation of why an individual or community favors a particular scientific theory. Interests and political jockeying work together with the more traditionally recognized cognitive processes of observation and reasoning.[11] He is at pains to emphasize that truth and falsity, rationality and irrationality, are not meaningless in the Strong Programme analysis but that they are always only locally meaningful distinctions. Thus, in intention, this relativism is severely attenuated, more resembling contextual empiricism. Nevertheless, the actual case studies offered as exemplars of Strong Programme analysis concentrate their attention on the social factors to the detriment of the cognitive. They are paraded as support for the view that social, rather than cognitive, factors are responsible for the resolution of controversy. In practice, then, Strong Programme analysts vacillate between the A and B readings of the three theses listed earlier. In spite of stated intentions to offer a more integrated account, the approach is still hamstrung by its commitment to the rational-social dichotomy. As a consequence, Strong Programme theorists give us no account of how epistemic or cognitive considerations might play a role in a social account and emphasize only one sort of cause of belief.

One of the most celebrated products of the Strong Programme approach is Steven Shapin and Simon Schaffer's *Leviathan and the Air Pump*, an account of the dispute between Robert Boyle and Thomas Hobbes regarding the probative value of experiment.[12] The dispute was focused on Boyle's instrument for creating a (near) vacuum, the air pump (which extracted air from an enclosed space). Boyle is often credited as the founder of modern experimental science. Not only did he carry out

---

[11] Bloor 1992.
[12] Shapin and Schaffer 1985.

experiments with instruments of his own making (or design), as had been done by sixteenth-century Italian scientists like Torricelli and Galileo, but he wrote extensively about the theory and practice of experiment. Where Boyle located cognitive authority in the piecemeal deliverances of nature revealed via experiment to multiple witnesses, Hobbes, impressed by the Euclidean style of geometric demonstration, located such authority in deduction from first principles, themselves beyond question. Hobbes argued vigorously, if not successfully, against Boyle's methods and his conclusions. Shapin and Schaffer situate this dispute in its larger historical context: the English Civil Wars; and identify the contrasting scientific epistemologies with contrasting approaches to the problem of social order, about which both Hobbes and Boyle also wrote extensively.

Hobbes's method is a decision procedure that leaves all propositions either true or false—nothing is left to contingency, nor are any propositions undecidable. Belief in all true propositions is compulsory; recalcitrance regarding any one of the body of truths imperils the security of all true beliefs. Boyle's method, on the other hand, treats as decided (and decidable) only what can be demonstrated by experiment. These will be matters of fact, and assent to such matters is compelled by their being observed either directly or by a properly constituted surrogate (the famous "modest witness"). What cannot be so demonstrated are matters of opinion regarding which belief cannot be compelled. Hobbes thought that leaving some matters open to opinion was the basis for civil unrest, for as long as individuals were logically entitled to different opinions, they would advocate for them. Hence philosophically eliminating diversity of opinion was part of the solution to the problem of civil order. Boyle, on the other hand, thought that confusion about what was demonstrable and what was properly a matter of opinion was a contributory factor to social division. Clarity about the distinction and tolerance regarding difference of opinion, where diversity was licensed by the available facts, contributed, in his view, to social harmony.

Shapin and Schaffer's thesis, articulated early in their book, is that this episode demonstrates that "solutions to the problem of knowledge are embedded within practical solutions to the problem of social order and different practical solutions to the problem of social order encapsulate contrasting practical solutions to the problem of knowledge."[13] Because they represent themselves at the outset as hoping to understand how it is that experiment obtained its privileged status as the arbiter of scientific truth, they are therefore claiming that this approach to experiment is an outcome of a particular solution to the problem of political order. In this they mean something other than what Jacob Bronowski claimed in his

---

[13] Ibid., 15.

Science and Human Values.[14] Bronowski argued that the successful conduct of science requires a certain kind of (liberal democratic) social organization in the scientific community as well as in the larger political community. Shapin and Schaffer's point instead is that it could have been otherwise: that Hobbes offered another way, not just of doing politics, but of doing both politics *and science.* The authoritarian way of life he offered, though viable, was not chosen. The experimental method championed by Boyle became the accepted way of obtaining knowledge of the natural world, not because it was a superior way of obtaining knowledge about the natural world, but because the parliamentary form of political life associated with it emerged victorious from the English Civil Wars.

Shapin and Schaffer go beyond earlier SSK in arguing not that particular episodes within particular sciences are socially valenced and socially resolved, but that one of the methodological cornerstones of modern science itself, the nature and authority of experiment, is so valenced. Their account brilliantly demonstrates the parallels between conceptions of political authority and cognitive authority and the importance of these parallels for Hobbes and Boyle. Their causal argument is, however, unsatisfactory. Part of the problem is the claim of the existence at the time of an alternative way of conceiving cognitive authority capable of generating a different natural science (or natural philosophy). That things could have gone otherwise, however, does not show that a viable natural philosophy on the Hobbesian deductive model could have emerged or have accomplished the same kinds of practical ends as the experimental method. Even if the latter is too strong a demand, such a natural philosophy would have to be successful by some criterion of success. What is missing from Shapin and Schaffer's presentation is an account of the workings of a Hobbesian epistemology re natural phenomena and some argument that it would have offered a comparable and effective natural science even in its own terms, whether that means pragmatically successful, metaphysically comprehensive, commanding general assent, or whatever other measure of effectiveness was implied by the Hobbesian way of life.

Even if they were successful in making the case for the viability of Hobbesian science, the supposition that the case shows that the legitimacy of experimental science depends on the mode of resolution of a political conflict presupposes the kind of arguments offered by Barnes and Bloor. These, as we saw, are intended to be general arguments against explanations of change of belief (or theoretical commitment) that appeal to the inherent truth, plausibility, or reasonableness of the belief or theory. If no such explanations can be forthcoming, they claim, then

[14] Bronowski 1956.

we must accept the alternative, which is causal explanation in which a social element will occupy a significant part. This is especially the case in science, which is practiced in highly organized social settings (universities, government laboratories, industrial research centers) and depends on a variety of social mechanisms (journals, professional associations, conferences, peer review, funding agencies, etc.). The difficulty with this argument is that it fails to show what it purports to show. I have already indicated that the particular arguments they deploy do not warrant the conclusions they draw, at least not in their strong forms. The philosophical arguments offered or invoked by Barnes and Bloor do not support a radical relativism that renders cognitive explanations moot. These arguments are familiar as antifoundationalist arguments, having been deployed since the 1950s against conceptions of knowledge that required genuine knowledge to rest on a base of indubitable beliefs or propositions (usually sense data propositions). Most of those deploying such arguments—John Austin, Willard Quine, Ludwig Wittgenstein, and others—were arguing that knowledge does not require such foundations. They were not arguing that the lack of such foundations means that we don't know what we think we know, or that the impossibility of indubitable foundations supported any kind of relativism.[15] In this context what is needed from the Strong Programme advocates is an account of the relevance of their antifoundationalist arguments to the claims they are advancing, in particular, to the symmetry thesis in its strong interpretation and their implicit denial that cognitive accounts—that is, accounts that appeal to agents' reasons—have explanatory value. What is required, in other words, is a demonstration, first, that all cognitive or epistemological approaches are committed to foundationalism and, second, that the cognitive and the social mutually exclude each other.

To be fair, it must be recognized that the Strong Programme theorists were working out their philosophical-historiographical views when the mainstream in history and philosophy of science was dominated by rational reconstruction and a strongly "internalist" Whig history. The ideal of the various versions of rational reconstruction from Reichenbach to Lakatos and its current practitioners was to show how scientific reasoning (theories, explanations, etc.) conformed to some philosophical ideal of reasoning (theories, explanations, etc.). The point of "Whig" history of science is similar: to show how various presently acknowledged scientific triumphs (e.g., Lavoisier's quantitative and analytic chemistry) were the result of the scientist's correct application of scientific methods in response to problems generated within the research context and contributed to the progress of knowledge as seen from the point of view of the

---

[15] For discussion of this point, see Friedman 1998. See also the appendix to this chapter.

present. Against the hegemony of such a view it may well seem imperative to develop an argument applicable to science or reasoning in general. However, the failure to question the deeper conceptual underpinnings of the internalist and whiggish view drives the argument from observations of the complex multidimensionality of scientific debates to philosophical conclusions as extreme and as fragile as the ones rejected. The sweeping generality of these conclusions leaves the distinct impression that practitioners of the Strong Programme are not only offering an argument for the legitimacy of social history in the history of science, but that they are undermining (or attempting to undermine) the cognitive authority of contemporary sciences as well.[16] This reading explains both the ire directed at the Strong Programme from some quarters and the welcome extended to it in others. According to the analysis offered here, however, it is a seduction representing the wrong lessons to draw from the case studies.

COLLINS'S PROGRAM OF EMPIRICAL RELATIVISM

Harry Collins has focused on contemporary experimental science, challenging, among other things, customary notions of the role of experimental replication. He has developed his analysis of the role of experiment in the course of extended observation of those physicists researching gravity waves.[17] He has also analyzed other episodes in contemporary science that seem to him to confirm the analysis.[18] Collins argues that in a new and controversial area, which is just the kind of area in which replication seems called for, scientists do not, in fact, follow a formula ("algorithm") for replicating an experiment whose purported outcome or interpretation is under challenge. Instead they alter the experiment in various ways, by designing slightly different detection apparatuses, for example. In a new area of research, Collins argues, standard criteria of success, such as "working," have not yet been operationalized. This view is supported by the analysis of case histories, such as the experimental detection of gravity waves and the production of surplus heat from fusion. The discussion regarding the value of one another's experimental setups, the significance of variations, and the relative importance of different segments of the experimental procedure should all be interpreted as negotiations concerning what will count as a replication of the original experiment and as competent experimentation

[16] See Schmaus, Segerstrale, and Jesseph 1992 for such an interpretation of the Strong Programme and other work in social studies of science.
[17] Collins 1975, 1985.
[18] Collins and Pinch 1993.

in this field and what will count, on the other hand, as incompetent experimentation. Collins draws attention to the invocation of prima facie extraneous considerations, such as the style in which findings are presented or the personality of the experimenter, in determining whether to accept the reported results of an experiment. This and similar rhetorical maneuvers he takes as evidence that there is no independent set of scientific criteria that can establish the validity of findings. These criteria are what will emerge when disagreement stops. Such cessation of disagreement, were it based solely on what nature determines, would be elusive. Instead, it is achieved, when achieved, socially, and our conception of nature emerges *from* these discussions, rather than being imprinted by nature itself. As Collins put it in "The Seven Sexes," "scientists' actions in the field may then be seen as negotiations about which set of experiments in the field should be counted as the set of competent experiments. In deciding this issue, they are deciding the character of gravity waves."

Collins represents himself as trying to undermine a certain kind of naive faith in science and scientists. Rather than treating science as an unquestionable authority, we should treat the sciences as human activities, subject to the same limitations as any other human activity. He decries a philosophical image of science that mystifies rather than informs about the real character of scientific inquiry. Like Barnes and Bloor, he characterizes the situation as one in which there are two opposed views. Either nature imposes its character directly on our (or on scientists') cognitive processes and representational mechanisms, or our (or scientists') cognitive processes and representational mechanisms are mediated in various ways . If the former, our theories, when they are the outcome of uncontaminated methods of inquiry, are direct, accurate, complete representations of that part of nature of which they are theories, and our adopting those theories is explicable by their truth, or by their being the most plausible in light of the evidence available. If the latter, our theories are not direct, accurate, complete representations of that part of nature, but constructions of nature adopted as a consequence of social negotiation and reflecting the interests of the victorious parties in these negotiations.

Collins calls his oppositions the algorithmic and the enculturational model, Barnes and Bloor label theirs the rationalist and the sociological. These dichotomies imply that rationality is algorithmic, the application of rules to a situation, or the use of rules to arrive at solutions to a problem. Rationality is represented as rigid rather than flexible, as transcendent rather than contextual, so that to show that a situation has not been resolved by context-independent rules is taken to show that rationality has not been in play at all, and that it has been displaced by social interests or negotiation. As I indicated in the introduction, one might reject the characterization of rationality that underlies this dichotomization and argue that reasoning is flexible, that it makes use of heterogeneous elements, including both the evidential and the pragmatic, the logical and the local. One might point out that rules of validity do not dictate what gets included in the premises of reasoning, and that conclusions that follow in the context of one set of assumptions, may not follow in the context of another set, that ideas that seem evident in one context are inconceivable in another. The sociologists of science can make or be read as making what seem extravagant claims about science and philosophy of science because they themselves are in thrall to a rigid conception of rationality and the cognitive. Rather than develop (or find) alternative conceptions of knowledge, rationality, and the like, which are more sensitive to the social processes observed to be instrumental in settling scientific questions, their focus is on the inadequacies of the traditional approach. In spite of their protestations, and even intentions, to the contrary, therefore, their rhetoric leaves no room for a third way, one that would employ a less formalistic conception of rationality and be part of, not opposed to, a social analysis.

Additional objections have been addressed to both British schools by Bruno Latour. He claims that, while their work purports to overturn an inappropriate asymmetry in the treatment of belief, it embraces an even more pernicious one. SSK analyses make our beliefs about nature problematic, but rely on our beliefs about social matters (power, interests, etc.) being unproblematic. They presume knowledge of the social in order to destabilize knowledge of the natural. As objects of inquiry in empirical social science, however, social categories are just as subject to question as are natural categories.[19] There are really two asymmetries here. One is epistemological: between the transparency granted to our knowledge of society and social processes, and the social mediation or opacity of our knowledge of nature. The other asymmetry is causal: the sociologists grant all the causal efficacy in closure of controversies to social processes and none to nature. Latour argues in his review of *Leviathan and the Air Pump* and subsequent work that the sociologists have simply reversed the philosophers' or rationalists' asymmetry.[20] What really requires explanation, he claims, is how science (or nature) and society became separated so that one could be seen as explaining the other, whether one uses society to explain science-nature or nature to explain society-science.[21] And he argues that Shapin and Schaffer, in particular,

[19] This point is also developed by Steve Woolgar 1983, 1992.
[20] Latour 1990, 1992, 1993.
[21] One can see in this formulation another articulation of the problem: science is identified with nature in one approach and with society in the other.

have failed to notice what, in his view, their work on Boyle really shows: not the construction of nature by society but the simultaneous coconstruction (and separation) in the seventeenth century of the natural and the social. To understand both society and nature as constructions completes the symmetry called for by the sociologists. In their responses, Collins and Yearly and Shapin acknowledge the asymmetry that remains in their accounts but claim that without it no understanding is possible, and that the Latourian form of symmetry of natural and social is itself pernicious and nonsensical.[22] The first part of this response demonstrates the trap into which the rational-social dichotomy has led the sociologists: in rejecting the self-ratification of reason, they embrace an equally problematic transparency of the social.

LABORATORY STUDIES

The Edinburgh Strong Programme and Collins's "empirical relativism" emphasize what they perceive as the indefinite flexibility and relativism of cognitive processes in the sciences and the role of professional interests and political ideologies in the persistence and closure of scientific controversy. A family of different analytical approaches, inspired partly by ethnomethodology and partly by cultural anthropology, can be grouped under the rubric of laboratory studies. Practitioners of laboratory studies include among others Karin Knorr-Cetina, Michael Lynch, Bruno Latour, and Sharon Traweek.[23] Their hallmark is close observation, assuming a naive perspective, of laboratory interaction. Knorr-Cetina, Latour, and Lynch are interested in how the work of science is accomplished. Traweek is interested in the culture of high-energy physicists, the parallels in their cosmologies and forms of social organization. Wisely, perhaps, she stays clear of the epistemological confrontations into which her colleagues have charged, although the ironic voice of her texts suggests that her epistemological sympathies are closer to those of social constructivists than to those of scientific realists or traditional empiricists. In the discussion to follow, I focus on Knorr-Cetina and Latour because they have been most explicit about the challenges they (hope to) pose to philosophical approaches to understanding science.

Karin Knorr-Cetina

Knorr-Cetina's early book, *The Manufacture of Knowledge*, is based on a year of field research conducted at a federal research facility in Berkeley,

---

[22] Collins and Yearly 1992b; Shapin 1988.
[23] In addition to the texts cited elsewhere in the chapter, see Lynch 1985, 1992.

California.[24] The particular unit she studied was concerned with plant protein. Knorr-Cetina observed scientists' interactions with their instruments and materials, with each other, and with others connected with or relevant to their research (scientists outside the lab, industrial representatives, etc.) In addition to watching, recording, and interviewing, she collected laboratory protocols, drafts of papers, and published results. The methodological point for the ethnographic researcher of assuming the naive perspective is to avoid excluding via one's preconceptions factors that are relevant to a full description of the causal patterns in the phenomena being observed. For example, a philosopher interested in social aspects of cognition might be predisposed to identify moments of hypothesis justification and analyze these. If as a consequence she were to neglect problem formation and selection as irrelevant to justification, she would remain ignorant of facets of scientific activity that could have an important bearing on the phenomena in which she is interested. The naive observer (ideally) collects everything indiscriminately and only later tries to make sense of it. Of course, no observer is truly naive. What the ethnographer of science wishes to avoid is an uncritical reproduction of a picture of scientific activity purveyed through its legitimating or idealizing representations. The observer is naive in the sense of not sharing the scientists' own understandings or their concepts, instruments, and practices.[25]

In *The Manufacture of Knowledge*, Knorr-Cetina argues that what are conceptualized by philosophers as occasions of theory validation analyzable by the tools of logic are better understood as complex processes constituted by various kinds of selection. Philosophers, she claims, take theory acceptance to be a matter of opinion or consensus formation, a process occurring outside the laboratory itself. But, Knorr-Cetina asks, "what is the process of acceptance if not one of selective incorporation of previous results into the ongoing process of research production?" What is important is the process "in which certain results are solidified through continued incorporation into ongoing research. . . . consequently, it is the process of production and reproduction in the laboratory we must look at in order to study the very 'context of justification.'"[26] Part of her point can be made by observing that even published results count for little unless they are taken up and used by other researchers. Scientific knowledge emerges not from explicit theory testing by attempted experi-

---

[24] Knorr-Cetina 1981.

[25] The reading of a narrative offered by an observer so constructed should also produce in the reader an awareness of the encrustation of values, assumptions, and expectations that shape our unstudied perceptions of scientific activity. At the very least it should challenge those assumptions and disrupt those expectations.

[26] Knorr-Cetina 1981, 8.

mental replication but from the implicit testing that occurs when one's results are relied upon or incorporated into another's research. If the reliance is misplaced (i.e., the results don't work in the new setting), or the incorporating research goes badly, one's results wither on the page as researchers abandon them or even disavow them. And if one's results are not so used, then they wither from lack of attention and fail to be incorporated into the "body of scientific knowledge." Generalizing from this account of justification through incorporation, Knorr-Cetina finds it fruitful to conceive all scientific decisions as selections—of instruments, of techniques, of problems, of "scriptural" resources. One way to understand the shift Knorr-Cetina is proposing is to remember that selections are performed with an end in view; they are not themselves accomplishments or ends. Science is conceived as an ongoing and self-perpetuating activity, not individual contributions to a potentially completed text.

To Knorr-Cetina this interactionism is an alternative to both individualism and wholism, because it focuses on the individual in interaction with others (including the ethnographer). Neither the individual nor the collectivity are independent causal agents. The locus of significant activity in the processes of scientific selection is interaction.

Knorr-Cetina employs two primary evidential resources in the construction of her argument in *Manufacture*. One is documentation and analysis of scientists' responses to questions and situations; the other is the analysis of one of the papers produced in the research unit. Both of these show what she calls the contextual and opportunistic character of scientific reasoning. The considerations brought to bear on selections depend on various features of the context and on perceived opportunities provided both by the material under investigation and the known or expected client (potential industrial uptake, patents, etc.). There is no pattern—each situation differs in its details from others. In explaining their decisions to the outsider, scientists make no effort to purge contextual considerations. For example, during the period of Knorr-Cetina's investigations there was a drought in northern California and the energy crisis was in full swing. Decisions about what procedures to use were deeply influenced by these factors—procedures using less water or less energy being favored over those requiring more. In response to the sociologist's question about how to identify successful ideas, one of the researchers said:

> You try to discriminate. You can get one idea a day, or . . . or one a week, and you discriminate (in terms of) your time and your ability to use it. You know, we have idea files, either in our minds or on paper, but you can't spend a lot of your time on things you don't have the opportunity to perform, or to prove, or to verify. So you try to limit your interest to the idea you know is

going to be most productive as quickly as possible within the frame of facilities at hand.[27]

This kind of pragmatism is actually a rather constant feature of the responses to this question (as distinct from invocations of the intrinsic challenge of an idea, the probability of making a major advance in knowledge, or other more prototypically "cognitive" features).

In one case a researcher dropped one line of inquiry when his industrial contact indicated lack of interest and reoriented it until client interest and research direction were united. This is an example of what Knorr-Cetina, following Michel Callon, calls "fusion" of interests. Strong Programme sociology appeals to antecedently shared interests grounded in shared material and social circumstances of thought. Knorr-Cetina argues, to the contrary, that commonality of interests is not a given and that it takes work to make and maintain a fusion of interests. Such fusion is fragile and very situation-dependent. The individual scientist creates and operates within a network extending beyond the immediate context of research to users (both industrial and scientific), funders, and the like. Again, the precise character of such networks ("variable transcientific fields") is dependent on the particular situation. Although Knorr-Cetina does not stress this point, one may also suppose that networks crisscross one another, so that any given individual is located in a number of different networks, in one of which she or he may be a sender of material or ideas, in another a recipient of material or ideas, in another a translator.

The one place in which contextual factors are purged, claims Knorr-Cetina, is in the preparation of articles for publication. The impersonality of the research article is an artifact of its preparation, however, not a reflection of the actual history of the experiments. In the second main line of her argument, Knorr-Cetina traces a paper from its beginnings in the laboratory, through its fifteen drafts in response to internal and external peer review. The agency of the experimenters is progressively eliminated as is any evidence of choices they made regarding, for example, procedures or reagents. The relation of the work to prior work by others is carefully presented. The earlier work is cited where necessary as background but not featured as inspiring or prompting the work being presented. The article is rewritten to incorporate peer reviewers' suggestions, as well as to transfer responsibility for the conclusions drawn from the researchers to their results. The problem, not the researchers, determines the tools; the results, not the researchers, determine (or "suggest") the conclusions. The outcome of this process, a piece of exposition that thoroughly cleanses traces of its origins from the

[27] Ibid., 75.

account of the research, is highly deceptive if taken as a record of the actual work. Of course, everyone within the sciences knows the difference. Only the outsider, who bases her understanding of science on such artifacts, will be misled. As Ken Waters has remarked, however, this process is not so much a *de*contextualization as a *re*contextualization.[28] The rewritten article is deliberately placed in specific relation to other work via the pattern of citations and announces its belonging in that body of work via its form. It has been relocated from the very local context of the group and its laboratory to the broader context of accepted public scientific knowledge.

The erasure of local context and particular agency in the final, public, draft of the research article, however, does encourage the belief, among scientists and lay persons alike, that the sciences aim for and achieve an exact representation of the natural world, that nature writes itself into the tables, graphs, figures, and their textual interpretations. "Getting it right" is transformed from making everything in the laboratory work as needed for a successful result to cutting nature at the joint. The first term is equated with the third, making the work of getting it right invisible. One of Knorr-Cetina's aims in her analysis is to undermine this equivalence, and she equates this undermining with a repudiation of the philosophical approach to understanding scientific inquiry. She makes this clear in a slightly later essay outlining the elements of her constructivist approach, in which "the study of scientific knowledge is primarily seen to involve an investigation of how scientific objects are produced in the laboratory rather than a study of how facts are preserved in scientific statements about nature."[29] The implication is that the philosopher is trying to study how facts are preserved in the scientific process, thus assuming they preexist that process and are the determinants of its success. The contrasting investigation of how scientific objects are produced brings us to see that "[t]he indexicality and the idiosyncrasies of scientific work jeopardize the hope of the philosopher of science to find once and for all the set of criteria which rule scientific selections."[30]

In this early work she was concerned to show how the discursive community of science extended beyond the borders of the laboratory to include state and commercial funders, users, and others. Knorr-Cetina's recent work focuses more closely on interactions inside the laboratory.[31] In what might be termed middle-stage papers reporting on studies in molecular biology laboratories, she emphasized the role of discursive

[28] In comments on an earlier draft of this chapter.
[29] Knorr-Cetina 1983, 119.
[30] Ibid., 134.
[31] Amann and Knorr-Cetina 1990.

interactions among laboratory scientists and technicians in determining what the (in themselves indefinitely flexible) data are.[32] "Indefinite flexibility" might be taken to mean that you can make the data do anything. This is probably too strong. But "indefinite flexibility" may mean that, given a range of possible values, the data will resist indefinitely fixation at any one of those, thus requiring input from the scientist.

The most recent work draws attention to what Knorr-Cetina calls the differing "epistemic cultures" of particle physics and molecular biology.[33] In this work she seeks to show the limitations of both philosophical and economic conceptions of rationality. Both philosophy and economics, she claims, posit a uniform rationality which can be characterized independently of contexts in which it is employed. This uniformity, however, is for Knorr-Cetina an illusion fostered by an illicit separation of context and content. Looking at problem-solving strategies in the laboratories of these two sciences, she says that instead of a uniform reason one finds disunity in what she calls their modes of "truth-finding navigation." Rational procedures are invoked in the face of dilemmas (e.g., the circularity of the relationship between methodology and outcome) that affect each science equally, but what counts as rational, what works as a solution, is radically different in the two contexts. As an example, in physics one finds a framing strategy in which results from one detector are used as a frame for another. This provides stabilization and solidification, but as Knorr-Cetina notes, the grounding of empirical findings, the interpretation of instrument-dependent traces, is therefore accomplished through self-reference, self-contextualization, and self-organization. Physics, that is, depends on itself for validation. By contrast, in molecular biology, the individual researcher is counted on to develop a sense for a reasonable challenge and a reasonable solution. The successful researcher has developed a "feel," for example, for when to turn the gel run off and when to keep it going. Scientists and the objects they study are joined in "interactional/behavioral" circuits in which neither scientist nor object behaves independently or completely dominates the other.

One can read Knorr-Cetina either as trying to reconceptualize rationality and to treat reason as situated reason or as dismissing rationality and reason as unfit for the analysis of scientific practice. For example, she characterizes the epistemological question as "how is that which we come to call knowledge constituted and accepted?"[34] Answers to this question are best provided by what she calls a sensitive methodology. This involves, "methodological intersubjectivity," the achievement of communication with the subjects of research, a "methodological relativism" that

[32] I return to the implications of these papers in later chapters.
[33] Knorr-Cetina 1999.
[34] Knorr-Cetina 1983.

gives voice to the subjects in construction of knowledge about them, and a "methodological interactionism," which focuses the ethnographer on "the practice, rather than the cognition, of its subjects." The application of this methodology leads us to answers to the epistemological question that invoke the social processes and interactions in the laboratory and between the laboratory and its worldly environment. This analysis, she claims, "defeat[s] the hope of the philosopher of science to find the set of criteria that govern scientific selections." This "defeat," however, is guaranteed in advance by her characterization of methodological interactionism as focusing on "the practice, rather than the cognition, of its subjects." This is just another way of expressing the dichotomy of the rational-cognitive and the social, assuming, as it does, that practice excludes cognition.

Read through the lens of the dichotomy, her empirical analysis does seem intended to show the irrelevance of reason to science. Read without such a lens, it is less a defeat or displacement of philosophical concerns, as a proposal to change the field on which such concerns are engaged. Philosophers are concerned both with the meaning of normative concepts and with the articulation of their criteria of application, the norms themselves. Knorr-Cetina's work can be read as urging us to shift our attention from a body of literature that can be analyzed with the tools of logic to a study of the processes by which that literature (and the understanding it expresses) is produced. The danger of the logical analysis is that it is confused with description of actual reasoning practices. If we understand the actual practices—social and material—by which scientific knowledge is produced as themselves cognitive practices, the field of philosophical analysis shifts not so much from texts to practices, as from texts abstracted from their social-historical intellectual and material contexts to texts embedded in those contexts and understood as outcomes of complex cognitive practices. It expands rather than excludes the domain of reasons. In this reading Knorr-Cetina's work is an empirical collaborator with philosophers seeking to represent norms of reason as complex, plural, and nontranscendent. Rather than showing that the philosophers' concerns with such matters as justification and knowledge are misplaced and misrepresent an activity at base irrational, one can see Knorr-Cetina's work as urging a rethinking of how we characterize rationality, and how we understand its expression in the processes of science.

Bruno Latour

In the first major work to come out of their joint field study at the Salk Institute in the 1970s, Latour and Steve Woolgar also adopt the narrative pose of the naive observer.[35] The neuroendocrinological unit headed by Roger Guillemin was engaged in fierce competition with another laboratory over the identification and analysis of the neuropeptide, thyrotropin releasing factor (TRF). Latour and Woolgar focus on what they call the "traffic in inscriptions." Inscriptions range from recordings produced by bioassay instruments that get passed around in the lab to the research articles that come into and are sent out of the lab in which the bioassay marks internally circulated are embedded for external circulation. These inscriptions can be understood as tokens exchanged in an ongoing economy of credit in which the aim of individuals is to amass credibility. Credibility is accrued through the production of information, the costs of challenging which are prohibitively high. The cost can be the discrediting of too much other research that has been integrated with the bit of information in question or the material and intellectual investment needed to build new instruments or design new experiments with which to challenge the information. Credibility issues in credit in the form of citations and other acknowledgments of indebtedness. This credit can be invested in projects whose outcome will bring more credibility, which can in turn be reinvested resulting in an accelerating and expanding cycle of production and reproduction.

This economic model of scientific activity allows us to see the embeddedness of that activity within the more encompassing world of capitalist investment and commerce. The idea is less that science is literally a matter of investment, exchange, and profit taking, but that both the economy and science are realizations of the same abstract model. Like Knorr-Cetina's work, the model directs our attention away from the content of theories and the manifest reasons (observations, experiments, etc.) scientists offer for them. The process of justification stops when it becomes too expensive to try to disconfirm, not when nature has been correctly cut at the joints. Knorr-Cetina, however, argues that the economic model is misleading or only incompletely realized in science. In particular, she criticizes Latour and Woolgar's model for omitting the idea of exploitation and the individual appropriation of surplus value in the form of profit and their correlates of class structure and alienation.[36] We might also note that it treats the scientist as independent entrepreneur, ignoring the complex dependencies and hierarchical structures of government and industrial research laboratories and of universities. Paradoxically, it promotes an internalist conception of science, in that the primary agents are

[35] Latour and Woolgar 1986.

[36] Richard Levins and Richard Lewontin (1985) use an explicitly Marxist economic model to characterize contemporary science. Class structure and alienation play major roles in their analysis.

scientists, and the scientific process is explicated without reference to other factors.[37]

In subsequent work, Latour has abandoned the economic model for a much looser framework. Latour's interpretation of Pasteur's accomplishment in the nineteenth century makes clear that he is actually trying to abolish the kind of internal-external distinction just invoked.[38] The accomplishment is not (or not just) the establishment of the germ theory of disease but the transformation of agriculture and veterinary and human medicine by microbiology. Rather than trying to understand Pasteur's work in terms of antecedent interests and a fixed context, Latour proposes that we first focus on a series of displacements and translations. Pasteur's encounter with the anthrax bacillus offers a good example. According to Latour, Pasteur first takes his technicians out to the field where they collect infected matter and establish identities between field entities and laboratory entities. Latour calls these translations, to reflect their partiality and strategic character. The farmer's infected fields become the laboratory's dormant spores. Pasteur then brings back and recreates only selected portions of the farm conditions in the laboratory. Specifically, he can create an outbreak of anthrax. Applying what he had learned from work with chicken cholera about variations in virulence, he is able to weaken or strengthen the microbe and thus ultimately to create a vaccine. The effectiveness of the vaccine is not demonstrated simply by shipping vials of it from the laboratory to veterinarians, saying "try this." Instead the laboratory conditions that support the vaccine's effectiveness in the lab must be recreated in the field—that is, the laboratory must be extended to the farm.

There is no outside acting on an inside, or an inside acting on an outside, according to Latour. Rather, there is traffic between specific sites, which brings elements of the one to the other, what he calls displacements, and translation, not just of concepts, but also of interests. The interests of the French farmers in economic success are translated into interests in the success of the experiments in Pasteur's laboratory, and thus into interests in its maintenance and support. This laboratory is a place where many trials are conducted and mistakes made (away from the public eye). The key to its success is the inscription devices, the techniques for measuring and recording the substances and processes the lab is working with. Their power lies in their ability to make the natural objects and processes whose effects and traces they record easily read-

---

[37] Knorr-Cetina (1981) develops an extensive critique of general economic models as adequate representations of scientific activity but proposes that the economic language they do use be interpreted as referring to a market, but a market in which the commodity traded is scientists, not what scientists produce.

[38] Latour 1988.

able. Only when a new configuration of actors-objects and powers is created in the laboratory, and a way developed to extend the relevant conditions of the laboratory into "society," does its work go public. For Latour, the laboratory is not a place where preexistent social forces interact but a place where new forces are created, "where the composition of the social context is metamorphosed."[39]

In *Science in Action* Latour offers a more general account of this approach, illustrated with a variety of examples.[40] He retains the idea in *Laboratory Life* that justification is accomplished by making it just too costly for competitors to attempt disconfirmation or the advancement of alternative models.[41] He adopts the sobriquet, "Trials of Strength," for the process by which competition makes disconfirmation or alternatives too costly. He also adopts and adapts notions like Michel Callon's field and network, ideas we saw also employed by Knorr-Cetina. Scientific knowledge production is represented as the hegemonizing of models through the stabilization of alliances and networks constituted of human and nonhuman actors or "actants." Stabilization is achieved when results either in the social world or in the natural (really, laboratory) world can be reliably reproduced, when a laboratory has won in the trials of strength. But this formulation would be problematic to the extent that it suggests that the social and the natural constitute separate domains. Adoption of a result is a social matter that simultaneously contributes to making of that result a fact. As is evident from the discussion of Pasteur, the point is not that the social interactions construct a fact out of thin air, but that, unless a laboratory artifact can be given life outside the laboratory, as Pasteur's anthrax vaccine was, it is of absolutely no interest and does not make it into the body of public knowledge or into the common world. Both raising the costs of challenging a formulation and bringing others to adopt one's interests as their own (Callon's fusion again) are processes of stabilization.

Latour is targeting two kinds of explanatory asymmetry: the asymmetry of those philosophers who claim that social causes can be invoked only when demonstrations of rationality fail, but also the reverse asymmetry produced by the distinction between nature and society that he sees as the dogmatic heart of social studies of science. Latour's suggestion that the stabilization of networks requires the cooperation of the nonhuman actants (sheep brains, enzymes, silicon chips, scallops) has been received with outrage by some readers who find the implicit attribution

---

[39] Latour 1983, 158.
[40] Latour 1987.
[41] Latour 1983.

of intentionality to nonhumans ridiculous.[42] One can, however, read this as a playful way to press his doubts regarding the nature-society divide that plays so prominent a role in the Strong Programme. He challenges philosophers explicitly. In a reversal of the rational-irrational asymmetry, he proposes that philosophers pursue his kind of social account of scientific knowledge production as far as it can go, and only then turn to cognitive accounts, that is, to accounts that appeal to reasons. The clear implication is that if one is really thorough in one's social explanation, there will be no more work for a cognitive account to do.

It is possible to read Latour as making a move similar to the philosophers' response to the Strong Programme, for his insistence on the role of "nonhuman actants" is also a way to bring nature back into the construction of knowledge. The conceit of the network is a way to make the contribution of the natural and the social equivalent in weight, or at least not specified a priori. It also decenters the theoretical products on which philosophers have placed so much weight. What we distinguish as natural and social are equally elements acting and interacting in a web of relationships. In this web, there are not privileged directions of causal influence, just successive states in which the elements relate to each other as in an unchoreographed dance. Certain sequences may be stable across successive states owing to the cooperation of all the elements involved. The parallel to the philosophers' response is in the insistence that it is not possible to create knowledge by fiat; the natural world must have some input.

But Latour is not allying himself with the philosopher, at least not with that philosopher. He seems to be saying that theory choice or acceptance is the wrong problem to start with in understanding science. In "Give Me a Laboratory," he puts it this way:

> The specificity of science is not to be found in cognitive, social or psychological qualities, but in the special construction of laboratories in a manner which reverses the scale of phenomena so as to make things readable, and then accelerates the frequency of trials, allowing many mistakes to be made and registered. . . . the mystification of science comes most often from the idea that scientists are able to make "predictions." They work in their labs and, sure enough, something happens outside that verifies these predictions. The problem is that no one has ever been able to verify these predictions without extending first the conditions of verification that existed in the laboratory.[43]

[42] Collins and Yearly 1992a.
[43] Latour 1983, 165–66.

The formulas by which the philosopher represents verification, justification, and theory choice, whether these are confirmation schemata, falsification and corroboration schemata, decision matrices, or other models, simply fail to express what is significant about the construction of scientific knowledge: the transformation of the world it is about.

On the reading of network theory I have just given, theories, models, explanations are just by-products of this complex process of displacements and translations rather than vehicles mediating the relationships between humans and nature or, as some philosophical accounts would have it, the point of the whole exercise. The student of science, then, can only document the step by which any set of agents has arrived at the configuration in which it finds itself, "follow[ing] scientists and engineers around." If this is what Latour has in mind, then cognitive accounts are unnecessary because there is no cognition. But this seems to me simply to step off a precipice created by the dichotomization of the rational and the social that haunts the other science studies work discussed in this chapter.

In his most recent book, Latour emphasizes even more strongly the role of the external world (or "reality") in determining the outcome of inquiry.[44] At the same time he struggles to articulate how the anthrax bacillus both does and does not preexist Pasteur's attempts to isolate it. Human and nonhuman interact in the production of knowledge; the trick is describing that interaction without overstatement or understatement. Latour might prefer to say the production of a world in which a microorganism isolated and brought under control in the laboratory is understood as the cause of anthrax. If the only role accorded cognitive rationality is testing and proof of a hypothesis about the cause of anthrax, then Latour is right to disparage it as ex post facto, but surely this is not the only place for rationality. It is expressed in the countless microcognitive acts by the Pasteurians that go into this production of knowledge (or new world). Their embeddedness in pragmatic contexts does not make them any less cognitive. The kind of cognitive account Latour is rejecting is the same kind the Strong Programme theorists reject in rejecting rationalism, an account that treats the truth of a belief as explanatory of its being believed, and thus treats reason and justification as separable from the messy social activities that occur in the transactions between the laboratory and its world.

But a cognitive account can also be one that treats scientists' reasons as explanatory of their beliefs. And surely the activities in which Pasteur and his technicians engage—growing the bacillus, determining in which media it grows more rapidly, and in which less, observing and recording

[44] Latour 1999.

which cows get sick, and which escape the disease—are at least partially cognitive processes. Only the dichotomy of the rational and the social compels one to treat this as noncognitive. Noticing the social and contextual embeddedness of scientists and of their reasoning practices does not banish reason from science, nor does it mean that cognitive accounts have no work to do, nor does it mean that human rationality is not a key element of science. It does mean that cognitive (or rational) accounts that take no account of the social and contextual character of actual scientific practice, or that, even worse, assume an independence of science from its context, will be inadequate and may even misrepresent the role and character of scientific rationality. But, as in the case of the Strong Programme, to assume that cognitive accounts must of necessity be insensitive to contextual matters, or must divorce the properly scientific from everything else that is going on, is to embrace the same rigid conception of rationality that supposedly characterizes the philosophical opposition.

TAKE HOME LESSONS

The sociological work reviewed in this chapter shows that an adequate representation of scientific practices must situate scientists in their communities and situate those communities in the larger and partially overlapping communities of clients, funders, consumers, and citizens that sustain them. These communities are characterized by heterogeneous, sometimes conflicting, interests and allegiances. The researchers whose work I have surveyed differ in their accounts of the mode of interaction and on the appropriate target and level of analysis. They agree that what they identify as the philosopher's approach—one characterized by normative concerns about the nature of knowledge—misrepresents the scientific process. Case studies show that social interests have been part of deliberative processes that result in the acceptance of a given theory or experimental result in even the model instances—for example, the political dimension of Boyle's experimental method provided an incentive to adopt it. Case studies show that negotiation—discussion and argument— can determine what counts as evidential in a given community. Case studies show that the expectation of uptake or neglect in the receptive field plays a role in the design of research, as in Knorr-Cetina's studies of the plant protein group. Case studies show that clever cultivation of allies (including the nonhuman objects of research) can ensure a provisional consensus around a result, as in the cases studied by Latour. If we try to represent scientific practices with a model of knowledge drawn from midcentury analytic epistemology, that is, with an abstraction derived from a priori models and principles of argument, we will only succeed in offering a caricature. At the same time, to argue that the case studies show that scientific practice is not rational, that evidential reason and reasons have no place in scientific practice, or that theory or hypothesis choice is always or by necessity determined by professional or political interests overstates the case. It accepts the "rationalist" view as an adequate analysis of reasoning and other cognitive concepts, and argues merely that it does not fit the actualities of scientific practice, rather than calling into question the rigid characterization of reasoning and rationality. But the fault may lie in the unquestioned dichotomy between the cognitive, or rational, and the social, not in the claim that the sciences are expressions of human rationality or cognitive capacities.

Sociological study of science asks, What is the character of the work of producing scientific knowledge? Knorr-Cetina's epistemological question ("how is that which we come to call knowledge constituted and accepted?") and Latour's injunction to follow scientists around are directed at characterizing this work. An answer to the question, How was this instance of scientific knowledge constituted and accepted? or to the question, What did the scientists do, where did they go, in the course of producing this bit of knowledge (or introducing this new object and interactions into the world)? is not , however, an answer to the question, In virtue of what is it knowledge? To say that scientific knowledge is whatever scientists say is knowledge, or whatever wins in trials of strength, addresses the questions about the work of producing knowledge, but leaves unanswered what we mean by treating a claim as knowledge rather than as opinion. Philosophers have started epistemological analysis with this question. Naturalist philosophers have answered it by describing procedures or processes that individuals perform or undergo in coming to beliefs, perceptual processes, reasoning procedures, and the like, in virtue of which we are inclined to call what they believe knowledge.[45] These are treated as justificatory in nature. By describing processes of belief or claim acceptance that do not include what have been traditionally understood as justificatory (or knowledge-constitutive) processes, the sociologists seem to have displaced the philosophical question. But the original question, which is a question about the *meaning* of a normative or norm-laden expression (i.e. "knowledge") remains. It may be that its answer does not lie in the processes of justification described by the philosopher and displaced from their causal status by the sociologists' explanations, or that it lies (contrary to the assumptions of both) in properties of at least some of the procedures and processes described by the sociologist. Unless it is answered, however, it is not clear what gen-

[45] Kitcher 1992.

eral point can be drawn from the sociologists' empirical studies. The sociologists have succeeded in casting doubt on the adequacy of the philosophers' rational reconstructions of scientific judgment as representations of cognitive processes. They have not dispelled the concerns that give rise to such reconstruction—questions about the nature of knowledge and about the power of scientific inquiry to produce knowledge.

_____ *Appendix* _____

I HAVE ARGUED that twentieth-century analytic philosophers had developed antifoundationalist arguments that did not lead to Bloor's Pyrrhonian conclusions. Bloor has, in fact, used versions of the antifoundationalist philosopher's arguments. In "Durkheim and Mauss Revisited" and elsewhere, he cites a form of the underdetermination argument attributable to Quine and developed also by Mary Hesse.[46] This form of the argument concerns the meaning and extension of category terms. Bloor sees Hesse's application of the argument in her network model of scientific inference as offering a philosophical, theoretical justification of the claim by Durkheim and Mauss that "the classification of things reproduces the classification of men," that is, that such classifications reproduce social patterns of inclusion and exclusion. The basic idea is that our judgments regarding the extensions of categories, what counts as a member or even exemplar of a category, are indefinitely revisable, the primary constraint on such judgment being maintenance of the coherence of the network of judgments. Because not every aspect of the network can be retained when confronted by anomalous experiences, belief revision is guided by coherence conditions that prescribe which parts of the network must be maintained and which are expendable. One condition is maintenance of correspondence with the world, but because this can be achieved in multiple ways, additional constraints on how coherence is to be achieved must be in operation. Where Hesse invokes "culturally conditioned metaphysical principles," Bloor cites Mary Douglas's proposal that metaphysical principles and conceptions of nature constitute polemical weapons with which to control others. Thus, as Durkheim said, "the classification of things reproduces the classification of men," or the conditions by reference to which coherence of a network of laws, singular empirical descriptions, and the like, is maintained, include (value-laden) beliefs about social order. One could see this as the claim that one coherence condition is that our beliefs about nature preserve the naturalness of our social arrangements. What Hesse's conception of theories adds to Durkheim's view, in Bloor's reading, is its extension to scientific theories.

The difficulty here is that the underdetermination argument together with Hesse's solution to it itself underdetermines the thesis about scien-

[46] Bloor 1982. The underdetermination argument is the argument that data do not fully constrain theory choice, leaving scientific judgment underdetermined by evidence.

tific knowledge that Bloor hopes to draw from it. The underdetermination argument is about the insufficiency of empirical data alone to constrain theories or hypotheses to one. Bloor's argument purports to be a priori but, without further premises, fails to constrain us to the conclusion he seeks. That some coherence conditions are required does not indicate what their content must be. Moreover, the fact that in some cases these conditions have included the preservation of social beliefs does not show that in all cases preservation of social beliefs or "the classifications of men" will be involved. Bloor sometimes invokes the fact that categories are conventions maintained and revised by the social institutions of language to support the claim that the content of belief is socially determined. But it does not follow from the fact that categories are maintained by social convention that their content is itself social or determined by the social relations prevailing in the context of that use. The conventional nature of categories is compatible with heterogeneous modes of fixation. To say this is in no way to detract from the historical work Bloor seeks to validate. And, indeed, the Strong Programme may better be understood as a historiographical program, as a philosophical view whose purpose is to direct the historian to certain facets of an episode in the history of science. But the resulting account must stand or fall on its own merits and is not a consequence of the philosophical thesis, so much as an empirical demonstration of it.

CHAPTER THREE

The Philosophers Respond

THE PHILOSOPHICAL response to sociological approaches to scientific knowledge ranges from outrage to selective incorporation. Like those approaches, it can be both temporally and thematically partitioned. Early response focused on the Strong Programme while later responses have taken on the microsociological approach to laboratory life. The hostile reception, whether early or late, attempts to refute what are seen as wrongheaded or perverse epistemological theses. The more welcoming reception draws attention to resonances of details of the sociological approach with their own historical and philosophical views. Often setting aside or reinterpreting the more controversial philosophical theses, sympathetic philosophers have either embraced ways in which the sociological approach shows up shortcomings of traditional philosophy of science or have identified (at least partial) compatibilities of aspects of one or another of the sociological approaches with aspects of their own noncanonical philosophical approaches.

Larry Laudan, Susan Haack, Alvin Goldman, and Philip Kitcher are among the most prominent philosophical critics of the sociologists, seeing in their work a dangerous defense of relativism.[1] Mary Hesse, Steve Fuller, and Joseph Rouse have been among the most welcoming, although in very different respects.[2] Ronald Giere and James Brown have offered mixed assessments.[3] Giere shows how elements of the sociological account can be incorporated into his decision-theoretic approach to scientific judgment, thus implicitly taking compatibility with some sociological view as a condition of adequacy for any philosophical account of scientific inquiry. Like those of Haack, Goldman, and Kitcher, however, his approach is shaped by a deep commitment to individualism. Brown has been concerned to rebut some of the more extravagant claims of the sociologists while nevertheless recognizing the importance of the implicit critique of individualism. Finally, some philosophers have offered social approaches to scientific knowledge or inquiry independently of the sociologists. David Hull's *Science as a Process* combined a history of biological systematics in the twentieth century with a theory of selection intended

---

[1] Laudan 1984a; Haack 1996; Goldman 1995; Kitcher 1993.
[2] Hesse 1988; Fuller 1988, 1989; Rouse 1987.
[3] Giere 1988; Brown 1984, 1989, 1994.

to apply both to biological change and to conceptual change.[4] The history of systematics was used to give empirical heft to the theory of conceptual change, as well as being of interest in itself. He thinks he can dispense with epistemology altogether by treating the sciences as an interactive selection process. Miriam Solomon's social empiricism sees communities acting rationally through the epistemic irrationality of individual members.[5] Solomon has looked to cognitive science but found there material for a social epistemology that breaks radically with traditional individual-centered approaches to scientific knowledge.[6]

Much of the philosophical criticism of the sociologists is directed at a reconstruction of the sociologists' philosophical conclusions, which, as seen in the previous chapter, are often extravagantly expressed. The debunking tone of the sociologists evokes an equally extravagant defense of the integrity of scientists, of the authenticity of science, and even of Western values.[7] Although some critique of standard modes of defending these is distributed through various sociologists' work, their most interesting point concerns the social and historical contingency of the particular accounts of nature developed in contemporary science. This very general claim can be understood in many ways, but the philosophers considered here all seem to assume that Western science represents *the* pinnacle of human intellectual achievement and that treating it as anything other than the expression of a rationality guided by sound epistemic norms is to open the gates to the barbarians. Rather than focus on the tone and subtext of these responses, I attend principally to the soundness of the arguments advanced against the sociological positions by three philosophers: Alvin Goldman, Susan Haack, and Philip Kitcher.

Larry Laudan's objections were directed largely at the early ideas of Barnes and Bloor and centered on their symmetry thesis and use of underdetermination.[8] Because both Goldman and Kitcher offer arguments that incorporate the points made by Laudan, I do not treat his arguments separately. Haack offers general arguments against treating scientific knowledge as social. Goldman and Kitcher both take social epistemology seriously, but both tend toward what Kitcher calls a minimalist social epistemology, one that treats the social as an aggregation of individuals and public knowledge as the additive outcome of many indi-

[4] Hull 1988.

[5] Ibid.; Solomon 1994a, 1994b, 1995. I take up Solomon's work in chapter 7.

[6] Solomon 1992, 1994a, 1994b, 1995; Goldman 1994.

[7] The so-called science wars in which scientists and some philosophers have taken up the defense of science against constructivists, deconstructionists, cultural theorists, etc., seem primarily exercises in public relations and obscure rather than illuminate the philosophical issues at stake.

[8] Laudan 1984a.

viduals making sound epistemic judgments. Some features of this approach are discussed in an appendix to this chapter. All three philosophers assume the rational-social dichotomy. All three are also committed not just to realism but to a monistic form of realism, that is, to a view that for any natural process there is one and only one correct account of it.

GOLDMAN

Alvin Goldman interprets the sociology of scientific knowledge[9] as claiming that science is "just politics."[10] He contrasts this view, which he vigorously rejects, with his own epistemic approach: scientists are persuaded by what they regard as the best evidence or argument, the evidence most indicative of the truth by their lights. To see this epistemic view threatened by the sociologists' work is very clearly to read that work through a lens that is both individualist and shaped by the dichotomy between the rational and the social. Goldman's view reduces the sociological analysis of the formation of public knowledge to a claim about individuals, in particular to a claim that individuals allow personal interests to overcome (their better) epistemic judgment. This treats the sociological view as a critique of the moral and intellectual probity of scientists, rather than as a view about the shortcomings of a purely logical approach to knowledge production or a view about the need for a more complex representation of science than has been forthcoming from mainstream philosophy of science.

To set up the version of the thesis he argues against, Goldman quotes passages like the following: "He who has the most and most powerful allies wins," from Shapin and Shaffer;[11] or "going from outer layers of an article to its inner parts . . . is going from authorities to more authorities, from numbers of allies and resources to greater numbers," from Latour.[12]

Taken out of context, these quotations can be read in many ways. For example, the power of the allies might mean brute force or it might

[9] I use "sociology of scientific knowledge" to refer to both the Edinburgh, Strong Programme, style characteristic of Bloor and Shapin and their colleagues and to the microsociological approach chracteristic of Knorr-Cetina and her colleagues and of Latour and his colleagues. For lack of a better term, I use "sociologist" to refer to members of those or related schools of thought. There is also quite a bit of sociology of science that is less philosophically controversial and that the philosophers discussed here would not find problematic. I do not mean to deny its existence by my restricted use of "sociologist" and "sociology." The sociologists criticized by the philosophers also have their sociological critics. See Schmaus, Segerstrale, and Jesseph 1992.

[10] Goldman 1995.

[11] Ibid., 279.

[12] Ibid., 280.

mean scientific, intellectual, prowess. It might also refer to the greater saliency or manipulability of one natural process as against others. The authorities in the "inner parts" of an article can also be read as referring to other scientists sharing the authors' views or to other scientists employing their cognitive abilities to the utmost. The allies may be non-human, in which case "allies" might mean the parts of nature that the authors can make evident through inscription devices. Certainly, Latour, as we saw in the previous chapter, makes no distinction between human and nonhuman actors recruitable as allies in a network. Goldman, how-ever, treats these as claims about persuasion and distinguishes three dif-ferent theses that he attributes to the sociologists. The noxious versions of the first two can be replaced by an innocuous epistemic version. The import of the sociologists' more radical claims is articulated in the third thesis, which, according to Goldman, is just false. The first of these is

PT1: Scientists are persuaded by the force or weight of greater numbers.

Goldman claims that to the extent scientists do respond to numbers—that is, to endorsements of a result or a view by a significant number of peers—it is because they think such numbers are a reliable guide to truth. Thus, he says the truth of PT1 can be expressed epistemically as

ET1: To the extent that scientists are persuaded by the force or weight of greater numbers, this is because they judge majority opinion to be a reli-able indicator of truth.

So the sociologists are understood as making a claim about the bases on which individual scientists come to accept a claim. The sociologist is represented as mistaking an evidential judgment (about who is a reliable authority) for a political maneuver. Goldman treats authority similarly. The sociologist is credited with

PT2: What persuades scientists is the power or influence of superior scien-tific authorities.

This, too, has an epistemic version:

ET2: To the extent that scientists are persuaded by authority, what promotes conviction is (primarily) the judged credibility of an authority, that is, the hearer's judgment of the likelihood that the authority is right.

Finally, Goldman extracts a third thesis,

PT3: What causes a hearer to believe or disbelieve a speaker's claims are the hearer's political and professional interests.

And, this, he says, is simply false.

Goldman's distinction between the P and E versions is a direct product of applying the rational-social dichotomy to the quotations from Shapin and Schaffer and Latour. And he clearly interprets the sociologist to be intending to make the P version. Although this is a possible reading of some of the sociologists' work, especially of sentences taken out of context, it is not the most useful approach. Goldman thinks that having made the distinction between P and E versions, we can see that the E theses are true and the P theses false. He supports his epistemic rewriting of the authority thesis and his rejection of the interest thesis by appealing partially to anecdotal examples and partially to psychological studies. Watson and Crick were not high-status scientists, yet their double-helical model was very quickly accepted. It was the character of their reasoning and data that won the day for them. Cline gave up a career-long opposition to the existence of neutral currents when faced with overwhelming reasons and results that supported them. Any sociologist could quickly contextualize these examples and dispel their purely epistemic aura. The point to draw from the sociological studies, in any case, is not about individuals but about the social processes that make ideas and results both available and salient. That someone can change her or his mind faced with what she or he takes to be appropriate evidence does nothing to undermine claims about the social character of the development of science or of cognitive processes in science (unless one believes that cognitive processes are internal to individuals).[13]

The psychological studies do more work. In addition, they help us understand the nature of Goldman's thesis and the focus of his concerns. He cites a psychological model of persuasion that distinguishes between "central" and "peripheral" routes to persuasion, where central routes involve such activities as a hearer evaluating the arguments contained in a message and peripheral routes involve factors such as speaker likability or credibility.[14] No data as to usage of central and peripheral routes are reported, but another of the studies he cites involves actual subjects and

[13] David Hull, while avoiding the rational-social dichotomy elsewhere (1988), treats the thesis that social ideologies play a role in science just as does Goldman and argues in exactly parallel fashion, citing individuals whose scientific work is in conflict with the interests of their social class. Hull also claims that the social interactions he does describe will eliminate any influence of social factors in the outcome of research. This point should be the principal response he makes to work in the social studies of science, because his selectionist view ought, in principle, to countenance any variation in the scientist-interactors. Even so, it ignores the way in which a commonly shared ideology may be part of the selective environment, restricting which ideas will be taken seriously, or even tolerated. The move to clear scientists of the purported imputation of explicitly trying to incorporate their social values into the content of science shows that Hull, too, succumbs to interpreting the claims of scholars in social studies of science as moral accusations.

[14] Credibility, Goldman underlines, is judged by competence and trustworthiness, and hence is largely epistemic.

the relative roles of interests and evidence. One study involves coffee drinkers' response to evidence that caffeine is harmful. Correlations are drawn between extent of coffee intake (heavy, light) and response to studies showing coffee's harmfulness. The psychological studies show that while personal interest that a given conclusion be true or false has some effect on belief, these effects are mitigated or constrained by knowledge or evidence to the contrary. Interest does not overcome reason. Indeed, reason constrains interest, and the epistemic is vindicated.

But what has really been accomplished? Goldman has told us that ordinary people attend to evidence, and hence it is likely that scientists do, too. But surely that's not the point. The issue is not whether scientists blind themselves to evidence in order to advance and establish those theories that will most advantage them politically and personally. We know that some have gotten away with such behavior temporarily (inventing twin data, painting mice, fudging in the notebooks) but not for long. The appeal to studies showing how individuals for the most part deal with data or evidence that is inconvenient or unwanted casts the issue as one of individual psychology and moral probity. On Goldman's psychological picture, the spread of knowledge is a matter of persuasion, and, in science, persuasion involves first one individual or group coming up with D/A (a set of data or a sound argument or both) and communicating it to others who consider the argument in light of epistemically respectable criteria and (let's say) accept it. Gradually this process radiates out from its originating point. If authorities examine and endorse D/A, its acceptance can be even speedier. Eventually, a plurality of members of the community have examined and endorsed D/A. At this point, ET1 kicks in, and majority opinion wins the day. This, as I indicated, is to trivialize the numbers thesis, to embrace the rational-social dichotomy, and to remain firmly in the grip of a methodological individualism.

The numbers thesis might be understood better as a constitutive than as a causal thesis, in spite of Latour's Anybodies and Manybodies. Success just is being accepted by the most numerous and most powerful faction. It is not an effect of such acceptance. Persuasion is (part of) what goes into producing that acceptance. Goldman's focus on persuasion directs him away from other dimensions of the sociologists' claims. His reliance on psychological studies burdens him with an unrealistic model even for individual scientific belief formation.

Consider again Goldman's empirical evidence for the claim that individuals modify their beliefs in response to evidence in spite of their interests in not doing so. The difficulty with psychological experiments designed to ascertain the role of epistemic versus nonepistemic factors is that, in order to produce clear results for statistical use, they must revolve around fairly simple beliefs (articulated against a background of

monistic realism). We must assume that caffeine either is (P) or is not
(~P) harmful for one. Heavy coffee drinkers who assign a lower level of
credence to P in the face of good reasons for believing P (e.g., a study
conducted by reputable authorities) are swayed by their desire to continue drinking coffee in good conscience. Interpreted in the context of
monistic realism, they are willing to sacrifice rationality or truth to pleasure (or withdrawal avoidance). If, presented with stronger evidence or
with evidence of greater harm, they come to accept P, then rationality
overcomes pleasure. (Plato would be relieved.)

But monistic realism imposes unrealistic constraints on these situations: we must make three suppositions: that the satisfactions of drinking
coffee do not lead to the same outcomes as do acting on the (allegedly)
true belief that caffeine is harmful, that is, that pleasure and what is good
for us are opposed; that there are no studies showing beneficial or neutral
effects of caffeine on aspects of health; and that the experimental subjects
and the populations they are taken to represent can set aside one meta-
inference from contemporary science, that studies are contradictory.
None of these suppositions is self-evident, and the second is actually
false. So, it is misleading to say, as Goldman does, that these experiments
can measure the degree to which epistemic considerations weigh against
desire and interest considerations. The epistemic considerations themselves, when suitably inclusive, are not unambiguous enough to permit
the required exclusive and binary classifications. Furthermore, the experimental setup is unrealistic to the degree that it forces subjects to attend
to the challenging claim.[15] In the real world there are multiple things
vying for our attention, which means that much more than dispassionate
(or impassioned) weighing of the evidence is involved in our believing or
not believing any given bit of information.

All of this is even more the case in the contexts of evaluation and
choice that are of interest to students of science. In these contexts, there
is no obvious best (epistemically) choice. Scientists are neither irrational
nor unreflective automatons. The social studies theses Goldman opposes
are advanced against a background of epistemic indeterminacy. There are
multiple factors having some epistemic weight at work in the internal
reflection of scientists and in the contexts in which their work is assessed,
and, frequently enough, there is more than one scheme for the assigning of relative epistemic weight. Hence the factors cannot be treated
additively. And objects of attention have to be selected from the array of
possibilities. So, while any given individual may be following the epistemically best course for herself or himself, it does not follow that any

---

[15] It is, of course, very like the stereotypical epistemic situation contemplated by analytic
philosophers offering definitions of knowledge or characterizations of justification.

set of individuals using the same data, will, by following the epistemically best course, arrive at the same set of beliefs. It is these descriptions of the context of scientific judgment and persuasion that Goldman must address, if his epistemic theses are to have any utility in explaining individual scientific behavior, let alone the development of scientific knowledge.

Goldman assesses social studies of science within the confines of a one-dimensional epistemic landscape, which involves collapsing theses about epistemic complexity into theses about the relative effectiveness of epistemic and nonepistemic factors in individual change of belief. Absent a demonstration that the scientific context is adequately represented by the scenarios he considers or presupposes, and hence that his reconstruction of the sociologists' positions as PT1, PT2, and PT3, is warranted, Goldman's objections to the social studies of science miss their mark.

Because the normative tasks Goldman assigns to science studies rest on the results of the descriptive or explanatory work, I do not consider them here, except to note that Goldman, like other philosophers to be discussed subsequently, acknowledges the role of credit motivation in science and argues that credit motivation can advance the goal of truth acquisition. I discuss this proposal along with the similar proposals of Hull and Kitcher in the appendix to this chapter.

HAACK

Susan Haack shares some of Goldman's concerns but develops her critique in a different way. She does not attempt to analyze any particular argument or position, but purports to refute a family of (quite disparate) positions having in common the claim that science is social. If science is social, she says, it is so only in a modest sense that does not subvert conventional epistemology. The general argument strategy Haack adopts is to offer several interpretations of the claim in question and argue that one or more of these are tenable but inconsequential, while the rest are consequential but untenable.

Haack situates her arguments about the social character of science as part of a criticism of feminist uses of underdetermination and of contextualism. Her principal fulcrum in "Science as Social?—Yes and No"[16] is the distinction between acceptance and warrant. Warrant is an epistemological notion (warranted belief is belief based on good evidence) in contrast to acceptance, which is a psychological and sociological notion. In general, she says, the radical and false interpretations of "science is

---

[16] Susan Haack 1996.

social" focus on acceptance rather than warrant. One interpretation is that social values are inextricable from inquiry. This claim rests on underdetermination arguments—that is, arguments that theories and hypotheses are underdetermined by data. Haack points out that if evidence is insufficient to warrant a hypothesis, one can simply refrain from believing it. Even if some form of underdetermination is true, one need not decide between alternatives on the basis of which is politically preferable. One can wait until there is decisive evidence. Furthermore, she says, choosing a theory is not equivalent to deciding it is true; one may decide merely to act as if it is true. So social values are not inextricable from inquiry. And inquiry can be purified without being eviscerated.

Haack's arguments apply only to the most superficial understanding of underdetermination and she treats the value-laden thesis as an essentialist claim about science. These are easy targets but made of straw. The version of the underdetermination argument on which I have relied elsewhere points out that a semantic gap between statements describing data and hypotheses must be bridged by substantive background assumptions establishing the evidential relevance of the data to hypotheses. The *de re* version of the point is that the facts requiring explanation and serving as data or evidence are different from the facts and processes postulated as explaining or supported by them. Bubble tracks in a compressed gas are different from the particles whose passage is postulated as producing them, and can serve as evidence for claims about the particles only in light of causal or statistical assumptions about the relation of tracks to particles. It is an oversimplification to suppose that there is a clear point at which the scientist is faced with a choice between relying on a value-laden assumption while going on or refraining from such reliance and withholding belief. Scientists come to the assessment of experimental and observational situations already informed by assumptions with both substantive and value-laden dimensions. Many of these are "second nature," and not the sort of thing about which one deliberates in the ordinary course of procedure.

One of the main lessons of the underdetermination argument is that there are no formal rules, guidelines, or processes that can guarantee that social values will not permeate evidential relations.[17] If this is so, then it is a contingent matter whether a given theory produced according to the best rules is value-laden or not. There are two consequences: it can be asked about any given theory whether it is value-laden and, if so, with which values; and it becomes imperative to produce an analysis of objectivity (understood as social value management rather than absence of social values) that does not invoke formal rules. By addressing only the

---

[17] This argument is developed in Longino 1990, chaps. 2 and 3. See also chapter 6 in this volume.

most simplistic versions of the theses she rejects, Haack's arguments ignore three different points made by advocates of the sociality of science.

1. Value-ladenness does not mean that social values outweigh other considerations, but that they interact with data and hypotheses in determining evidential relevance.

2. If the value-ladenness of a theory is a contingent matter, then whether values are extricable or inextricable from inquiry is not a matter for general a priori argument but case-by-case analysis.

3. Contextual or social values are not just negative features in inquiry, but can have a positive role in grounding criticism of background assumptions and in fostering the development of empirical investigation in directions it would not otherwise go.

Although the Strong Programme theorists might balk at the second, all of these points have been advanced in some form or other by thinkers she seeks to rebut.

Haack's arguments require us to ignore the sociologists' claim that inquiry takes place in a value- or interest-saturated context as well as the often made observation that inquiries are judged by how satisfactorily they answer questions. Haack herself acknowledges that the aim of inquiry is not just truth but significant and substantive truth. But she seems to assume that significance and substantiveness are not a matter of context and that they are given by the material apart from context.[18] By simply assuming what requires analysis and argument, Haack has failed to show that there is no acceptable radical interpretation of "science is social." Her inability to perceive interpretations that escape her criticisms is, I think, a function of a dichotomous bifurcation of value-laden and disinterested ("honest") inquiry, which is in turn a function of the dichotomy between the rational and the social. She seems to think that value-laden inquiry cannot be honest inquiry. But this is just false: one can be honest and subscribe to value-laden assumptions. The problem for epistemologists and philosophers of science should be how to articulate norms of inquiry (and warrant) in the face of this fact, rather than to deny it.

KITCHER

Perhaps the most extensive rebuttal of social constructivist claims is that offered by Philip Kitcher in the second half of *The Advancement of Science*.[19] In this book, he aspires to offer an alternative both to what he calls

---

[18] For a more extensive elaboration of this point, see Anderson 1995.
[19] Kitcher 1993.

"Legend," the triumphalist account of science associated with whig history of science and some versions of logical empiricism, and the sceptical antirealism of social constructivism. Because this alternative, a "minimal" social epistemology, is intended to integrate the (tenable) historical and sociological insights of the constructivists with the normative concerns of (some) philosophy of science, Kitcher's arguments here are worth studying in some detail.

Kitcher's aim in these sections of the book is to articulate acceptable versions of sociologists' claims and incorporate them into an account that preserves the (his) intuition of the rationality (and cognitive superiority) of science. His reconstructions of the sociologists' positions are more alive to the complexity they have made salient and more cognizant of the philosophical arguments on which they rely than those of Goldman and Haack just considered. Nevertheless, Kitcher, like Goldman, seeks to defend the rationality and cognitive progressivity of science against what he perceives to be the sociologists' attack. There are three elements in Kitcher's positive account: a view of inquiry, a set of normative concepts, and a proposal for what ought to constitute social epistemology.

Kitcher rejects the logical empiricist static representation of science as a set of logically related propositions with a dynamic view of scientific inquiry. Inquiry is a process that takes place in time; successful outcomes of inquiry are the product of struggle and hard work. Theories and hypotheses do not arrive on the scene fully formulated and ready for confirmation or refutation, but are changed and refined in the course of debate. The key notion here is that of a practice. Individuals and communities have practices. Consensus practice, according to Kitcher, consists of a language, a set of questions impersonally identified as the significant problems of a field, a set of accepted statements (or, more generally, representations) together with a justificatory structure, a set of explanatory schemata, a set of paradigms of authority and criteria for identifying authorities, a set of exemplary experiments, observations, and instruments, together with justificatory criteria, and a set of methodological exemplars and principles.[20] Individual practices are just person-specific versions of these components of a practice. Kitcher uses the distinction between individual and consensus practice to account for change and variation in a scientific community. Kitcher-type practices seem to combine elements of the logical empiricist view of theories with elements of Kuhnian paradigms.

The second element of Kitcher's view is a set of normative epistemological concepts to use in providing accounts of success. These are "significance" or "significant truth," "cognitive progress," and what

[20] Ibid., 87–88.

Kitcher calls "the external standard," a criterion of rationality that works with the first two concepts in the assessment of episodes of scientific change. Cognitive progress is articulated in relation to what he takes to be the aim of scientific inquiry: uncovering the structure of nature. As we make cognitive progress we become (more) able to refer to natural kinds and to specify referents (of our natural kind terms) descriptively; to construct a picture of the objective dependencies (inclusive of causal relations) in nature; and to accomplish both goals within a unified framework.[21] Significance is attributed both to questions and to truth to the degree that they contribute to progress so understood.[22]

The third element of the view is Kitcher's proposal for what constitutes social epistemology: the use of decision theory and neoclassical economic modeling to specify optimal organizations of scientific communities (discussed in the appendix).

Kitcher's overall argumentative strategy is to defeat the antirealist and underdeterminationist bases of the constructivists' approach and replace them with historically and sociologically sensitive accounts of reason and observation that nevertheless support or require scientific realism. These accounts are then used to provide retellings of key constructivist case studies that locate them in the following grand narrative of cognitive progress. Individuals and communities start with some view or set of views, either arbitrarily chosen or socially determined. Repeated encounters with nature produce two sorts of convergence: of beliefs among individuals, and of those beliefs and how nature is. Put in terms of practices, this comes out as a convergence of individual practices into a consensus practice, and the convergence of (the referring and descriptive elements of) consensus practice with how nature is. This narrative is occasionally

---

[21] Ibid., 93–95.

[22] David Hull (1988) adopts a similar view of scientific progress. But his commitment to the progressivity of science sits in sharp tension with his antiepistemological selectionism. While both biological and conceptual evolution are locally progressive, he says, only science is (or can be) also globally progressive. Because environments are constantly changing, there can be no goal of perfect adaptedness for all species. By contrast, there is a goal in the case of science and it makes sense, Hull thinks, to see the sciences as progressive in relation to that goal. There are laws of nature and we can meaningfully think of scientific inquiry as moving ever closer to their correct articulation. This is reasonably close to the conception of cognitive progress advanced by Kitcher. But whether one can understand science as progressive within Hull's overall anti-intentional selectionist framework is not clear. Presumably the self-correction provided by checking is supposed to eventuate in progressively more approximate articulations of the laws of nature. But no reason is given for thinking it would do so. For simple selection to work the selective environment would have to include the goal of uncovering laws of nature either as a feature of the scientific community, or of the society that supports the activity of scientists. But, then, why laws of nature? Why not pragmatically useful models, and why only one goal? Hull cannot avoid the epistemology he has so resolutely eschewed.

placed within an origin story which has hominids exercising primitive, basic, cognitive propensities. So, from whatever position we have as a culture or species started, we are making progress toward a unified true account of nature. Kitcher's task is to display the processes that make this possible. In the execution of this task, he is resolutely and explicitly individualistic and psychologistic. That is, he treats individuals, individuals' beliefs, and individuals' change of belief as the primary, or basic, elements of his epistemological ontology. Collective states, or carriers of content other than belief, are treated as causally or definitionally dependent on individuals and their beliefs.

Kitcher's account is certainly more nuanced and sensitive to historical and social dimensions of science than the view he rejects as "Legend." In the end, however, his effort relies on crucial ambiguities in the normative terms he proposes to use as well as on fairly crude readings of the constructivist position. The social in constructivism, for example, is, when it is explained at all, identified with ideological bias or professional (self-)interest. But although this may characterize the meaning of "social" for some sociologists of science—for example, the advocates of the Strong Programme, as we have seen in the prior chapter—it does not characterize the sense of "social" used in microsociological studies. And one of Latour's central arguments against the advocates of the Strong Programme, that it presupposes a distinction between the natural and the social that is itself a legacy of the philosophical tradition they reject, could equally well be directed against Kitcher. I will elaborate these points by reviewing in some detail the principal arguments Kitcher offers to support his view of the progressivity of science against the challenges of the sociologists. My aim is to show that his attachment to a qualitative distinction between the cognitive and the social prevents him from drawing the appropriate lessons from the sociologists and sociologically oriented historians and, thus, undermines his attempt to offer a more philosophically palatable alternative.

Realism and Antirealism

Kitcher discusses two philosophical arguments for antirealism before addressing the constructivists directly: Laudan's historical arguments and van Fraassen's epistemological argument. Although each is in his way hostile to social approaches to science, the work of both of these philosophers has been invoked by scholars attempting to show the relevance of social analysis for understanding science. Regarding Laudan's "pessimistic induction" from the history of theories successful in their time but whose postulates have been later rejected, Kitcher makes two points: the history of science can as easily be read as evidence for an optimistic induction because some successes have persisted; and the appeal to cases in the pessimistic induction must distinguish between "working posits" and "presuppositional posits." Only if it can be shown that a theory's "working" posits (i.e., those essential for making the theory's predictions, etc.) are or were nonreferential can the theory be used as evidence for the pessimistic induction. This response of Kitcher's succeeds in underlining the contingent character of any antirealist or realist theses based on cases and also in raising the bar for any argument of the sort Laudan makes, but it does not refute antirealism or establish scientific realism.[23]

His response to van Fraassen's epistemological arguments focuses on the distinction between observable and nonobservable that supports van Fraassen's antirealism. Kitcher claims that it is not possible to make this distinction without invoking some part of "scientific lore." But if one does invoke any part of scientific lore, then one is committed to observing the standards of scientific explanation set by the scientific picture. If we are so committed, then there's no way to distinguish commitments to the observable things with which science says we have physical interactions from commitments to genes, subatomic particles, and so on with which science also says we have physical interactions. But then observables are not distinguishable from nonobservables in the requisite way and the argument from the distinction between observable and nonobservable subverts itself. This rebuttal of van Fraassen, however, makes some dubious assumptions. It assumes one scientific picture and one set of standards of scientific explanation, such that accepting any part of current science commits one to accepting all of it, and the methodology that supports it. Also, and more crucially, Kitcher's claim that one cannot make a distinction between what is observable and what is not without invoking "scientific lore" assumes that the distinction rests on some scientific basis—for example, that we accept that those things we call obser-

---

[23] In their paper, "The Flight to Reference," Bishop and Stich (1998) take on the argument for scientific realism that Kitcher develops in this section. They identify a pattern of reasoning shared in a number of philosophical programs. This pattern attempts to draw ontological or metaphysical conclusions from premises about reference. Kitcher, for example, claims that some instances of use of "working posits" in past, failed, theories are or were referential in a sense he terms "baptismal"—that is, i.e. used with the intention to refer to something thought to be present regardless how it might be characterized. This encapsulates the first two stages of the "flight" described by Bishop and Stich. The third stage uses the first two as premises in an argument about truth or ontology. But this stage requires reliance, usually tacit, on one of a family of principles about reference. These are principles that connect reference and truth. The flaw in these arguments is that they fail to establish that the characterization of reference in the first stage of the argument satisfies the principle about reference being assumed in the third stage of the argument. Without such an argument, no conclusion about truth or ontology can follow.

vable exist because the best scientific explanation of our sensory experience is that it is the result of causal interactions between ourselves and objects in the external world. But this causal belief is not a deliverance of science but at best a presupposition of scientific investigation of perception. That objects in the external world somehow cause our perception of them is held quite generally and not as a consequence of being convinced by some scientific account. Furthermore, if we look at contemporary science there is not one scientific theory of perception but many—both David Marr's computational theory and J. J. Gibson's ecological theory have their followers among psychologists and philosophers, and theirs are hardly the only ones around.

Kitcher is here, as elsewhere, investing "common sense" or (in the case of the causal theory of perception) a philosophical reconstruction of it with the status of science. This is continuous with an apparent commitment to seeing science and ordinary, everyday, human cognition as qualitatively the same. While logically independent of it, these commitments are more plausible in the individualistic psychologistic framework he adopts than they might otherwise seem, for if some cognitive processes are irreducibly social, then the commitment to qualitative uniformity of all forms of cognition is less plausible. But the assumptions of Kitcher's rebuttal themselves require argumentation if they are successfully to destabilize the epistemological argument for antirealism, or the same argument used more modestly as an argument against scientific realism.[24]

The final sections of the chapter on realism and antirealism are addressed to sociological antirealism. He is concerned, here as in his other discussions of social constructivism, to rebut radical versions of the sociological critique without erasing the roles of history and social interaction in the production of scientific knowledge. The realist thesis he has defended earlier in the chapter does not imply that there are no biases but only that they don't overpower. Thus, he attempts an account that both accords with accounts of the social lives of scientists and supports the claim that we gain knowledge of "independent reality." In this discussion, Kitcher explicitly equates social forces with "bias." Indeed, the section is entitled "Social Interference." Thus, "social force" in this discussion, as in those of so many philosophers, comes to mean anything deflecting from pure pursuit of truth. Any account that sees social interaction as integral to justification is made invisible by this construal of the social, as is any specific meaning the sociologist might have for "social."

---

[24] Fine (1984) offers a "third way" with his Natural Ontological Attitude. He argues against any grand hermeneutical strategies such as scientific realism or scientific antirealism. He recommends instead a local, particularist, approach that does not add a metaphysical fillip to whatever existence claims are made by any given theory.

Kitcher's conception of the social as a foil to the epistemic affects the structure of the argument he develops against the constructivists. He first distinguishes between two theses: the radical and false and the conservative and plausible. The radical and false thesis is that social forces are so strong that the same changes will occur in individual practice no matter what the stimuli are. The fact of disagreement among scientists, he says, shows this is false. Of course, he must presume here (highly counterfactually) that only one social force acting equally on all is involved. Otherwise, the social theorist can invoke multiple, conflicting social forces to explain disagreement. The plausible conservative thesis has two parts. Kitcher proposes a distinction between *framework* and *filling*, understanding by *framework* the general theoretical frame within which some bit of research is pursued and by *filling* the articulations of that framework achieved through experiment and observation under the guidance of that theoretical frame. The plausible thesis, then, is that where social forces are understood as affecting the framework of inquiry, while nature fills in the details, social forces may be so strong as to prevent different effects of different stimuli produced in individual practice from being absorbed into consensus practice. In cruder terms, it is plausible that social forces reinforcing a particular framework might be so strong as to prevent disconfirmations of elements of the framework (or of the filling) evident to some individual(s) from being generally accepted as such. Against the background of this thesis, Kitcher articulates the ideal—no framework is so inviolable that input from nature cannot displace it—and claims the compatibility of part of the plausible view of social effects (i.e., that they affect frameworks) with his concept of cognitive progress. Social forces (including such innocuous forces as tradition and education) supporting a framework of inquiry may resist the truth, but not indefinitely. This represents an initial articulation of the integration of the historical and sociological with the philosophical and normative.

With this integrative alternative to what he regards as implausible forms of constructivism in place, Kitcher can turn his attention to cases. Of Latour and Woolgar's study of the work at Roger Guillemin's laboratory at the Salk Institute, he says that their claim that the structure of TRF (thyrotropin releasing factor) was constructed, that "out-thereness [or reality] is a consequence of scientific work," requires a demonstration (not provided) that the structure would have turned out the same no matter what nature had done. Absent this demonstration, the case of TRF as so far described by Latour and Woolgar supports neither the strong (and implausible) thesis nor the weaker (but plausible) thesis. Kitcher's earlier discussion of the reception of Darwinism is advanced as a model for the treatment of any other cases. The sociologist is first imagined as claiming that the cognitive propensities present in nineteenth-century naturalists yield no resolution of the question whether organisms are related by descent with modification, and that the actual resolution was brought about by social causes. Kitcher's alternative involves three steps: articulate ideal experiments and clear statements of the outcomes realists and constructivists would expect;[25] bring people's actual behavior in different contexts to bear on studying the episode;[26] and, if there are general considerations (like underdetermination, which he addresses in the following chapter) that suggest a decision might not or could not have been determined through a recourse to nature, consider whether there are reliable processes that would deliver a verdict.

Read as an appeal for more thorough case study work, this model has much to recommend it. As a rebuttal of the sociologist, however, it, again, rests on problematic assumptions. This response, first of all, assumes that when Latour and Woolgar say that the structure of TRF was constructed in the laboratory, they mean that there is nothing answering to that structural specification in the real world. Though possible, this reading is not the only, and certainly not the most fruitful, way to interpret their constructivist claims. Second, Kitcher's response assumes that Latour and Woolgar are claiming that cognitive practices are insufficient to settle disagreements and that social factors bring about an end to dispute. But Latour and Woolgar may be better read as claiming not that our cognitive practices are inadequate, but that our characterization of cognitive practices is insufficient to capture what is going on in the laboratory. They could be read, that is, as claiming that our (cognitivist philosophers') characterizations of cognitive practices cannot sustain the conclusion that scientific inquiry ultimately succeeds in getting at the real structure of the natural world. (And because only scientific inquiry can tell us whether there is such a thing as the real structure of the natural world, those characterizations make presuppositions that they are not entitled to make.) Third, the response assumes that present judgments regarding the availability at the time of a decisive process are relevant to historical understanding of a particular episode. But what can be concluded from the availability of "reliable processes that would deliver a verdict" in the case (e.g., as to whether the structure of TRF is really x,y,z, or whether organisms are really related by descent with modification)? Indeed, what does the assertion of their availability and reliability and of the inputs from nature rest on? If Kitcher's alternative model is an idealized reconstruction of the argumentation, the sociologist can reply that it is at best partial if it fails to address such matters as how the

---

[25] This can be read in several ways depending on whose experiments are understood, the scientists' or the historians'. The ambiguity is not important to the outcome of the argument, however.

[26] This, too is ambiguous. The protagonists' behavior in different contexts, or that of others who are in different contexts, could be meant.

reliable process became available, why it was deemed reliable, and so on. The sociologist is not the only protagonist who must give a more detailed story. Furthermore, the availability of a process is no guarantee of its employment. It does not follow that Darwin's argument in *The Origin of Species* was decisive because, from a logical or epistemological point of view, it had the capability of being so.

Even more problematic is the earlier noted framework Kitcher imposes on this entire discussion and which forces the interpretation he thinks must be refuted. Because the social (as bias) is represented as working against the true, and the true is identified with nature, any constructive role that the social might play is eclipsed. But, in the form of bits of organic or inorganic matter, nature does not, cannot, act alone in the laboratory. The "out-thereness is a consequence" thesis of Latour and Woolgar could be interpreted quite differently than as either the radical or the conservative thesis Kitcher is concerned with. For example, a more fruitful interpretation is that the end of controversy and stabilization of the structure as x,y,z are a consequence of scientific work, which includes the availability of a chemical theory classifying molecules, their constituents, and interactions; having people in the lab who know how to bring the theory to bear on a substance; having or developing reagents of the kind necessary to isolate or break down the molecules of the substance; having or developing a community beyond the lab interested in the molecule and placed to make use of a characterization of its structure; and so forth. In other words, it may mean that the information necessary to characterize the structure of TRF as being a certain sequence of amino acids is not sufficient by itself to become part of scientific knowledge but needs a whole social and institutional structure in order to be deployed. The sociologist would reject Kitcher's plausible thesis, arguing that it is precisely the provision of "filling" that requires sociological explanation. The challenge is to see how the social and the cognitive interact or even fuse, not to engage in a partition of effects. And, to use Kitcher's language of effects and practices, why can we not also see the social as facilitating the selective absorption into consensus practice of some (nature-induced) differences in individual practices over others? If the social includes the pragmatic as well as the ideological, this seems an equally plausible view of the role of the social, but one that is eclipsed by the Manichaean representation of the social and the cognitive that Kitcher favors.

Underdetermination

Chapter 6 on "Dissolving Rationality" and chapter 7 on "The Experimental Method" together develop an apparatus designed to undermine and deflect sociological or constructivist arguments that rely on the logical underdetermination of hypotheses by data. Like the chapter on realism and antirealism they contain much unexceptionable common sense, but they, too, fail to establish the cognitive progressivist thesis or to rebut constructivist alternatives.

Kitcher proposes that rationality be analyzed as applying to change of belief (as distinct from the content of beliefs) and articulates what he calls "the external standard" (ES), which will be invoked in offering alternative models of debate closure and of solutions to underdetermination situations. The topic of controversy closure was of great interest in social studies of science during the 1980s because scientific controversies were thought to offer a valuable window into the true character of scientific inquiry, and scientific debate and controversy are crucial elements of particular or local underdetermination stories. Thus, an account of rational belief change that is to replace the radical constructivist accounts of scientific change must apply to the cases of closure invoked as evidence. According to ES, a shift from one individual practice to another is rational if and only if

> the process through which the shift was made has a success ratio at least as high as that of any other process used by human beings (ever) across the set of epistemic contexts that includes all possible combinations of initial practices possible for human beings and possible stimuli (given the world as it is and the characteristics of human recipients).[27]

After articulating rationalist (right methods) and antirationalist (social power) models of debate closure, Kitcher offers his compromise. In the early phases of a debate, the processes undergone by the ultimate victors may be no better designed for promoting cognitive progress than those of rivals. Nevertheless, debates are closed

> when there emerges in the community a widely available argument encapsulating a process for modifying practice which, when judged by means of the External Standard (and other standards) is markedly superior in promoting cognitive progress than other processes. Power accrues to the victor in virtue of the integration of this process into the thinking of members of the community.[28]

In other words, at the outset of a controversy, positions, favored methods, criteria, and the like may be influenced by all sorts of factors. Controversy about a domain, however, is resolved by the emergence of a

---

[27] Kitcher 1993, 189. Kitcher acknowledges that this articulation of the External Standard is too strong and proposes relaxing it to specify specific contexts of comparison, rather than including all possible human practices.
[28] Ibid., 201.

process that is superior at revealing natural kinds and objective dependencies in the domain. Those who have embraced or advocated the process achieve power in their communities as a consequence of the adoption of the process by community members rather than vice versa.

But this model, which is social at the outset and rationalist at the conclusion, raises a number of questions. I concentrate on two. One problem is how it is to be interpreted. Is it normative or descriptive? On neither of these alternative readings is the model going to be persuasive to the sociologist. If it is understood as a descriptive thesis, then the relevant evidence is historical and sociological. Disputes between the sociologist and the philosopher must be settled by more mucking about in the archives, more observation of live controversies. Mere articulation of an alternative to the model attributed to the sociologist is not enough to persuade her that the model is realized. In any case, one wants an account of how the superiority of a process relative to ES is determined in order to apply the model. If it is understood as a normative thesis, that is, as a model of how debates should close, then the sociologist can argue that real cases do not satisfy it, and that it is therefore of no help in understanding the resolution of actual controversies. And still, one requires an account of how the superiority of a process is to be determined in a noncircular way in order to use the model to distinguish the cases of rational debate closure from the irrational or nonrational ones. How, for example, is it determined that a process is revealing genuine natural kinds and objective dependencies rather than spurious kinds and illusory dependencies? Neither on a descriptive nor on a normative reading does this model put to rest the questions raised by the sociologist.

But perhaps the proposal of the compromise model is analytic in character. Two possibilities suggest themselves. First, what counts as debate closure is the emergence of an argument or process that is markedly superior to alternatives. This, however, can not be right, because the emergence and availability of an argument or process do not guarantee its widespread adoption, even if it is superior (supposing we know how to determine this). Second, what counts as debate closure is the integration of a markedly superior argument or process into the thinking of the members of the community. This seems closer to right. But notice that this interpretation foregrounds a social process: integration into the thinking of members of a community. Surely this *is* what the end of controversy consists in. But presumably both good and bad (relative to ES) processes can be integrated. To use Kitcher's language, we may have rational or irrational debate closure. The rational one integrates the superior process. But simply stipulating this fails to specify how marked superiority is ascertained. Without such specification, it is an open question whether there have ever been any cases of rational debate closure.

But this is just what Kitcher wanted to settle with the compromise model.

The second main problem lies with the assumption that good or ES-satisfying cognitive practices yield a unique resolution to debate. The External Standard itself, however, offers no assurance that any single argument to a single conclusion will or ought to emerge, or any reason to think that there is a single set of cognitive goals that will uniquely select an argument as superior. Debate may come to an end with more than one process capable of promoting cognitive progress, and the fact that a community might come to closure regarding an argument or its conclusion via processes we judge to satisfy some criterion of epistemic success means very little for a claim of unique correctness.[29] There may be another equally (potentially) successful argument that drops out of contention for reasons other than epistemic ones. This doesn't mean that the closure, or end of controversy, is *ir*rational or *a*rational, but that factors in addition to the epistemic rationality enshrined in the compromise model may lie behind the emergence of a theory or approach as the consensus view. This is enough for most sociologists. In order to complete his rebuttal of the sociological approach to scientific knowledge, then, Kitcher must hold the underdeterminationist challenge at bay.

The version of the underdetermination problem that engages Kitcher's attention is the one attributed to Duhem. A Duhemian predicament is a situation in which (1) a scientist or community of scientists S accepts a hypothesis H and accepts auxiliary assumption A; (2) H and A together imply observation O; but (3) following normal observation procedures, S would accept ~O (not O) on presentation of the relevant stimulus (e.g., performance of the relevant experiment). The predicament consists in not knowing (logically) which of the three possible producers of the contradiction to modify: H, A, or the procedures underwriting acceptance of ~O. Analysts, such as David Bloor, have exploited underdetermination to argue that it leaves scientists attached to H, free to replace A or to blame the observational procedures for the untoward result. Thus, any H can, in principle, escape falsification. Kitcher's general response to underdetermination is that, while it is a global, logical feature of empirical reasoning, individual cases can be satisfactorily resolved. Kitcher's treatment of underdetermination is intended to acknowledge the logical point, while blocking any value this might have for what he understands to be the sociologists' claims.

[29] Furthermore, Kitcher, relying on evolutionary hypotheses of dubious credibility, is assuming a high degree of cognitive uniformity in this exposition. Variations in metaphysics, cosmology, or politics are not seen as generating cognitive diversity that would obstruct comparisons across rival theoretical frameworks.

The principle tool Kitcher introduces to accomplish this task is the concept of the *cost* of amending an underdetermination situation by dropping one of the auxiliary assumptions A_i (which includes here assumptions about the reliability of supporting chains of reasoning for A_i for which no error can be diagnosed). This cost is measured by the number of apparently acceptable explanations and predictions that have to be sacrificed if A_i is dropped. The notion of cost enables Kitcher to restate conditions of falsification: when H and A_{1-n} imply O, $\sim$O counts as a crucial falsification of H if the observation rules of prior practice require acceptance of $\sim$O, and (for any admissible cost function) the costs of any amendment to A_{1-n} are greater than the costs of abandoning H. By the same token, underdetermination arises if (1) for the same admissible cost function, there are equally good alternative ways to amend the set {H, A, $\sim$0} to make it consistent, or (2) there are different admissible cost functions that single out rival emendations as optimal. Kitcher argues that underdetermination is always eliminable when the costs of abandoning assumptions are accounted for.

Regarding the claim that the first case always holds—that is, that there are always equally good alternatives to the one chosen in the face of underdetermination—Kitcher points out that choosing such hypothetical alternatives is only cost-free if one overlooks the fact that observation rules and auxiliary assumptions are constrained by the explanatory dependencies and views of projectibility present in prior practice. If one understands these constraints (if one is properly historical), one sees that there is no quick argument to widespread underdetermination. Kitcher is certainly right to point out the dependence of reasoning or evidential relations on the fabric of theory enshrined in current practice. But while this may reduce the number of realistically possible selections, it does not guarantee that there is one best. No one supposes that underdetermination means judgment is free of constraints. It means that the constraints of data are not sufficient to compel judgment. The relevance of the logical fact of underdetermination is, then, not that scientists must make, for the most part, arbitrary or venal decisions, but that analysts of particular episodes must attend to *how* the logical gap is bridged—for example, to what assumptions are used to confer evidential relevance to data. To put this in Kitcher's terminology, analysts must attend to *how* the costs of amending rules and auxiliaries are calculated. Calculation of costs may include social considerations and may be accomplished socially. To say that costs must be assessed is not yet to eliminate the social.

Regarding the possibility of alternative cost functions as in the second case, Kitcher acknowledges that while there can in principle be such situations, the resulting inconclusiveness is temporary and is resolved through the "provision by the victor of success in the terms demanded by the rival." That is, in cases of multiple contesting solutions, debate eventually comes to an end, as described in Kitcher's compromise version of closure. ES-satisfying reasoning about all of the elements in the situation (hypotheses, observations, assumptions, constraints, and cost functions) ultimately wins the day. But the performance of ES-satisfying reasoning does not guarantee the end of debate—that is, the claim that inconclusiveness is temporary, that ES-satisfying reasoning will converge on a single set of cost functions, is an empirical claim in need of empirical support. Kitcher gives no arguments to show that ES-satisfying reasoning ultimately wins the day. Furthermore, how should "success in the terms demanded by the rival" be understood? Why is this not a social process in which cognitive agents assess the multiple dimensions of their differing cost functions and negotiate as to what will count as terms of success. And, again, why can cost functions not have social and pragmatic dimensions? Kitcher's analysis shows that underdetermination cannot be used to support an unconstrained relativism; it does not show that all underdetermination situations can in principle be resolved in favor of one of a set of rivals.

One of the appealing features of Kitcher's proposed solution to claims of global underdetermination is the exhibition of the sheer hard work and the time that are involved in scientific inquiry. But not even hard work and additional analytical apparatus can support the kind of progressivist story he wants to tell. As I argued earlier, Kitcher's compromise model of debate closure does not rule out the possibility of more than one argument satisfying the external standard. The examples discussed throughout involve an outcome in which one theory or theoretical approach emerges victorious over rivals, so one could say that Kitcher has proposed an alternative account of iconic examples for the constructivists, rather than trying to give a model that holds for all cases of controversy. But the prescriptive interpretation of his model assumes that all cases will resemble those he has discussed. Furthermore, bringing in the costs of amending elements of prior practice, while it does make for a more realistic account of the work of resolving local underdetermination situations, assumes that prior practice is sufficiently tight and uniform so that costs will be similarly assessed by individual cognitive agents, or that there is a way to constrain admissible cost functions if agents are cognitively diverse. Kitcher's models for closing controversy or resolving underdetermination situations involve the invocation or assumption of a uniquely correct solution, whether in the form of a process for modifying belief or for assessing costs and cost functions in the case of multiple processes. But what the models fail to do is show how such a solution is or could be arrived at. In particular, they fail to show that such solutions are not achieved socially. Kitcher's implicit equation of the social with

(distorting) bias, and hence with the noncognitive—that is, his acceptance of the rational-social dichotomy—leads him to overlook gaps in his
account and to assume that the cognitive account he does provide eliminates the social. But if the social includes more than individual bias, he
has not succeeded.

Kitcher's account of scientific inquiry is certainly richer and more sensitive to the details of historical cases than those of many philosophers
who simply overlay models of (good) reasoning on highly abstract
accounts of historical episodes. But because he reduces the sociologists'
view to claims about bias, he has not succeeded in refuting the sociologists' arguments. Moreover his version of a rational, but socially and historically sensitive, account fails to ground the claim that science does
make cognitive progress. There are several reasons for this failure.

One is his conception of cognitive progress itself, that is, the idea that
progress is progress toward the goal of uncovering the structure of
nature. This presupposes, of course, that there is such a thing as *the*
structure of nature. For the squeamish about metaphysics, he offers unification as the goal, suggesting that the structure will be whatever the
unified account says it is.[30] Monism, then, is a given. But the belief in
monism is not grounded in any empirical data, but serves as an a priori
condition of adequacy for his accounts of scientific reasoning. The a priori nature of the commitment to monism can be seen in his defense of
his system against an imagined skeptic in the final section of the chapter
on "The Experimental Philosophy."

The skepticism he feels it important to address is one that claims that,
"when judged from the scientific perspective to which they have given
rise, the methods actually employed by scientists are too weak to show
the correctness of that perspective."[31] There are two stages to Kitcher's
answer. The first locates scientific inquiry as a natural continuation of
primitive thought processes of our hominid ancestors. Contemporary science is the outcome of repeated modifications of some aboriginal set of
categories and explanatory schemata achieved via successive application
of inductive and eliminative strategies subject to the principle of unification. And even without engaging in detailed historical study, we have
ordinary grounds for thinking that the varieties within our ordinary clas-
sificatory groups—for example, the factors affecting the behavior of met-
als and the colors of bird plumage—are well understood. I can only read
this as saying that contemporary science in the form of particle or atomic
physics and genetics (or maybe the neo-Darwinian synthesis) is roughly

[30] This does sound rather close to Latour and Woolgar's (1986) view that "out-thereness
is a consequence, and not a cause, of scientific activity." (Cf. 1986, 25–31.)
[31] Kitcher 1993, 302.

correct and represents the stage of belief to which our processes of self-correction practiced through the aeons have led.[32] The second stage is to point out that we can "give an account of scientific reasoning that resolves those situations in which underdetermination is supposed to be present." So, we have ordinary reasons for thinking that the sciences we rely on now provide a correct understanding of processes in which we are interested, and an account of reasoning that shows how convergence around such correct understandings and the practices that have produced them is achieved.

Are skeptical worries really to be resolved by these means? (Should the skeptic fold up her tent and sign on for a position in the research management unit that will deploy the apparatus of chapter 8?) Certainly this depends on just what the skeptical worries are. First of all, it is not clear what the real question is. Is the skeptic supposed to be concerned about particular scientific theories? If so, the correct response is to point to the practices and procedures through which the particular theories were developed and address any specific evidential challenges. But this localized doubt is not a philosophical form of doubt, nor is the answer needed a philosophical answer. To be concerned about particular theories is just to wonder, in the context of some evidentiary standards, whether they meet those standards. Skepticism about science grounded in either antirealist arguments or underdetermination considerations is not doubt that a given bit of research satisfies evidentiary standards or that scientific practice generally satisfies its own evidentiary standards. Rather it is doubt that science satisfies evidentiary standards articulated by philosophers or doubt that anything can be concluded from satisfaction of scientific or philosophical evidentiary standards apart from the fact that they are satisfied. Bootstrapping from parts of physics and biology and the cost-sensitive resolution of underdetermination can not help us reach anything more stirring. But the sense that they should is what motivates Kitcher's analysis. Thus, he accepts the presupposition of his imagined skeptic's question, instead of challenging the idea that in order to legitimate scientific inquiry we must demonstrate that the methods of science are sufficient to show that the scientific perspective is correct.

Why should we demand of science that its methods be adequate not only for producing accounts of nature that meet certain specified criteria but for proving that those methods are the correct way to produce such accounts? Kitcher demands this because he wants to tell a story of science that is not just about the self-correcting procedures of science but

---

[32] If this is a correct reading, I wonder if these achievements of modern science are supposed to be direct descendants of animism and other forms of belief attributed to early humans. And whether they and contemporary science are to be judged by exactly the same criteria, functionally as well as empirically.

what he terms an optimistic story, without resorting to suspect transcendental principles. This optimistic story is one of self-correction leading to progress in charting the true divisions and recognizing the genuine explanatory dependencies in nature. He is, that is, a philosophical naturalist, albeit one committed to a progressivist account of human rationality. But his conception of rationality is articulated against the background of scientific monism, such that rationality that achieves cognitive progress is rationality capable of ascertaining a uniquely correct account of the natural world. He is not just assuming that the aforementioned parts of science are roughly correct, but that they (or close approximations of them) will be integrated into a unified account that captures *the* structure of nature. I have argued, by contrast, that once we remove that element from Kitcher's definitions of rational procedures nothing in them guarantees that rationality will arrive at a unique or uniquely correct account. It is a quasi-theological commitment to monism that leads Kitcher to drive out the social, but as I argue later, only the social can rescue rationality (and realism) once metaphysics and theology are abandoned.

If cognitive processes and practices applied to the world as it presents itself to us cannot guarantee monism, absent a prior commitment to unificationism, and communities nevertheless tend to converge to one theory or approach, then there is more to that story than self-correction, even self-correction as elaborately described as in these chapters. For example, the purported successes (in physics and biology) that are supposed to show that there has been progress from hominid ignorance to genuine knowledge may be limited to those aspects of the phenomena that are of interest to us (or those of us relying on contemporary Western physics and biology). Our resulting ability to predict and manipulate may be a function of our intervening in processes of whose fundamental nature we (or the scientists who are our surrogates) remain ignorant, even while guided by nature's response at a phenomenal level.[33] And if communities tolerate more than one approach or multiple theories of common phenomena, then a story that depends on unification cannot account for the whole of scientific practices.[34]

CONCLUSION

Kitcher's account of reason is intended to show how cognitive practice narrowly construed eventually achieves the best theory (the one that

---

[33] Fundamental here may mean at a deeper level, or of greater complexity.

[34] For accounts of specific areas of inquiry in which pluralism is either the norm or the best resolution of debate among multiple approaches, see Cartwright 1995; Ereshevsky 1992; Waters 1991; Dupré 1993; and further discussion in chapter 8.

belongs in the progressive lineage). I have argued that his account fails to show this and that his attempts to control the social only obliterate it. Goldman and Haack share Kitcher's view of the rational, the social, and of their relation to the each other. The rational is truth seeking (or cognitively progressive), while the social is equated not just with bias, but with what deflects from truth. A rational belief change is one in which reason overcomes the social. This dichotomy shapes their interpretation of the sociologists' claims and their responses to them. Their commitment to cognitive individualism further reinforces the assumption that cognitive processes are always opposed to social processes and obscures the possibility that some cognitive processes may *be* social processes. But this strong social epistemology, already advanced in other philosophical circles, is the most fruitful way to read the work of the sociologists. It is also the best way to understand the cognitive practices of the sciences.

Appendixes

Goals and Significance

KITCHER TAKES on Laudan's reticulation model of scientific change in order both to defeat the view that the goals of scientific inquiry are internal to scientific practice, and hence adjustable parts of the network, and to support his alternative view that there is one overarching goal of scientific inquiry, which serves as an external criterion of evaluation. Laudan proposes that Kuhn's notion of a paradigm be replaced by the notion of a network constituted of three sorts of elements: substantive claims, methodological prescriptions, and goals. Scientific change is a matter of adjusting any one of the elements of the network in order to preserve its overall consistency. This gradualist model of scientific change is intended as a successor to the cyclic revolutionary model of Kuhn. Kitcher claims that even if we accept Laudan's picture of the constituents of inquiry, the need for consistency is insufficient to explain the kinds of change that actually occur. If consistency were the only desideratum, then one could just eliminate offending elements and maintain a minimal set, instead of replacing or adding members. Because change is characterized by replacement and addition, something besides consistency must be driving the process. Kitcher claims that one must suppose enduring, context-independent goals to explain the kinds of change that take place. Change in formulation of aims can be understood as "expressions of the enduring goal of discovering significant truth in light of changing beliefs about what is significant, what nature is like, and so forth." [35]

There are two difficulties here. First of all, if one grants the point that merely preserving consistency in the tripartite set is insufficient to explain change, this still does not indicate what more is required. Why could not the goal be self-perpetuation of a form of intellectual play, a form that requires a rich and complex theoretical matrix rather than a stripped down one? Or one can put this sociologically—that the goal is self-perpetuation of a community of designated inquirers whose size is justified by the richness and complexity of the scientific world view it is their task to elaborate. The conclusion that scientific change must be understood as successive expressions of the enduring goal of discovering significant truth rests on a false dichotomy. Heretical as the alternatives

[35] Kitcher 1993, 160.

just articulated may sound in a philosophical context, once scientific inquiry is located in history and society, the philosopher cannot simply ignore them. But there are also problems with Kitcher's use of significance. Kitcher wishes to insist that the goal of inquiry, that is, the achievement of significant truth, remains the same through change, but that *beliefs* about what is significant can change. This formulation is ambiguous and provokes a dilemma. If the second proposition means that the particular kinds of truth held to satisfy the criterion of significance change, then more needs to be said about significance in order to make sense of the claim that a kind of truth does or does not meet it. But this more will make significance too specific and hence itself subject to change or challenge.[36] Alternatively, the concept of significance may be itself variable and plural, so that while there is general agreement that significance is aimed at, there are multiple context-specific articulations of what significance consists of. Thus, significance is either too empty or too particular and context-relative to function as the external context- or practice-independent goal required here.

Managing Scientific Communities

PROGRESS AND THE INVISIBLE HAND

Goldman and Kitcher, along with David Hull, agree that the pursuit of credit (recognition for one's scientific work) is a feature of science. They further agree that the desire of individual scientists for credit, far from showing science to be as corruptible as any other human institution, can enhance the pursuit of truth. While Hull thinks that attention to the reward structure of science makes epistemology unnecessary, Kitcher and Goldman seek to incorporate it into epistemology through the use of economic models. This is a reasonable enough procedure if one thinks the maximization of utilities or desired consequences is illuminated by economic, or more precisely, decision-theoretic, modeling. What the decision-theoretic approach does is to treat both credit and truth as utilities and then show how the constraints of the scientific situation can have the consequence that actions designed to maximize credit also maximize truth. This kind of demonstration is a part of the general enterprise Goldman and Kitcher assign to social epistemology. Kitcher says that

> the general problem of social epistemology . . . is to identify the properties of
> epistemically well-designed epistemic systems, i.e. to specify conditions

[36] Kitcher seems to think that treating unification as an overriding cognitive goal will neutralize this problem, but then much more argument regarding unification is required.

under which a group of individuals, operating according to various rules for modifying their individual practices, succeed through their interactions in generating a progressive sequence of consensus practices.[37]

Goldman's characterization is similar:

> The proper domain of social epistemology ... is the social processes and institutional provisions that standardly affect belief formation. ... social epistemology should evaluate various social processes and institutional arrangements in terms of their promotion of true rather than false beliefs.[38]

These descriptions of social epistemology indicate that epistemology is, for both authors, a normative enterprise—distinguishing those social processes and structures that enhance the acquisition of true beliefs or cognitive progress from those that do not. Goldman's approach is essentially a formalization of Hull's: a system that rewards individuals who contribute toward the attainment of systemwide goals needs only individuals motivated by the rewards and does not require that they be motivated directly by the goals. Kitcher's approach is more elaborate, but it enables identification of the limitations of their shared conception of social epistemology. He focuses on two general areas: issues of trust and authority and issues connected with the distribution of effort—that is, the division of cognitive labor. Both are treated from the point of view of individual scientists deciding on a course of action and from the point of view of communities. In addition, Kitcher distinguishes between epistemically pure agents and epistemically sullied agents. Epistemically pure agents are cognitive agents whose primary goal is "to reach an epistemically valuable state," whereas sullied agents are cognitive agents driven by other than epistemic goals, such as priority or credit. This enables him to show that the issues are decidable (though differently decided) whether communities consist of epistemically pure or sullied agents.

TRUST AND AUTHORITY

In their interactions with each other scientists (must) accept claims made by some of their peers and ignore those of others. Given multiple claims for one's assent, how are those worthy of trust distinguishable from those not so worthy? The simplest case consists of an epistemically pure agent deciding whether to rely on the work of another, the potential authority. The agent's goal is to reach an epistemically valuable state. While this is

---

[37] Kitcher 1993, 303.
[38] Goldman and Cox 1994, 190.

left uncharacterized, let us say it is an answer to some question Q. The factors that are brought into the calculation include the agent's total resources, the resources needed to answer Q, the cost of acquiring those resources directly, the cost of acquiring them indirectly (i.e., from the potential authority), the agent's error rate (or reliability), the potential authority's error rate, and the probability that a correct answer to Q will be deployed at the use stage (the value of a correct answer). If the agent is sullied, that is, is motivated by goals other than epistemic ones, such as a desire to be first with the answer, then additional factors must be brought into the calculation, for example, how many others are expected also to rely on the potential authority. The formula will recommend different strategies for agents who either assess the error rates differently, or have different levels of resources, or both. Kitcher considers a number of different scenarios and concerns about them, showing how to adjust the formulas appropriately. For example, it is possible to set parameters in such a way that even in situations in which some individuals wield a high degree of unearned authority (on the basis of power, name recognition, institutional affiliation), the outcome of decisions taken by agents in those situations can foster cognitive progress.

The community-level question that he uses the authority formula to address is what the proper response should be to announcements that challenge the current consensus. Individual options include adopting the challenging result, ignoring its announcement, or attempting to replicate the result in question. A community strategy will be the assignment of each member of the community to one of the options. In the simplest case, one replication is sufficient for all members to adopt the result and for it to be absorbed into consensus practice. Then the community's options are that everyone ignore the result (I), that everyone modify their views to adopt the result (M), or that one person attempt to replicate it while the rest ignore it (R). I will be preferable to M when the community has a low error rate and the value of the finding's being true is also low. R is preferable to M when the reliability of the replicator is high, and is preferable to I if the challenger is reliable, the replicator is reliable, and the cost of replicating is not too high. I is preferable to R if the challenger is not reliable. Once the structure of the simple case is clear, it becomes possible to demonstrate more complicated decision problems, such as how many individuals to assign to the job of replication. Kitcher concludes:

> The exact relation between the actual distribution of effort and the community optimum will depend on the values of various parameters, but even in communities [characterized by intuitively worrying forms of authority], it is quite possible for those parameters to be set in ways that make for good

epistemic design. To understand how well a particular community is likely to do, one cannot rest with simple descriptions of it as "authoritarian" or "individualistic." There is no substitute for looking at the types of models I have surveyed.[39]

In spite of the exuberance of calculation, it is still a little difficult to understand how this apparatus should be deployed. Kitcher does not, for example, apply the models to the case studies discussed earlier in his book. We do not learn how the debates about natural selection in the nineteenth century are illuminated by the formulas for attributing or withholding authority, or what Guillemin and Schalley might have gained from taking Kitcher's decision-theoretic approach to replication decisions. This leaves us free to think about how the calculations might be deployed in the near future. One possibility, that implied by the language of "assignment," is that there is a centralized decision-making system. But so far as I know this exists only in Bacon's New Atlantis. The closest approximation is national funding bodies, and they depend on proposals for research coming up from the "grass roots" (and in the United States, at least, are themselves multiple and decentralized). There is no doubt that funding bodies engage in some kind of cost-benefit calculations in making funding decisions. It would be interesting to know what goals they try to optimize and whether their decision making is adequately modeled by Kitcher's formulas. Otherwise these models apply to individual decision makers. Thus, for example, there is a formula for an individual to use in deciding whether or not to replicate a challenging result. Depending on whether the agent is pure or sullied, various parameters will be differently weighted. It is not made clear how different individuals maximizing their desired outcomes contributes to the attainment of systemwide goals. Although there are certainly distributions of parameter settings that could achieve this, it is not clear how those distributions are to be achieved, and what we can say if they are not.[40] Even more problematically, Kitcher does not explain how to obtain parameter settings whose correct estimation is crucial to the utility of these models. The initial calculation of trust requires an estimate of the resources needed to answer question Q. But a reliable estimate of this parameter is only possible for very well-defined and restricted questions articulated in the context of an assumed theoretical framework and for which the general shape of the answer is already anticipated.

[39] Kitcher 1993, 342.

[40] A Panglossian epistemologist of the kind envisioned by Steve Fuller would recommend that one determine just what is maximized by the system in order to learn what its goals are, rather than imposing one of one's own or relying on participant avowals.

THE DIVISION OF COGNITIVE LABOR

The conceit of this section is that it is possible to find optimal community strategies for dealing with unclarity or difference of opinion. A community that "is prepared to hedge its bets is likely to do better than one that moves quickly to a state of uniform opinion."[41] How is this hedging of bets to be achieved? That is, in the language of earlier chapters, how can premature closure be avoided? Kitcher maintains that if all the agents in a community are epistemically pure, it is likely that the outcomes of separate decisions will eventuate in an epistemologically homogeneous community. The solution to maintenance of diversity lies in organizing a reward system that will encourage the epistemically sullied to participate. As long as there are conditions under which the rewards of success outweigh the risks of being wrong for enough participants, initially implausible ideas can get a run. And as long as the overall goals of the system remain the attainment of truth, then the choices of individuals will be constrained and chaos will not rule. This much was claimed by David Hull. What does Kitcher's more formal treatment show?

The specific situations he addresses include choice of method and choice of theory and within each of these, individual decision problems and community decision problems. Formulas are offered for the epistemically pure and the epistemically sullied, as well as for hybrids. Suppose there are two methods that might work in a given research context. There will be some parameter settings that, in epistemically sullied communities, produce stable and attainable distributions of effort that offer a higher probability of community success than the distributions in epistemically pure communities. Theory choice is treated similarly. The theory that solves all its problems is correct and is the one that individuals and the community should choose. But as long as there are unsolved problems and two theories, then the optimum is a stable distribution of effort between them.

The condition of two (or more) competing methods or theories is a classic underdetermination situation. But Kitcher does not show how the decision-theoretic calculations should affect our assessment of the underdetermination situations he discusses earlier in the book. Indeed, there he leaves the impression that ES-satisfying reasoning is sufficient to resolve underdetermination situations. It is not clear what these calculations regarding the distribution of effort are intended to add to the earlier discussion. Furthermore, as is the case in the authority formulas, except in the most pedestrian sorts of cases, the actual calculations

---

[41] Kitcher 1993, 344.

require that we have knowledge we are not likely to have. In the case of the division of labor, this is the probability that for any given number of individuals or resources devoted to it, a method will arrive at the correct answer to a problem or question.

WHY GO NEOCLASSICAL?

Both sets of discussion are characterized by an odd distinction between the pure and the sullied.[42] The pure epistemic agent not only is not motivated by greed or ambition, but does not bring any metaphysical assumptions to her work either. But this seems just to replicate the false dichotomy Susan Haack relies on between honest and value-laden inquiry.[43] To take only the most salient example from Western science, I see no incompatibility between metaphysical commitments either to reductionist simplicity or to antireductionist complexity and the desire to attain "an epistemically valuable state." But as long as both of these metaphysical positions are represented in the community, there will be some diversity, probably sufficient to prevent closure on theories or methods incorporating those metaphysical biases. That both metaphysical perspectives are also sustained in the culture at large by their perceived social implications is irrelevant to the motives of any given individual. Furthermore, the social views with which those perspectives are associated may also be held as truths. The distinction between the pure and the sullied (or the honest and the value-laden) suggests that either inquirers have no preconceptions or they are deliberately trying to insinuate their social views where they do not belong (or to advance their careers). This reinscription of cognitive Manichaeanism presupposes a simplistic account of cognitive agency and misunderstands what social and cultural analysts, including feminist scholars, of the sciences have been claiming: that values and social preconceptions are embedded in scientific concepts and practices and are carried, for the most part, unconsciously by scientific practitioners.

One might say, on Kitcher's behalf (and Goldman's), that what they have demonstrated is that cognitive progress does not require that all of the individual members of a community be motivated by a desire for truth, that even in the unrealistically simple model cases to which decision-theoretic calculation can be applied one can find parameter settings in which individuals differently motivated or communities consisting of

---

[42] Deconstructionists, cultural anthropologists, and psychoanalysts could make much of the distinction whose self-evidence is assumed here. I leave those forms of interpretation to the practitioners of those disciplines.

[43] Haack 1996.

individuals differently motivated, do as well or better at achieving cognitive progress than individuals or communities motivated purely by the desire for truth. Thus, they might be seen as having taken on board the sociological-historical observation that scientists are often motivated by ambition or other worldly goals. By showing that issues of cognitive progress or truth are not thereby banished from an understanding of scientific practices, the decision-theoretic scenarios show that philosophers' normative concerns are compatible with social studies of science (properly understood). But this relies on a crass interpretation of the notion of credit, as used by a Knorr-Cetina or a Latour, which not only leads to prizes or other rewards, but is also necessary for the continued pursuit of research. They use a different kind of economics, the economics of capital investment, as their model for understanding science. Goldman's and Kitcher's interpretations put a moralistic spin on their claims and, in doing so, narrow considerably what philosophers can learn from this work.[44]

---

[44] I cannot resist commenting on another result of applying the dismal science to understanding scientific practices. Scientists become single-minded maximizers (whether of truth or credit or whatever else they seek), making of science a grim pursuit indeed. Gone are joy, delight, and playfulness. These economic models may fit today's "big science" better than the science of the early modern period, but this in itself should give us pause. For a different use of economics to understand science, see Mirowski and Sent, forthcoming.

CHAPTER FOUR

Disassembling the Rational-Social Dichotomy

IN THE debates about the role of the social in scientific knowledge, and the relevance of social studies of science to philosophy of science, the various sides share a common, but implicit, premise—that the rational and the cognitive, on the one hand, and the social, on the other, constitute exclusive zones or sets of processes and practices. The rational and the social are dichotomized and the debate is about which ought to be given primacy in accounting for scientific knowledge. Another feature of the debate, and one that promotes a communicative impasse between philosophers and the social, cultural, and feminist theorists of the sciences is ambiguities of the term "knowledge." Although significant substantive differences exist between the approaches reviewed here, some of the details of debate trade (unintentionally) on equivocations. "Knowledge" and its cognates, "knows," "known," etc., are used and conceived, in these debates, in relation to different dimensions of the cognitive. When these are distinguished, they can be seen to require different sorts of account. Failure to distinguish the different senses undermines efforts to make the case for the sociality of knowledge. I distinguish some of these senses—showing how they are differently understood by the sociologists and the philosophers and emphasizing their collision in debates between proponents of empirical and philosophical approaches to understanding knowledge—before focusing directly on the dichotomy that yields these divergent understandings. Once its assumptions are identified and discarded, it becomes possible to give accounts of knowledge in its different senses that express the empirical and normative concerns otherwise so much at odds. I also consider how this social account embraces the relation between the epistemological project and one of the more controversial theses—pluralism.

THREE SENSES OF "KNOWLEDGE"

At least three distinct senses of knowledge are embroiled in debates about the sciences. "Knowledge" can be used to mean sets of knowledge productive practices; knowing, that is, the relation of a cognizer to some content; and the outcome of knowledge-productive practices. Each sense involves some contrast or distinction, but the contrasts are not the same, and there are multiple contrasts within each sense reflecting the different philosophical and empirical uses of the term. I will display these different senses in a series of tables, a kind of progressive disambiguation grid.

Knowledge as Knowledge Production

One of the questions a theory of knowledge should address is that of how knowledge (or what comes to be treated as knowledge) is produced or generated. The contrast is between efficacious and inefficacious production methods, but how efficacy is understood depends on whether the context is empirical or normative. In an empirical sociological context, the contrast is between practices or processes that do and those that do not succeed in ratifying some content as knowledge—that is, having some content accepted as knowledge in a given community. In a normative context the contrast is between processes of belief acquisition that do and those that do not rationally justify belief. Philosophers are interested in conceptual analyses that incorporate the normative uses of the term, and often in spelling out what processes and practices satisfy those norms.

The question of the production of knowledge can be understood as a question about the transformation of initial inputs into representational outputs.[1] As such, it is a causal question, one answered in different ways, with different methodologies, by psychologists and social scientists. Part of the difference is accounted for by the different levels at which inputs and representational outputs can be identified. Psychologists and cognitive scientists are concerned with representation on the part of individuals: internal representations. Social scientists are concerned with representations that are the medium of intellectual exchange, with public, shareable, representations. In content, of course, internal and public representations may be the same, but different mechanisms are required to account for the generation and storage of internal representations and for the constitution of representations that come to be shared in various

[1] The inputs are usually conceived as sensory—the classic view, of course, was that knowledge is built up from sense data. This empiricist psychology has been superseded; it is at best controversial in philosophy, and contemporary psychology contains many different ways of characterizing the sensory inputs to an organism. See Grandy 1987. And inputs are conceived as sensory when the transformation is a "from the ground up" transformation, but, of course, many transformations occur across higher-level representations, thus taking representations as their inputs. For purposes of this discussion, I leave unspecified the precise form inputs and outputs can have. This is, at least in part, an empirical question to be investigated by neurophysiologists who can tell us what states of the brain constitute having a representation. In general, no particular theory of belief or representation is presupposed in what follows.

kinds of social groups. At the very least, internal representations have to be transformed into a medium that can be shared in order to be put into play in a common discursive space.[2]

What counts for the empirical investigator as producing knowledge is not the processes by which individuals are or become justified in their beliefs, but the processes of generating accounts and representations and having those accepted by the community. The model for the sociologist of knowledge is science, but science as a process of developing and distributing new accounts of natural processes in such a way as to effect general assent to those accounts, not science as the belief-forming or hypothesis-acceptance practices of an individual in the laboratory or in the field. The sociologist is interested in all the causal processes and interactions involved in the formulation of a model or in the discovery or construction of a hitherto unknown substance or process and in the processes and interactions involved in its acceptance-rejection in a community.[3] Thus the empirical investigator is interested in the processes by which cognitive authority or the status of legitimacy is claimed and constructed. But the philosopher recognizes that cognitive authority or legitimacy can be claimed and attributed without being earned and wants to identify those processes that can warrant such attribution. There are patterns of belief fixation or content acceptance that have epistemically worthy outcomes and some that do not. Divination, tea-leaf reading, the dictate of civil or religious authority are all methods of belief fixation that under most familiar circumstances issue in systems of representation that are less reliable than those resulting from sense perception or inductive inference. The normative philosopher wants to exclude those from the category of warranting practices. Thus there is a distinction between what the empirical investigator and the philosophical investigator treat as knowledge-productive practices. I call these the empirical and the normative account respectively. PP_e are those practices actually employed in a given context, while PP_n are those that are normatively sanctioned (see Table 1).

---

[2] If publicity of objects is required for science, the sciences may never really be able to get at subjectivity, because subjective states can only be studied in their public form. Jamesian introspection was supposed to be a way around this, but one lesson of Wittgenstein's private language argument is that we can only share information about our private states in a public medium. This does not mean that subjectivity and subjective states themselves are not real, but that they may elude, qua subjective states, a scientific accounting. What it is like to be in this room looking out this window can be partly conveyed by a very lengthy detailed verbal description or a photograph, but neither of these can convey fully and exactly what it is like for me to be in this place now. See Lloyd 1995a, 1995b.

[3] Given that sociologists differ as to what is relevant, "all" here must mean "all deemed relevant within the researcher's theoretical framework."

TABLE 1

	Empirical	*Normative*
Knowledge-productive practices	PP$_e$: processes or practices that succeed in fixing belief or in having some content accepted in some community	PP$_n$: processes or practices of belief acquisition that justify belief

Knowledge as Knowing

In this sense, we mean knowledge as a state of a person or persons (or of any creature or entity that can know) with respect to some particular object or set of objects. Knowledge, in this sense, is a three-term relation between (1) a subject or subjects, (2) a representation or some content, and (3) an object or objects.[4] Again the empirical and the philosophical investigator understand the relation differently. Empirical investigators are less interested in this relation, but to the extent they have a use for it treat it derivatively from the productive practices sense. Philosophers, on the other hand, have spent much effort on the analysis of knowledge as the subject's (complex) relation to some content. The goal of these efforts is to make explicit the grounds for an intuitive distinction between knowledge and opinion. These grounds are often spelt out in variations on the formula familiar to philosophers, which, while offered as a definition of knowledge, is really a definition of knowing:

S knows that *p* if and only if
i. S believes that *p*,
ii. *p* (or *p* is true), and
iii. S is justified in believing *p*.

These conditions correspond to the three senses of "knowledge" I am distinguishing: agency, content, and knowledge-productive practices. But they are treated as components of a definition, rather than as independent aspects of knowledge. As parts of the definition of "knows" they progressively narrow "knowing" to a particular relation among broader relations. They specify, first, a relation of the subject to some content—here, belief;[5] then, a relation of that content to its object—here, truth (or

---

[4] Some analysts (e.g., Rouse 1996) may wish to do away with the representational component, but this seems to be because they object to particular theories of representation.

[5] That we speak of subjects and objects is owing to the asymmetry of the relation of

satisfaction of p by its object); and finally a further relation of justification holding between S's believing p and something else (which justifies). The relation "S knows that p" is constituted by the intersection of the three defining relations. Each of these elements of the formula is the topic of philosophical investigation and debate, both on its own and as an element of the formula. Philosophers debate how to define belief, how to understand content, how to define truth, how to spell out justification. For the moment, though, I wish to focus on the element of justification as a source of misunderstanding between the philosophers and the social scientists.[6]

Philosophers understand "justification" in many different ways. In the broadest sense, a subject's being justified in believing that p in a philosophical sense (or a belief that p's having been legitimately acquired by a subject) consists in the subject being in an appropriate relation to p and to the object or state of affairs that p represents. We might signal this by saying that the subject's believing that p stands in the appropriate relation to p's truth (i.e., to that portion of the world that makes p true). Spelling out what counts as appropriate would then involve spelling out features of other relations in which subject and content, or content and object, or subject and object, stand to each other.[7] This could be a state of attention of subject to object, it could be an appropriate relation to someone else's attention to the object, or it could be being in a position to respond to questions about p and about the object. Typically, however, the appropriate relation has been spelled out in terms of having reasons, which is in turn spelled out in terms of being able to construct (or of its being possible for some third party to construct) an argument to p from certain propositions the subject believes and is (already) entitled to believe. One central task of philosophers has consisted in spelling out what can count as a reason. This can be expressed in the previously introduced rubric of normatively sanctioned knowledge-productive practices, PP_n (Table 1).

Foundationalists seek to identify what can serve as basic grounds in justification (i.e., grounds that themselves do not require justification).

---

representation. A subject represents an object. It does not follow that certain objects of representation may not in turn represent those who represent them. But each representation by a subject involves a unique point of view or perspective, the subject's point of view. Furthermore, the representation by a subject of another subject may eliminate the latter's having a point of view from the representation. This is what we call objectification. See Haslanger 1993.

[6] Because the formula is expressed in terms of belief, I shall keep with that expression in this discussion. Nothing is presupposed as to the correct analysis of "belief."

[7] Epistemologists have recently been divided into internalists and externalists. Internalists about justification require that the subject have some belief about what justifies, whereas externalists require only that the subject stand in some appropriate relation to the object of belief (e.g., having been caused to have the belief that p by the fact that p).

Coherentists spell out having reasons as coherence of the belief with the subject's other beliefs. Earlier philosophers such as Locke, "traditional naturalists" in Philip Kitcher's phrase, understood justification in causal terms, namely that the propositions that figured as premises in arguments to the conclusion that p, expressed experiences or mental contents (e.g., sense data) that caused belief that p. The causal interpretation of justification has persisted in some of the more recent philosophical accounts of knowledge.[8]

This view is one of the targets of the social scientists' derision. They claim that the causes of belief are not the sorts of thing that can figure in good arguments for some belief p. Real as opposed to idealized knowledge-productive practices do not justify in the philosopher's sense. Indeed, the factors that sociologists attend to are often explicitly discounted by philosophers. Either the causes of belief themselves do not possess the required character (the properly justifying relation to the subject's believing) or they are just not the sort of thing that philosophers have proposed as belonging in a good argument, being, say, what someone else told the subject, or the result of social influence or bias. Conversely, sociologists point out that the rules of good argument are not sufficient to provide a causal account of why some S comes to believe p rather than q on the basis of some set of beliefs r, because subjects may have what philosophers would consider logically compelling reasons yet fail to accept a belief on their basis. If one were to offer a parallel to the philosophical account, for the sociological investigator someone S counts as knowing that p if S accepts p, p is part of what is accepted in S's society, and there is a causal relation between S's believing and S's community or the processes by which S comes to believe are processes accepted in S's community. One might see both the empirical and the conceptual investigator as concerned with what counts as legitimate belief, but for the sociologist this is indexed to the subject's relations with her or his community, whereas for the philosopher the relations hold independently of any community. Thus, in the empirical world, the set PP_n is, or could be, empty, and in the ideal world in which PP_n is not empty, PP_n and PP_e are mutually exclusive. The second row in Table 2 reflects these different views.

Knowledge as Content

Finally, we also mean by knowledge that which is known: the content or a corpus of knowledge. Thus we speak of scientific knowledge, legal

---

[8] Hence, the equivocation on justificatory and causal senses of knowledge-productive practices noted in the previous section.

TABLE 2

	Empirical	*Normative*
Knowledge-productive practices	PP_e: processes or practices that succeed in fixing belief or in having some content accepted in some community	PP_n: processes or practices of belief acquisition or acceptance that justify belief
Knowing	S accepts that p, and p is accepted in C, and S's acceptance of p is acceptable in C	S accepts that p, and p is true, and S's accepting that p is the outcome of or accords with PP_n

knowledge, technical knowledge, historical knowledge. Knowledge is not, in this usage, attributed to any particular person, nor is it necessarily tied to any particular moment of the history of its production. In this usage, knowledge is what piles up in books and journals in the form of verbal or two-, three-, or four-dimensional visual representations.[9] Here, too, some distinction is intended between representations that do and those that do not count as knowledge. But several distinctions could be meant. One is a distinction between discourses that do and those that do not purport factuality, that is, between biology or history on the one hand and fiction or poetry on the other. Another is a distinction between what we—members of a society existing at a certain historical period—take to be correct representations contrasted with incorrect ones—for example, heliostatic as distinct from geostatic accounts of planetary motion; relativistic as distinct from classical physics; the sciences produced with our knowledge-making tools as contrasted with the science ("science" by analogy or courtesy) produced in another historical context with other and, to our way of thinking, inferior, knowledge-making tools.[10] Finally, there is a distinction between what is really true and what is merely believed, even with good reason, to be true. This latter is the distinction many philosophers have been concerned with. This distinction holds out the hope that there is a set of all truths, a subset of which is known at any given time. One can speak of the knowledge of an individual as the intersection of what the individual believes (justifiably) and the set of all truths, or the knowledge of a community as the intersection of what is accepted (justifiably, or as a consequence of normatively sanc-

[9] These days one might include audio and video tapes, compact discs and floppy disks, and the Internet.

[10] Of course, one might imagine a society with superior knowledge-making tools, although we would, ex hypothesi, not be able to imagine the science such a society could produce.

TABLE 3

	Empirical	*Normative*
Knowledge-productive practices	PP_e: processes or practices that succeed in fixing belief or in having some content accepted in some community	PP_n: processes or practices of belief acquisition or acceptance that justify belief
Knowing	S accepts that p, and p is accepted in C, and S's acceptance of p is acceptable in C	S accepts that p, and p is true, and S's accepting that p is an outcome of or accords with PP_n
Content	$Content_e$: what is accepted in some community C or the outcomes of PP_e in community C	$Content_n$: the subset of truths which is known (whether by an individual or by a community)

tioned practices) by a community at a time with the set of all truths. The empirical investigator instead treats whatever a community so designates as knowledge and is interested not in what makes (or would make) it knowledge independently of community practices, but in how said content acquires the status of knowledge in that community. The conceptual investigator is concerned with the relation of content to object; the empirical investigator, with the relation of content to users.

Table 3 enables a partial diagnosis of the communicative impasses between the empirical sociological investigator and the philosophical investigator. The empirical investigator starts her or his analysis with processes or practices. Her or his other uses of "know" are derivative from the account of knowledge-productive practices. The philosopher, on the other hand, starts from the content sense. Philosophical epistemology has been driven by a vision of the possibility of complete or total truth, and has concerned itself with the means of attaining such truth (or approaching it). The philosopher's other uses of "know" are derivative from, determined by, the account of the content sense. Even philosophers who might be skeptical or pessimistic about our ability to attain such truth are influenced by this conception of the ideal in their thinking about knowledge. For example, philosophers of science think of scientific knowledge as a set of theories, and many of them think of those theories as sets of propositions. Sociologists think of scientific knowledge as including theories, but also ways of doing things—for example, protocols of experimentation or observation, or tacit knowledge. The disembodied, detached character of the ideal corpus persists in philosophers' accounts of knowledge in the other two senses—in accounts of a subject's knowing and of knowledge productive practices—whereas the sociologists' initial focus on practices persists into the characterizations of knowing and of content.

Sources of Misunderstanding

One early debate between the sociologist and the philosopher clearly reflects these different starting points. Larry Laudan argued that David Bloor was mistaken in claiming that a scientific approach to understanding science required the symmetry thesis.[11] Laudan argued that explanation by appeal to reasons *is* empirical, that one simply offers different (causal) explanations for rational and irrational beliefs. But he went on to say that there is an adequate framework for explanation of why agents adopt the reasons they do in a (largely asociological) model of "good reasons," thus suggesting that the explanation of true or rational beliefs will still be different in kind from the explanation of false or irrational beliefs.[12] Using the disambiguation grid, we might say that the impasse here springs from emphasizing one or the other of the words in the expression "knowledge production." Laudan not only emphasizes "knowledge" but has a conception of knowledge as the true content as in the third row of Table 3. From this point of view it seems reasonable to demand, as Laudan does, an account of those mechanisms that produce true belief as distinct from unwarranted or false belief, that is, one might demand that the mechanisms must be justificatory in nature. If the emphasis is on "production," as in the first row of Table 3, then it seems reasonable to demand, as Bloor does, an account of the mechanisms that produce belief, no matter what their epistemic status. Bloor, of course, goes on to deny that there is any process, apart from social convention, that will distinguish true from false belief. But whether or not it is true that no such distinction can be made between causal processes, it does not follow that we cannot specify conditions that will distinguish that content which qualifies as knowledge from that which does not.

Just as starting from opposing places in the grid produces communicative impasses, failing to distinguish the roles of the different senses can produce problems. For example, if we think of the philosophical definition of knowing as the correct definition of knowledge, we become

---

[11] Laudan 1984a; Bloor 1984.
[12] Laudan 1984a, 64.

entangled with the conditions that define a subject's knowing (that something is the case). In consequence, those conditions are treated as defining knowledge (e.g., belief, propositional form, truth, and justifiability by appeal to a sound argument). When, in addition, insufficient attention is paid to the subject, and to the subject's membership in a society, these conditions are thought to hold independently of historically specific features of the putative knower's situation. Assuming this perspective ultimately restricts what can be known to a very small class: those representations that would or do occur in every system of representation and are produced by universally shared knowledge-making tools, that is, what will remain certifiable as knowledge across changes in context. But the content produced with other knowledge-making tools may be knowledge in our third sense nevertheless, as in "the state of astronomical knowledge in Ptolemy's time, or in Newton's time."[13] So perhaps the achievement of a society of inquirers working with a particular set of tools and a particular set of cognitive goals and associated criteria should not be analyzed in the same way we analyze a subject's knowing something about an object.

A different impasse is reached if we think of an account of knowledge-productive practices as specifying the meaning of knowledge in the third, content or corpus, sense. These practices, as we saw, issue in systems of representation of varying worth, and they are historically, socially, and geographically circumscribed. Foucault introduced the term "episteme" to refer to the systematically interconnected set of vocabulary, formation rules, rules of truth, and the like that constitute, generate, and sustain a discourse about a domain. The elements of the episteme constitute the objects of inquiry by determining the categories of object in the domain, the kinds of question it is legitimate to ask, and the criteria of what constitutes an adequate answer to those questions.[14] Objects so constituted may not be recognizable from within another episteme. The nineteenth century saw, for example, the emergence of a discourse of sexuality that introduced objects of inquiry that had not previously existed as objects of inquiry. A new science of sexology was born that both permitted the expression of and was constituted by a network of interests (anxieties?) around sex and reproduction. The claims that twentieth-century knowledge of sex coevolved with a network of practical interests, that it involved the emergence of a discursive practice that makes sense only in the context of these interests, and that it bore no relation to

---

[13] This is one of the lessons of Kuhn 1962. Another is that what the Ptolemaic astronomer knew cannot be separated from the entirety of Ptolemaic theory.

[14] Foucault 1970, 1972. Here I follow the reading given Foucault's ideas by Ian Hacking 1982.

previous modes of representing and explaining sexual behavior sound like claims that twentieth-century knowledge about sex is not really knowledge. From the point of view of the philosophical definition of knowing, Foucauldian archaeology looks like either a strategy for undermining all knowledge claims (good and bad) or, because every discourse has an episteme, a strategy for validating any knowledge claim whatever, provided it belongs to a discourse. This is, I think, to misunderstand the Foucauldian project, because within a discourse knowledge claims can be discriminated into the legitimate and the illegitimate, the true and the false.[15] Only from the perspective of eternally stable attributions of knowledge, that is, from the perspective of Content$_n$, does the discourse, or episteme, relativity of truth and falsity undermine the possibility of knowledge.[16]

Finally, debates structured by the rational-social dichotomy assume a conflation between reasons and causes that further vitiates attempts at their resolution. Satisfying the condition of being justified is interpreted by both sides as a claim about knowledge production: knowledge is produced by the movement of a subject through a temporal (or causal) sequence of beliefs, some of which are premises, the last of which is the conclusion—that is, by movement through the steps of a (valid) argument. In other words, being justified is interpreted as having performed a (logically sound) transformation of some set of inputs into an output or set of outputs.[17] The disagreement, then, is over whether this describes how persons actually come to hold beliefs. But being justified may not necessarily mean that one has reasoned one's way to a conclusion or performed a transformation on a subset of one's beliefs. Perhaps on certain occasions we do perform such a transformation, but more often than not, we do not, or at least not one we can reconstruct.[18] Nevertheless, even when there's no reconstructable causally effective argument, that is, one that records the actual steps or stages of internal processing, we can on

[15] This point is stressed by Hacking 1982.

[16] This is not to minimize what may have to be given up in taking this sort of approach. For example, one may have to give up the idea that scientific knowledge is knowledge of natural kinds, in some strong sense of natural kinds.

[17] I think this approach to justification is partly responsible for the idea that epistemology is centrally about appraising and improving human cognitive performance (whether generally or in the sciences). See, in this connection, Kitcher 1992. But restricting the theory of knowledge to this narrowly conceived normative endeavor is to deprive oneself of many interesting philosophical questions about knowledge and to place oneself in an unnecessarily antagonistic relation to an important contemporary direction of empirical study. It is also to engage in a hopelessly quixotic enterprise: the prescriptions of epistemologists have had little effect on change in belief in the last 2,500 years. There's no reason to think the next 2,500 would be any different.

[18] See Kaplan 1994.

request specify reasons, the propositional versions of which would figure in good arguments. Perhaps a transformation involving these reasons has occurred, perhaps not. Its occurrence or nonoccurrence is irrelevant to our assessment of whether the reasons cited in response to questions are justificatory. One may have good reasons for believing something even when those reasons are not causally involved in one's having come to believe it. But, if this is so, then the fact that the processes by which belief that p was induced were not themselves justificatory processes may be irrelevant to the question whether a given individual is justified in believing that p and hence to the question whether that individual knows that p in some philosophically robust sense of "knows."

A moral I draw from this is that the justificatory condition in the definition of knowing should be kept (analytically) distinct from the procedures involved in knowledge production. The specification of what counts as being justified should not a priori be identified with the specification of what counts as producing or causing knowledge.[19] The specification of nonjustifying causes of belief should not be interpreted as meaning the irrelevance or undermining of justifying reasons of belief. And the specification of justifying reasons of belief should not be interpreted as meaning the irrelevance or nonapplicability of explanations invoking nonjustifying causes of belief. We should treat causes and reasons of belief as distinct aspects of knowledge (knowing) that may sometimes in fact coincide, but not necessarily so.

The Challenge

This differentiation of conceptions of knowledge shows that there are different senses of *knowledge* that shape the accounts that will be given of this concept. Philosophical and scientific debates about the nature of knowledge arise in relation to each of the specifiable senses: processes or practices, agents' knowing, content. In addition, debates and puzzles arise from crossed wires, when the analytic or explanatory expectations generated for accounts of knowledge in one sense are applied to assessments of

---

[19] Internalists in epistemology would take exception to such detaching. Strict internalism which requires that a justified belief is one whose cause is the believer's reason, however, carries its own liabilities. For example, if the cause of a belief must be a reason, what does the internalist say about a case where the cause of S's belief p is not a (good) reason (e.g., one's advisor said "B"), although S is in possession of good reasons for p. Similarly, the testimony of another may cause me to know something, in the sense of articulating it to myself or bringing it to my attention, without necessarily being what justifies me in my belief. To maintain the internalist thesis would require contorted redefinitions of belief and reasons that are not necessary on the account to be offered here. Testimony will receive more attention in chapter 7.

accounts in a quite different sense. In order to avoid getting tangled in these wires, a theory of scientific knowledge should have something to say about knowledge in all of these senses or should at least acknowledge the differences between them.

Acknowledging these different senses of knowledge is not to say that there are entirely different phenomena answering to these senses. The differentiated definitions demonstrate their interdependence. It is, however, to acknowledge the complexity of talking about knowledge and to recognize a challenge. Is it possible to offer accounts that will not result in communicative impasses? Is it possible to talk about, to analyze, knowledge in any of the empirical or philosophical senses in ways that remain open to the meanings of each of its counterparts? This challenge is similar to the challenge posed to epistemology and philosophy of science by recognizing the locatedness of knowing subjects, which also produces a clash between causal and logical or rational approaches to knowledge. Distinguishing these different senses of knowledge is a first step in the task of responding to the challenges to philosophy articulated by social and cultural studies of science. The second is to address the dichotomy framing their disputes about all these senses.

DISSOLVING THE RATIONAL-SOCIAL DICHOTOMY

The rational-social dichotomy, like any dichotomy, is sustained by a set of underlying binaries. Three major binaries are in play in the construction of the rational-social dichotomy. These are individualism versus nonindividualism, monism versus nonmonism, and relativism versus nonrelativism. Individualism and nonindividualism are views about the agents or subjects of knowledge, monism and nonmonism are metaphysical views about the character of the known (or knowable), and relativism and nonrelativism are views about the character of epistemic warrant or acceptability. These correspond to aspects of the three senses of knowledge just distinguished. At least partly because these senses are not distinguished, the dichotomizers do not always explicitly distinguish monism from nonrelativism, but these are different kinds of position and they play different roles in the arguments, especially in those of the philosophers. Similarly, individualism and nonrelativism are not distinguished from each other. This is presumably because individualism is also identified with universalism—that is, the individual is, insofar as it is a knower, like all other knowers and thus subject to the same epistemic rules. Although differently salient in different analyses, these binaries were aligned in the same way in the empirical sociologizers' and the normative rationalizers' discussions: individualism, monism, and non-

TABLE 4

The Dichotomizers' Way	
Individualism	Nonindividualism
Monism	Nonmonism
Nonrelativism	Relativism

relativism are treated as different aspects of a single position. I call this the dichotomizers' way (Table 4), a way shared by the empirical and normative investigators examined in chapters 2 and 3.

The dichotomizers seem to think that the binaries are such that the third element on the left side (nonrelativism) implies the other two on that side (monism with regard to content and individualism with regard to agency, while the first element on the right side (nonindividualism) implies the lower two on that side (nonmonism with regard to content and relativism with regard to warrant). The sociological dichotomizers embrace the right side as an integrated set; the philosophical dichotomizers embrace the left side as an integrated set. Thus, a philosopher like Kitcher thinks he has refuted nonindividualism with arguments against relativism and sociologists seem to think nonindividualism implies relativism. Kitcher's arguments presuppose monism, as I argued in chapter 3, while the sociologist denies the monist claim that there is one and only one correct and complete account of (all or any) natural process. Once exposed, these alignments lose their self-evidence. I wish to contrast the dichotomizers' way with another that realigns nonindividualism, nonmonism, and nonrelativism as an integrated set (see Table 5).

As mere negations, the three components have no obvious interpretations. Each, as it turns out, admits of multiple interpretations. Advocates (victims?) of the dichotomizing way frequently identify only one possible interpretation, whose unpalatability reinforces their commitment to the rational-social dichotomy. There is, however, a set of positive interpretations that constitutes a constructive alternative to either path of the dichotomizing way.

Nonindividualism has at least three interpretations: wholist, eliminativist, and social. Wholism is the view that only a group qua group knows.[20] Another form of nonindividualism eliminates the knowing subject altogether: nobody knows. Knowledge is instead a detached product of col-

---

[20] This is the view advocated by Lynn H. Nelson 1993 and adumbrated, but rejected, by John Hardwig 1985. For further discussion, see chapter 7.

TABLE 5

The Dichotomizers' Way		The Nondichotomizers' Way
Rationalizers	Sociologizers	
Individualism	Nonindividualism	Nonindividualism
Monism	Nonmonism	Nonmonism
Nonrelativism	Relativism	Nonrelativism

lective practices residing in those outcomes rather than in the agents.[21] Each of these forms of nonindividualism emphasizes one or the other of the kinds or senses of knowledge just distinguished. Wholism extends the sociality of knowledge-constructive practices to the state of knowing, such that all those involved in the exercise of knowledge-productive practices are part of a collective subject of knowledge. The elimination-ist, on the other hand, takes the material embodiment of content (in books, journals, instruments, etc.), or the independence of content from any individual member of a discursive community, to indicate the super-fluity of the cognitive agent or subject. Both of these forms of nonin-dividualism simply erase the individual subject. A third form is neither eliminationist nor wholist, but socialist. It stresses, that is, the interde-pendence of cognitive agents and subjects. The differences between (as much as the commonalities among) such agents are what enables them together to generate and justify content. Their interrelations license the attribution of knowledge to any one of them. The characterization of knowing subjects as interdependent yields individual subjects without individualism (the view that individuals know independently of their rela-tions with others).

Nonmonism, a position about content, is a denial that there is exactly one (correct, complete, consistent) account. It, too, admits of three inter-pretations. The antirealist interpretation is what is commonly referred to as constructivism: multiple accounts of any natural process can be made compatible with whatever empirical basis one has and none of them cor-responds (or need correspond) to anything real. Constructivists can have a richer or poorer conception of the empirical basis.[22] There is an elim-inationist interpretation here, too: no correct accounts are possible. An eliminationist position distinct from constructivism might hold that there is a real-world or causal network, but no accounts can capture it.[23]

---

[21] This seems to be the view of Foucault (1972) and, minus the reference to practices, of Popper (1972).

[22] Both van Fraassen (1980) and Bloor (1992) would be constructivists in this sense. Where they differ is in their conceptions of justification.

[23] Cf. Rosenberg 1994.

Finally, the realist interpretation of nonmonism holds that while no single account, no single theory or model, captures the entirety of physical and biological processes operating in a single real-world system, each satisfactory account captures some aspect. Thus, multiple accounts (theories, models) are not just permissible but necessary. Realist nonmonism, then, is pluralism.

Nonrelativism, finally, is the denial that justification is as each sees it or, to put it another way, that warrant is arbitrary.[24] This, too, can be given three interpretations. The absolutist interpretation holds that justification is independent of context, and that the acceptability of procedures of justification is also independent of context.[25] The dichotomizers tend to identify nonrelativism with absolutism. An eliminationist version would hold that there is no justification of belief, either because justification is impossible or because it is unnecessary. The view that it is impossible is, in the empirical world, equivalent to relativism. The view that it is unnecessary might be applicable to entities capable of what Kant called "intellectual intuition," that is, direct insight into the truth of things. An epistemology for empirical (human) subjects can set this possibility aside. Finally, the contextualist interpretation holds that justification is neither arbitrary nor subjective, but is dependent on rules and procedures immanent in the context of inquiry. Contextualism is the nondichotomist's alternative to relativism and absolutism regarding justification.

Breaking out these multiple interpretations undermines the apparent self-evidence of the original dichotomy and frees us from the illusion that the dichotomy exhausts the possibilities. An additional benefit is the dissolution of the mutual support among individualism, monism, and nonrelativism on one side of the dichotomy and of nonindividualism, nonmonism, and relativism on the other. Multiple combinations of the conceptions of cognitive agency, content, and warrant are conceivable, even if not all, in the end, equally viable. Furthermore, it becomes clear that the nonrelativism of the rationalizers is an absolutist conception of justification and warrant. Rationalizers are committed to individualism, monism, and absolutism. Sociologizers, overlooking nonabsolutist interpretations of nonrelativism, are committed to nonindividualism, nonmonism, and relativism. As an alternative, I propose understanding and

---

[24] "Justification" is here, as earlier, used broadly and not in the sense of any particular theory of justification. "Belief," too, is used broadly, without reference to any particular theory of mental states or propositional attitudes or other vehicle.

[25] Both Goldman and Kitcher can be understood as subscribing to this kind of absolutism. Distinguishing between the metaphysical dimension of the dichotomy and its epistemological dimension shows the "realism versus relativism debate" to be a misnomer produced by collapsing monism and the absolutist interpretation of nonrelativism, as the dichotomizers have done.

adopting an interdependence interpretation of nonindividualism, a pluralist interpretation of nonmonism, and a contextualist interpretation of nonrelativism.

Nonmonism

Realist nonmonism is pluralism. One can be a pluralist for all of science, or just for some sciences. Pluralists have offered different kinds of arguments for pluralist conclusions, which amount to different versions of pluralism.[26] Some forms of pluralism pose no challenge to traditional approaches, such as are represented in the foregoing philosophers' column. Philosophers who advocate strong forms of pluralism, however, are claiming that the complexity of natural entities and processes (either all such or just organic entities and processes) eludes complete representation by any single theoretical or investigative approach. Any given approach will be partial and completeness will be achieved not by a single integrated theory but by a plurality of approaches that are partially overlapping, partially autonomous, and resisting reconciliation. Given that a phenomenon is modeled slightly differently in different approaches, quantitative measures will vary between approaches, so that comparing data descriptions will show inconsistencies between the approaches. Deep insight into a phenomenon will be purchased at the cost of losing unifiability with other approaches. The difficulty with strong pluralism, of course, is that it sits uneasily with standard ways of thinking about knowledge or about the world. One expression of this worry, which assumes that, in the long run, there is or must be a final set of data that can be reconciled in one framework, proceeds as follows.

If

1. different approaches or investigative strategies presupposing different theories or models result in nonreconcilable measures of what pretheoretically would be identified as the same phenomenon, and

2. there is one world and not many, and

3. all true statements must be consistent with each other,

then

4. those theories cannot all be true and some investigative strategies are simply wrongheaded and are to be rejected.

---

[26] Thus, Suppes (1984), Waters (1991), Dupré (1993), Beatty (1985), Cartwright (1995), and Ereshevsky (1998) can all be described as advocating pluralism, but pluralism of quite different varieties. Different versions of pluralism are discussed in greater detail in chapter 8.

The pluralist approach sees the trouble in statements 2 and 3. The problem is not that those statements are false but that they are ambiguous. "World" can mean the whole of all there is, in which case the pluralist would agree that there is only one of those. But it can also mean the collection of aspects of the world that is salient to those approaching it with a given set of assumptions and strategies for acquiring knowledge, not to mention a given sensory and cognitive apparatus. In this sense there are many worlds. The demand for consistency of all true statements is only problematic if one supposes that statements can be detached from their truth conditions and the contexts in which those are determinable. A contextualist denies that such detaching is possible without constructing a further or more encompassing context. A measurement made in the context of atomic physics is carried out in relation to standards of precision and comparison specific to atomic physics. It cannot be compared with a measurement made in the context of quantum chromodynamics or experimental high-energy physics without the construction of another context that provides criteria for the comparative assessment of measurements from the different approaches.[27]

The monist might object that we can surely evaluate such different approaches or investigative strategies. But by what criteria are we to evaluate investigative strategies? And if incompatible strategies nevertheless produce usable results, why should we insist upon the relinquishing of one or the other? Not only is the objectivity of the sciences at stake, so seemingly is the metaphysical unity of the world. How can we make sense of multiple, equally good theories (or approaches) without slipping into multiple world talk? Even Kuhn ended up suggesting that scientists holding sufficiently incommensurable yet incompatible theories occupied different worlds. If meant, literally, this is a recipe not for the disunity of science but for the fragmentation of sciences and worlds. The pluralism envisioned by theoretical pluralists is a pluralism of theories of a singular world. The pluralist claim, moreover, must be understood as an empirical claim, not as the expression of a necessary truth about the world. Pluralists in philosophy of science base their arguments on cases in contemporary science, not on a priori arguments.[28] If the eliminability of pluralism is a contingent fact, an epistemology ought not presuppose it.

Can our conceptions of knowledge and inquiry accommodate such a pluralism? I would like to suggest several guidelines to observe in thinking about this question.

[27] Paul Feyerabend (1962) emphasized such points in his arguments for incommensurability.
[28] I am grateful to Christopher Eliot for the comment that prompted this clarification.

1. The plurality of representations in the sciences may be a function of how the world is or of human intellectual equipment for and interests in understanding the world (or of both). Our epistemology cannot dictate which. Thus:

2. A satisfactory epistemology should be open to theoretical plurality *or* theoretical unity being the final result of inquiry, or what amounts to the same thing:

3. The issue of theoretical pluralism ought not be decided by one's choice of epistemology.

4. A suitable humility requires a modest epistemology. An epistemology— as a theory of human knowledge—does not have to promise complete knowledge (or trade in other absolutes, like certainty) but ought rather to give sense to the distinctions and normative judgments that are a part of epistemic discourse.

These guidelines amount to an injunction against presupposing either pluralism or monism. While I must confess to a partiality to pluralism, accommodating pluralism in epistemology requires only resisting an overhasty conclusion against it. Of course, not every pluralist relies exclusively on the evidence of contemporary science. Some logical features of inquiry also conduce to the pluralist position. They will be addressed in chapter 6.

CONCLUSION

I have diagnosed two obstacles in the way of reconciling work in social studies of science with the normative concerns of philosophers: equivocations on the multiple senses of knowledge and the binaries constituting the dichotomy between the cognitive or rational and the social. Rejecting the conceptual conflations generating both these obstacles means it should be possible to develop an epistemology for actual, empirical subjects, in addition to, or instead of, the epistemology for idealized subjects that characterizes much normative thinking. The diagnosis offered has some consequences for such a development:

1. The senses of knowledge for which empirical and normative thinkers give different accounts should be reformulated in ways that remain open to, or preserve, the insights of both parties.

2. Any reanalysis of the cognitive concepts should observe the differences among the senses of knowledge distinguished earlier. My dissolution of the dichotomy reinforces the observation that analyses of epistemic justification or warrant, of cognitive agency, and of the content of knowledge are at least partially independent of one another.

3. The evaluations implied by the normative epistemological concerns of philosophers should not foreclose metaphysical questions; nor should they be foreclosed by the empirical versions of cognitive concepts. In particular, they should not foreclose, without argument, the question of monism versus nonmonism with respect to the content of knowledge.

The way is open, then, for an account of scientific knowledge that features contextuality of justification, interdependence of cognitive agents, and (possible) plurality of content.

CHAPTER FIVE

Socializing Cognition

As a step away from the rational-social dichotomy and the communicative impasse associated with it, I propose to move the distinctions marked in the conceptual or normative column of the disambiguation grid (Table 3 in chapter 4) inside the empirical column. This may mean abandoning some notions involved in the elaboration of the various philosophical senses of "knowledge." But it may also mean letting go of some of the notions involved in the elaboration of the various empirical social senses of "knowledge." The question then is whether any recognizable concept of knowledge can be recovered from a more thoroughly social account of inquiry. The first stage in answering this question is the development of analyses responding to the different senses of knowledge that draw both on sociological observation and philosophical analysis. This task might be thought of as the development of an epistemology for empirical subjects.

My aim is to integrate the empirical studies of scientific practices with the conceptual and normatively responsive reflections of philosophical analysis. In order to do so, I make use of the tripartite semantics of *knowledge* discussed in the previous chapter. "Knowledge" and its cognates are honorific terms, designating success. The integration I envision requires that, in each case, the success picked out by the normative concept be explicable for the empirical social concept. In addition to arguing that central elements of the knowledge-productive practices of the sciences—observation and reasoning—are social (this amounts to an argument that cognitive processes in the sciences are social) I discuss the implications of the interpretation of sociality that emerges from this discussion for our understanding of the attributive or relational sense of knowledge and offer an account of knowledge as content with special attention to what might count as success of content. These three accounts amount to a socialization of cognition, which points to how success is to be understood.

KNOWLEDGE-PRODUCTIVE PRACTICES

The expression "knowledge-productive practices" refers to all practices—intellectual or material—occurring within a context of inquiry that have a bearing on the outcome of inquiry. Thus, particular ways of manipulating experimental materials—for example, transferring samples from vials to petri dishes, particular ways of measuring those samples, particular kinds of question about and particular categorizations of the samples, particular statistical methods—would count as knowledge-productive practices. Philosophers of science typically treat observation and reasoning as the main sources or bases of scientific knowledge. Theories are secured to the phenomenal world by chains of reasoning that trace logical connections between high-level theoretical principles, mid-level laws, and observation statements. In a philosophical analysis these tend to be abstracted from the context and circumstances of observation and reasoning and from the persons engaging in these activities.

The social analysts claim that when they situate observation and reasoning in their real contexts these practices do not look like the kinds of practices to which philosophers attribute justificatory import. That is, scientists do not just observe; they design and execute particular experiments on particular occasions for particular purposes, they count a particular set of specimens with particular measurement technologies, and they select particular sites for particular field studies. Scientists don't just reason; they interpret observations and experiments, they support or critique conjectures or hypotheses, they derive consequences, they extend models to new domains. They have multiple reasons for the particular choices and decisions they make in the course of all these activities, reasons that include feasibility, potential for application, aesthetic values, interest from other colleagues, interest from potential consumers, intelligibility to colleagues, resonance with metaphysical or ideological commitments. These are the kinds of factors included under the umbrella of "the social." The intermixture of such considerations in producing decisions, claim the sociologists, means that actual practices depart in one way or another from the idealizations described in philosophical prescription. The conclusion most frequently drawn by those analysts discussed in the first chapter is that either scientific inquiry fails to produce knowledge or knowledge does not have the privileged status traditionally ascribed to it by philosophers.

What is not investigated, of course, is whether these practices might nevertheless have cognitive, even justificatory, import. The philosophers referenced by social studies of science might be right that observation and reasoning are central to justification but mistaken about how or why this is so. One problem is that the model of justification as valid argument obscures the hard work that scientific inquiry actually involves. By the time an argument of the sort featured in rational reconstructions can be formulated, most of the hard work (that interests the historian and social scientist) has been done. But what matters from the (normative) philosophical point of view is that the argument be formulable, not that it represent the sequence of steps actually taken by the scientist. Such reconstructions represent, perhaps, why we laypersons should accept a scientific conclusion. It is a mistake to think such reconstructions represent the reasoning of scientists involved in the production of the knowledge represented in the reconstruction. The mistake is traceable to conceptions of cognitive activity that are so idealized as to be irrelevant to the epistemological analysis of actual scientific practices. If the social is thought of as a contaminant, then the social aspects or performances of those practices will be treated as compromising of their justificatory or status-conferring import. I propose, contrary both to many philosophers and to many social theorists of science, that when we understand observation and reasoning as social practices, their justificatory role becomes clearer. In particular, I propose to treat both observation and reasoning as dialogical, that is, as activities involving discursive interactions among different voices. "Social," here, does not mean "common," "collective," or "shared," but "interactive." Rather than sort through all possible social processes of belief fixation to ascertain which are successful (in the philosopher's sense), my strategy is to show that the practices that are generally accepted as yielding knowledge are social practices.

Observation

Ethnomethodologists and sociologists practicing discourse analysis have argued that establishing what the (observational) data are is a social matter. Ascertaining what the results of an experiment are, what is a real result and what an artifact of the experimental situation, what are new data (constituting a genuine anomaly), and what is an experiment gone wrong is accomplished by "negotiation," or critical discussions among group members.

Michael Lynch has used ethnomethodological analysis to uncover the conversational work that anchors the interpretation of data. In a piece on digital imaging in astronomy, he and Samuel Edgerton describe the intersubjective and socially interactive process of interpreting and clarifying the salient features of galactic images.[1] Karin Knorr-Cetina has engaged in similar sorts of investigations, although without the theoretical trappings of ethnomethodology. In a paper with Klaus Amann, she reports on a study of a molecular biology laboratory using gel electrophoresis techniques to identify the molecular constituents of a sample of

[1] Lynch and Edgerton 1988.

DNA.[2] The two sociologists identify various discursive interactions that propel a group of investigators to progressively more definite accounts of what is actually exhibited on a given film. At the outset, the film is seen as supporting a variety of readings, but eventually one is preferred. Amman and Knorr-Cetina's claim is that the changes that generate a stable unanimity are in the discursive interactions, not in the object of common perception—that is, neither the film itself changes, nor is there a sequence of better and clearer representations. The film remains the same, fuzzy, while the interpretation offered of it changes until the bands are seen as here and here, and not there. Not only is the reading of a single film social in this way, but the final representations, the ones used in publication, are constructed by synthesizing and abstracting the common features of a number of films thus interpreted—introducing a second level of integrative sociality into the construction of data. While the film excludes many possibilities, it leaves enough open that the ultimate reading agreed upon cannot be understood as forced by the film. There is no guarantee that the individuals involved would eventually and independently have arrived at the very same reading rather than one of the others compatible with the evidence of the film.

Of course, what happens in one or two laboratories is not evidence that scientific observation is intrinsically social, rather than contingently so on the occasions reported. But more conceptual considerations do support thinking of scientific observation as dialogical in nature. Observational data consist in observation reports that are ordered and organized. This ordering rests on a consensus as to the centrality of certain categories (the speed of a reaction versus the color of its product), the boundaries of concepts and classes (just what counts as an acid), the ontological and organizational commitments of a model or theory, and so on. Observation is not simple sense perception (whatever that might be) but an organized sensory encounter that registers what is perceived in relation to categories, concepts, and classes that are socially produced. Both ordering and organization are (dependent on) social processes. I leave open whether the sensory registering is linguistic; it does involve classification and categorization that notes similarity and dissimilarity with other items of interest.

This dependence on the social is reflected in Richard Grandy's proposal for the definition of that Quinean entity, an observation sentence:

O is an observation sentence for community C with respect to stimulation pattern class S of modulus M to degree n if at least n percent of C agree in their patterns of assent, dissent, and suspension of judgment for all stimuli in S of modulus M.[3]

---

[2] Amann and Knorr-Cetina 1990.
[3] Grandy 1992a, 198.

Grandy notes that variation in any parameter change will change the class of observation sentences. In particular, the smaller the community, the larger the class, and the larger the community, the smaller the class. Of course, a community of one is possible, but the point of this definition is that for any community numbering more than one, no single member can generate what will count as the observation sentences. Individuals will be differently placed, differently informed, and so on. What counts as an observation for community C will depend on how these differences are resolved in C. There is no court outside of C to make this determination.

Furthermore, not just any observation will do. To have value as data, observations must have a stability that allows their transfer from one laboratory to another, or comparability between different field sites. If we are going to treat observational data as data, we need assurances that an apparent or purported regularity really is one or at least that it can be made manifest in a relevantly similar but spatiotemporally distinct setting. The requirement of the repeatability of experiments is a requirement for the intersubjective accessibility and cross-subject invariance of data serving as evidence because it is a requirement that anyone similarly placed with similar equipment would see (perceive) the same thing. Nature has been "enrolled as an ally" when the experimenter has found a way to stabilize his or her results across different perspectives and settings.[4] Latour, for example, emphasizes that Pasteur's triumph over anthrax involved being able to recreate in the field the conditions he created in the laboratory.[5] Even when an experiment is not actually repeated (which is the case for the majority of experiments), the presupposition of its results being used as evidential data is that any one similarly placed would observe the same thing.

Harry Collins has argued that only in cases of controversial science (cold fusion, parapsychology, molecular memory) does anyone go to the trouble of actually trying to produce the same results with the same methods.[6] We might say, only in such cases does anyone attempt actually to determine the publicity or intersubjective accessibility of experimental results. Collins is trying to expose the repeatability requirement as window dressing not supported by actual practices. His view is that negotiation among scientists and *not* input from the world investigated determines what counts as a competent experiment, and hence what counts as an experimental outcome. But the infrequency of actual repetition undertaken as checking need not undermine its centrality to the

[4] The condition of reproducibility, which involves stability across different apparatus as well as across different observers, signifies an even stronger alliance than repeatability. See Cartwright 1991.

[5] Latour 1988.

[6] Collins 1983, 1991.

concept of observation and observability. On the view urged here, the invocation and application of the repeatability criterion in controversial cases demonstrate that the presupposition in the "normal" case of the *unchecked* taking of a set of observations or measurements as data is that they are and will remain stably accessible and invariant across changes in context or point of view. The presupposition is, that is, that the observations are repeatable, even if not repeated. In the case of doubt as to its satisfaction, the presupposition is tested by bringing different perceivers to the situation (identical or a replica) and ascertaining intersubjective invariance (or its absence), as was done in the case of cold fusion. Furthermore, in many cases, when experiments are repeated, the purpose is not checking but extending a result claimed to have been achieved in the first performance of an experiment. If they fail, among the factors called into question is the original result, even though this might not have been the main purpose of the new experiment. From this point of view, then, the studies of Lynch and Knorr-Cetina are not at all surprising. If intersubjective invariance is an important feature of observational data, then of course experimenters will consult with one another to establish or impose definiteness on initially "flexible" data. Indeed, because one of the professional aims of researchers is to get their data and interpretations taken up by others, the very kind of sociality to which Knorr-Cetina and Latour draw our attention guarantees that researchers will aim for intersubjective invariance of observation. Otherwise, their work will perish.

Miriam Solomon, whose social empiricism is discussed in chapter 7, has articulated another dimension of the sociality of observation in the view she calls "social empiricism."[7] She notes that in major episodes of theory change, such as the geological revolution, aspects of a complex phenomenon are differentially salient to different individuals and to different communities. For example, different geologic features were salient to geologists familiar with Southern Hemisphere phenomena than to geologists familiar with Northern Hemisphere phenomena. Some initially saw in their data reason to resist the plate tectonic view, whereas others saw in *their* data overwhelming reason to adopt it. What tipped the scales, she says, was when the different communities of geologists both had observational data specific to their hemispheres that they understood to support plate tectonics. In this story, different data accessible to different communities of investigators facilitate the development of a consensus view.

The point of emphasizing the sociality of observation is not that an individual could not engage in experimentation or record perceptions on

---

[7] Solomon 1994a. See Grandy 2000 for a different interpretation of this episode.

her own. Indeed, the manual and sensory capacities of individuals are crucial to the social practice of observation. The claim of sociality is the claim that the status of the scientist's perceptual activity as *observation* depends on her relations with others, in particular her openness to their challenge to and correction of her reports. This is what enables the transformation in assertability-status from "It seems to me that p" to "P."[8] The data are established socially through the interactive discursive processing of sensory interactions. There is no way but the interaction of multiple perspectives to ascertain the observational status of individual perceptions.[9]

Reasoning

The second main cognitive element in the production of scientific knowledge is reasoning, which traces lines of evidentiary support between data and theories and hypotheses. Individual brains or minds, of course, engage in calculation, but reasoning (at least scientific reasoning) is not mere calculation; it is combining different kinds of information in the production of conclusions, bringing the appropriate considerations to bear on judgments. Reason here has two senses. One is a constructive sense: reasoning is the combining of ideas or information to produce new ideas. Some of the ideas so combined may be value-laden or value constrained in ways that reflect views of the individual reasoner or the shared assumptions of a community, but the point of constructive reasoning is to increase the cogitative range of the reasoner. In the other, justificatory, sense, reasoning is the combining of ideas or information to support some other idea. Here, too, some of the ideas combined may be value-laden or value-contrained, but the point of justificatory reasoning is not to reach new ideas but to establish the plausibility or likelihood of one already thought or articulated. Where constructive reasoning is creative, justificatory reasoning is grounding. Justificatory reasoning can be understood as part of a practice of challenge and response: challenge to a claim is met by the offering of reasons to believe it, which reasons can then be challenged on grounds both of truth and of relevance, provoking additional reasoning. Justificatory reasoning, thus understood, gets its point in a social context, a context of interaction among individuals rather than

---

[8] Latour (1999) emphasizes that the status of *p* can also move back to an attribution from an affirmation, that is, from "*p*" to "It seems to me (or to S) that *p*." This is (part of) the point of his introduction of the "stabilization gradient."

[9] This is the epistemological dimension of what Joseph Rouse (1987) and Jerome Ravetz (1971) discuss as standardization, a practical aim whose satisfaction enables the transfer of results from laboratory to laboratory and from laboratory to the world outside.

of interaction between an individual and the object of her cogitations. What counts as an appropriate consideration, as a reason, is determined and stabilized through discursive interactions.

In the empirical sciences, observational and experimental data function as the appropriate sorts of consideration. But their precise relevance, even when described and categorized, to particular hypotheses and theories is not self-evident.[10] Both ascertaining the evidential relevance of data to a hypothesis and accepting a hypothesis on the basis of evidence require reliance on substantive and methodological background assumptions. Just as not any old observations will do, so not just any old assumptions will do. In general, the assumptions on which it is permissible to rely are a function of consensus among the scientific community, are learned as part of one's apprenticeship as a scientist, and are largely invisible to practitioners within the community. Although invisible, or transparent, to members of the community, these assumptions are articulable and hence, in principle, public.[11] For example, taking changes in properties like the texture or temperature of a substance as evidence that constitutive parts (e.g., molecules, atoms, subatomic particles) of the substance are undergoing rearrangement is to assume both that substances are composed of smaller elements and that the phenomenological properties of substances are a function of the properties of their constituents. The in-principle publicity of such assumptions makes them available to critical examination, as a consequence of which they may be abandoned, modified, or reinforced. Just as not all experiments are repeated, not all assumptions are in fact so scrutinized, but the presumption in inference is that they would survive scrutiny and criticism, if subjected to it.

Some other recent philosophical work points in the same direction. Both Stewart Cohen and David Annis have argued that what counts as

---

[10] None of this is to deny that theoretical considerations play a role in the selection, reporting, and description of observational and experimental results. For a good account of the role of theory in observation, see Hesse 1980. The point is reinforced, I think, by Miriam Solomon's observations about the role of psychological salience in determining to what observations scientists will assign evidential status. And the social interactions described as involved in observation may also involve application of theoretical considerations to the stabilization of data. We are inclined to extend a greater degree of epistemic privilege to observation, to the extent we think observations are more directly causally related to that of which they are observations than are the conclusions of inferences. Both inference and observation are mediated, but the degrees of freedom in inference or reasoning are greater than in observation.

[11] Eric Reck asked whether this articulability requirement ruled out criticism of items of "tacit knowledge"—for example, that the liquid in the flask has to be poured just so. On reflection, it seems that some of this tacit knowledge can be made explicit (as I have just done) and that the rest is subject to criticism by demonstration—for example, one takes the flask from the other and says, pouring, "Do it this way."

appropriate justification depends on contextual factors.[12] Both treat justification as a practice of meeting objections. The relevant level of objection and the obligations of a believer are determined by context. Annis offers his contextualist analysis as an alternative to both foundationalist and coherentist approaches to justification. Cohen is concerned to spell out a complicated set of relations between prima facie reasons (S has for belief that p) and defeators (objections to those reasons).

Annis analyzes being justified in one's belief that p as meeting or being able to meet two types of objection: those to the effect that one is not in a position to know, and those to the effect that what one purports to know is false. The objections one needs to be able to meet are limited in several ways: they must be appropriate to the "issue context," and they must be assigned a better than low probability by one's challengers. The issue context for a given claim is determined by features of the claimant and of the situation in which the claim is made. These determine the level of understanding and knowledge required of claimant and challenger and what the relevant objector group is. For example, different types of challenge are appropriate for a student in a sixth-grade science class who asserts that polio is caused by a virus and for a biomedical researcher who makes the same assertion at a virology conference. To be justified is to be able to meet objections in a way that satisfies the practices and norms of one's group. This conception of justification is social in two ways. Justification is itself located in the interactive context of challenge and response, and the norms regulating these practices are the norms of a particular social group. This is not to say that they are beyond criticism, but it is to deny that there is some context-free or transcendent set of norms that preempts or trumps the norms of a group. Those norms themselves develop in the course of a community's engaging in the practices of assertion, challenge, and response, and are a second-level product of such practices.

Cohen's essay is devoted to working out the relations of challenge and response in more detail. One significant difference from Annis's account is his introduction of a distinction between intersubjectively and subjectively evident or opaque defeators, which either undermine prima facie reasons (as objections) or restore them (as responses to objections). Evidence and opacity indicate the degree of obviousness of the relevance of defeators to their intended objects. Thus the relevance of a defeator to a given reason may be clear to most members of a community (intersubjectively evident), but not to one of its members (subjectively opaque) or vice versa. These distinctions permit more nuanced judgments of when one is and is not justified in one's belief but the overall approach is simi-

---

[12] Cohen 1987; Annis 1978.

lar to that of Annis's paper. Justification is a social practice and standards of justification (the appropriate degrees of opacity and evidence of defeators) are determined intersubjectively, that is, socially.

Mark Kaplan, in an article demonstrating some problematic assumptions common to naturalized and analytic epistemology, argues that the only way to retain the normative force of principles of reasoning is to regard them not as "rules for the direction of the mind" (to borrow a phrase from Descartes) but as grounds for legitimate criticism of beliefs.[13] This, however, is to locate the role of principles of reasoning in interactions and to see reasoning, insofar as it is subject to normative rules, as social, as proceeding in a context in which shared rules provide a basis for critical discursive interaction.[14]

In a scientific context, in which the interest is in extending knowledge and the means of obtaining it, not in justifying knowledge or cognitive tools already possessed by a community, competing interests must be reconciled. There is a need to go beyond the cognitive resources presently available, and hence to disregard the rules, but at the same time the new avenues opened up must be reliable—that is, dependable when used, invoked, or assumed by others. The subjection of assumptions to criticism is a way to assure their stability and, hence, requisite reliability. Just as the inferences that ground scientific knowledge are socially stabilized, so the inferences that build scientific knowledge are not the inferences made by individual researchers but inferences that proceed through discursive interactions.

These discursive interactions are integral to both observation and reasoning in the sciences. The results of both reasoning and observation, then, are socially processed before incorporation into the body of ideas ratified for circulation and use, or are treated as having been so processed. The critical dimension of cognition is a social dimension, requiring the participation of multiple points of view to insure that the hypotheses accepted by a community do not represent someone's idiosyncratic interpretation of observational or experimental data. If we regard observation and reasoning as consisting of families of cognitive practices, rather than as some idealized set of relations between subjects and the world or between the beliefs of a subject, then we can see that socializing cognition is not a corruption or displacement of the rational

---

[13] Kaplan 1994.

[14] While it is possible to abstract a set of statements that function as responses to objections to a claim and treat them as an argument, and further abstract from sets of arguments to patterns (and then principles) of validity, such patterns are not independent of the interactive, discursive contexts from which they are abstracted. Steve Downes (1993) sees the failure to observe this distinction as one of the major failings of philosophers using cognitive-science approaches to naturalize philosophy of science.

but a vehicle of its performance. The dichotomy between the rational or cognitive and the social has been left behind. The reason that the social practices and processes studied by the sociologists contribute to the production of knowledge is that they are both social and cognitive. They are social processes and practices aimed at producing reliable representations of or recipes for interaction with natural processes. Cognitive processes have a social dimension. Of course, while the sociality of cognitive processes is part of what grants them their warranting status, this social dimension can also be a source of difficulty. For example, the invisibility of many background assumptions as assumptions to a community means that a closed community will not be able to exhibit those assumptions for critical scrutiny. In addition, the degree of intersubjective invariance of a set of observations will be limited by the degree of perspectival variation. But the social is also the source of solutions to these difficulties, just as perception is both the source of cognitive difficulties and of the solutions to those difficulties.

COGNITIVE AGENCY

Understanding the cognitive processes of observation and justificatory reasoning as social in the ways just delineated has consequences for our conception of cognitive agents or subjects of knowledge. What is the S to which knowledge is attributed in the relational sense in which "S knows that p" if S and p satisfy certain conditions? In chapter 2, I argued that an important lesson from the sociological work is that the subjects creating scientific knowledge are located—historically, geographically, socially— and that their locatedness must be taken seriously. To acknowledge the locatedness of subjects is to reject what we might call an "unconditioned subject," that is, a knower guided only by context-independent and value-neutral methodological rules. As seen earlier, the dichotomy between the rational and the social is constructed partly by restricting the rational to rules or algorithms applicable to such neutral and disembodied subjects. The sociologists insist that individual knowers are instead conditioned by various aspects of their social location—from their dependence on government agencies and industry for funding, their location in an intellectual lineage, in a family, in a particular research group, to their position in the race, gender, and class grid of their society.

In particular, subjects are dependent on one another for the establishing and stabilizing of observational and inferential claims. Even philosophically conceived subjects are not disembodied, unlocated, and unconditioned. As is clear from the previous chapter, this does not force us either to holism (the community knows) or to eliminativism (there is no subject, only discursive formations). The account of cognitive practices reveals subjects that are neither wholly independent of others in their cognitive communities nor wholly determined by those communities. They are instead *interdependent*. It is the interaction of subjects exercising their cognitive capacities to observe and reason that stabilizes these processes in a way that permits inquiry or investigation to continue.

The problem with recognizing the social locatedness and, hence, conditioned character of individual epistemic subjects is that it seems to force us into choosing between relativism or demonstrating the epistemic superiority of one among the various social locations. The sociologists embrace relativism, and the philosophers embrace not just the superiority of Western science but are committed to the unique superiority of some one (as yet potential) set of scientific theories—that is, to monism. I wish to reject this choice, which I see as arising from the conflations examined in the previous chapter. Nonabsolutism, from the perspective of individualism, does seem to mean anything goes—to be unbridled relativism. This is because no constraints apart from rules binding on an, in principle, independent individual are recognized.[15] From a nonindividualistic point of view, however, nonabsolutism does not necessarily reduce to whatever the individual wants to believe. Constraints may be of various kinds, such that one might speak of knowledge relative to a given set of constraints or relative to a certain context. Then one could raise a question as to which kinds of constraint or context are more congenial to the distinctions the concept of knowledge is used to mark (see chapter 6). For the moment, it suffices to note that the attribution of knowledge in the relational sense must include some acknowledgment of the social (i.e., interdependent) character of the subjects to which knowledge is attributed.

WHAT IS KNOWN

In the third usage discussed, "knowledge" refers to content, whether an accumulation of representations or of skills, ways of doing things.[16] In this third sense, the distinction marked by using the honorific "knowledge" is a distinction between successful and unsuccessful content. Representational content can be stored—in documents, in memory,

[15] Concerns about relativism sometimes sound as though individuals are not cognitively trustworthy. This supports the unfortunate caricature of epistemologists as a self-appointed epistemic police force. I think the concern is rather that a theory of knowledge that has relativism as a consequence fails to capture the distinction it is intended to give sense to.

[16] This section benefited from comments by Lisa Gannett and Chunghyoung Lee on an earlier draft.

linguistically or imagistically—and is transmissible. The content of practical knowledge may sometimes, when codifiable, be stored and transmitted through documents, but it is also stored and demonstrated bodily. One might think that practical knowledge belongs with knowledge-productive practices, but there are many instances when what a group of scientists is trying to achieve is a method, a way of producing a certain kind of effect. A protocol for a practice, knowledge how to produce a particular effect, is, in such cases, the desired outcome of knowledge-productive practices.

How is success of content to be understood? The disambiguation grid (Table 3 in chapter 4) shows the differences between the sociologists and the philosophers.[17] In the sociologists' usage what is important is the relation between the representation and its users: successful content is content accepted in a community. Sociologists are quite content to call knowledge whatever the communities they study call knowledge. What is called knowledge is content that is used in certain ways by the community. In the philosophers' usage, what is important is the relation between representational content and the intended objects of representation. For philosophers there is a conceptual distinction between what any given community treats as knowledge and genuine knowledge, between what everyone accepts or believes and what is true. Knowledge as content is, first and foremost, a truth or set of truths. Is this an unbridgeable gap or is it possible to understand knowledge in this third sense in a way that can integrate the social and the cognitive?

For philosophers, it seems almost common sense that the meaning of "knowledge" includes truth of the content. Philip Kitcher, for example, has complained that we have a perfectly serviceable set of terms for evaluating purported claims about the natural world: true and false. Why abandon these for less precise and more subjective dimensions of assessment? When the genetic engineer succeeds in inserting a gene into a bacterial plasmid, he says, surely it is because the propositions she or he uses to describe what she or he is doing, including propositions about the molecular structure of the gene, are true. And true in the classical sense of correspondence: there are things just like the scientist's descriptions, and there being those things with the properties assigned to them is what explains her success in manipulating genes, atoms, and the like. Our homegrown notion of truth does just fine and does not require replacing. I would agree that we do have a homegrown notion of truth that functions quite well in those contexts in which we most commonly use it. I would, however, emphasize its homegrownness. We know what it means to call propositions such as "the cat is on the roof" true or false, and we

[17] See also Rediehs 1998.

know how to ascertain whether they are true. But when we extend this correspondence concept to sentences, propositions, or statements (in general—representational content) whose corresponding fact of the matter (in general—intended object) is not so easily ascertainable, we encounter problems. Whereas practical knowledge in science poses no philosophical problem over and above those posed by practical knowledge generally,[18] representational knowledge is another matter. Both Nancy Cartwright and Ian Hacking offer examples of problems posed by certain kinds of representational content in science.

Nancy Cartwright has argued that the laws of physics, strictly construed, are false.[19] In order to make something like Snell's law, or Boyle's law, true, an indefinite number of qualifying clauses, what Cartwright calls ceteris paribus clauses, must be added to the expression of the law. These include clauses stipulating perfect isotropy of the medium in the case of Snell's law, or restriction to ideal gases in the case of Boyle's law, and other clauses further restricting the class of phenomena for which the laws are, strictly speaking, true. Doing so, however, destroys the explanatory value of the laws which can no longer be used to explain phenomena in the real world of anisotropic media and nonideal gases. So correspondence to the facts will not do as an account of the success of the law or of the respect in which it is useful to us. The genetic engineer, if using lawlike statements at all, would describe what she has done with propositions about relationships between genes and phenotypic traits that are, strictly speaking, false, or not ascertainable in the same way that some facts about traits and some separate facts about genes are ascertainable. This point holds whether the trait in question is the sequence of amino acids for some protein or a higher-level trait. But it is not clear that we should deny her descriptions the status of knowledge. They are how the purportedly underlying phenomena are represented. The representations are supremely successful at what they are intended for—to guide our interactions with some messy tissue in glass vials and dishes in order to produce from it what we want. Indeed, they are essential in the practices of genetic engineers. But they do not need to be strictly true, they need only conform enough to the material interacted with to enable the engineer to succeed in getting the gene into the plasmid.

Ian Hacking offers another kind of example.[20] In an essay on what he calls the statistical style of reasoning, he contrasts two types of sentence, superficially the same: "The number of persons in this room at this moment is 30" versus "The population of Paris in 1800 is N" (where N

---

[18] The locus classicus for discussion of practical knowledge is Ryle 1946.
[19] Cartwright 1983.
[20] Hacking 1992b.

is a number in the tens or hundreds of thousands). To the first of these there does correspond a fact of the matter that makes the sentence true or false when uttered. In the second, there is no such fact existing prior to methods of counting populations. Because residency can be a social or a legal category, because city limits are social and legal constructs, because the actual number of people in Paris, whether claiming residence or not, changes over the time necessary to complete a count, the adequacy of the sentence is not its correspondence with some preexistent fact. Its adequacy is a function of the sentence's (proposition's, statement's) having been established in accordance with accepted procedures for verifying sentences of its kind. These procedures include or presuppose criteria of residency, methods of setting boundaries, and strategies of dealing with flux. Success of content, here, is dependent not on the relation of content to intended object, but also on conformity with the procedures adopted to generate content. Absent such procedures, absent the development and implementation of modern statistics, Hacking says, there are no facts of the matter, and the sentence could not be either true or false. This way of putting it makes it seem as though the fact is fabricated. Another way to put the point is to see the sentence about the population of Paris as ambiguous and having as many possible meanings as there are possible procedures. Then, there are many possible facts of the matter and the issue is to decide which of these facts is worth knowing. This is determined in the course of selecting procedures and criteria. There are two kinds of issue forcing choices and decisions. First, the matter of inquiry is itself a socially produced entity: decisions about criteria of residency and about boundaries are social decisions, not the discovery of previously unknown facts. Second, it is not possible to ascertain the matter within its time period of stability. On the microscale, births and deaths, immigration and emigration produce changes, and on the macroscale, there is either growth, decline, or stability in the population, which itself cannot be decided in the absence of a means of measurement more powerful than fingering each individual. This requires the development of a counting technology—of, for example, sampling—that will produce a number for N close enough to the actual range within which the number of people living in Paris (and satisfying specified criteria for inclusion) fluctuates in order to estimate demands on its infrastructure or engage in other tasks requiring some estimate of population size.[21]

---

[21] Indeed, this example helps draw attention to an important feature of scientific inquiry: that it is not about establishing isolated facts but patterns, relationships, and regularities. The population of Paris (or of any large political entity) is not of interest in and of itself but in relation to other such figures. What matters is less the absolute number, than the comparison between it and similar numbers generated by identical counting practices for similar entities: Lyons, Marseilles, and so forth in one comparison; Rome, London, Brussels in

In Cartwright's example, the role of laws in physics, and hence their utility, is such that they cannot correspond in the sense of directly conform to some single matter of fact or collection thereof in the physical world without forfeiting their utility. That utility lies in covering a range of related phenomena in which a similar principle is operating, but the cost of the range is expression of the principle for ideal and unrealized rather than actual situations. The mathematical precision of the laws masks their literal inaccuracy. Not only are laws, strictly speaking, false, but they are more useful in their false versions than in their indefinitely qualified, but true, versions. In Hacking's example, there is a constantly changing phenomenon such that, during the period of a description's adequacy, it will only precisely conform to its object fleetingly, if ever. A style of thought had to be invented to accommodate this measurement challenge. Furthermore, applying any method for obtaining descriptions adequate to the purposes for which they are sought involves an element of conventionality. Statistical representations of the population of Paris will contain elements systematically related to one another, some of which are stipulative (e.g., the definition of "resident") and some of which are, given a particular system of measurement, true. The stipulations may be arbitrary relative to "the facts," but not relative to the needs of the city's bureaucrats. They make perspicuous one set of truths obtainable within the measurement system. Rejected alternatives, while contradicting the perspicuous set, are not false, so much as unsuited to the particular needs for which the count is engaged.

In both types of example, truth is an incorrect description of that in virtue of which competitors are successful, and false is an incorrect description of that in virtue of which competitors are unsuccessful. Neither example, it should be noted, concerns the postulation of unobservable entities, like fundamental particles, which provokes most debates about the possibility of scientific truth. Idealizations, such as laws, bear a different relation to the observable. Both examples also demonstrate another feature that makes "true" or "false" unsatisfactory instruments for evaluation of scientific content. What we call scientific knowledge does not consist of individual propositions or assertions that can stand alone. Individual representations draw their significance from the larger systematic network of representations to which they are related. That Snell's law is, strictly speaking, false would matter if it were not part of a network of representations, some of those being particular measurements of the angle of refraction in particular media, others being higher level laws in optical theory. The whole network gets something right about

---

another. Statistics is ultimately about ratio, proportion, and frequency and distribution, about comparative information rather than categorical or absolute information.

light, but truth as correspondence is not even a desideratum for some elements of the network. Even though truth as correspondence to features in the world is not even a desideratum in those cases, we would not on that account deny that Snell's law or properly constructed estimates of the population of Paris constitute knowledge, nor would we deny that there are criteria for ascertaining their adequacy, in the sense of conformity to the degree required for the purposes at hand. Truth as correspondence then does not seem to express the kind of success that is intended in talk of scientific knowledge.

A further problem with using "true" and "false" as the primary dimensions of evaluation is that they limit candidate representations to the sorts of thing that can be true or false—linguistic entities like propositions or assertions. But much scientific knowledge is contained in images, in diagrams, especially, but also in the images produced by various imaging technologies.[22] These difficulties for "true" or "false" weigh against treating scientific knowledge as content that is true or false. Because propositions or statements are what are paradigmatically true or false, the possible alternatives would either treat content as something other than sets of propositions or develop an account of adequacy or truth that eludes the traps just outlined. In recent philosophy of science, the former strategy has been adopted by proponents of the model theory of theories—that is, the view that scientific theories of a phenomenon are best understood as models of the phenomenon—rather than a set of propositions about the phenomenon. The model theory (not to be confused with model theory in logic) has been advanced for a number of different reasons.[23] For example, Fred Suppe argues that it better captures the actual uses to which theories are put in the sciences. John Beatty argues for the view because the old axiomatic theory has led to the exclusion of some scientific theories (evolutionary theory) as proper theories. Ronald Giere advocates the model approach as more compatible with a cognitive science approach to scientific knowledge. The approach treats theories as models or families of models. There are, however, quite a few different conceptions of what a model is, ranging from a mathematical entity (i.e., a set of equations) to a two-, three-, or four-dimensional visual representation. What the conceptions have in common as treatments of scientific theories is a rejection of the standard view: that theories are sets of propositions, organized as axiomatic systems, that constitute comprehensive accounts of some domain, for example, the physical world or the living world or suitably broad aspects of these domains.

---

[22] See Giere 1988, 1999.

[23] Among the advocates of some version of semantic theory are Beatty 1981, 1987; Giere 1988; Grandy 1992b; Lloyd 1994; Suppe 1977; van Fraassen 1980.

On the standard view, the adequacy of a theory is a matter of the truth by correspondence of the individual propositions constituting the theory. A model, by contrast, is neither true nor false. Instead its structure, or the structure of a subset of its elements, may be identical to a structure in the world. This isomorphism permits the mapping of the relations, structures, and processes of the model onto some portion of the world. Isomorphism is just one of the possible relations between a model and some portion of the world. Homomorphism is another. While "isomorphic" and "homomorphic" refer to one-one relations between constituents of two sets of elements, many different models can be iso- or homomorphic to the same phenomenon, depending on how the phenomenon is parsed. At different levels of resolution (tissue, molecules, atoms; genome, genotype, allele) or from different points of view (structure, function) a phenomenon consists of different sets of constituents, and, hence, different structures, against which iso- or homomorphism of models is ascertained. This many-one (or many-many) character of isomorphism and homomorphism permits multiple, nonintegratable, models to count as successful content, making them much more flexible as instruments of evaluation than truth or falsity.

There is another reason to think of theories as models. Often research programs are guided not by an explicit theory, but by a sense of how things in the domain under study are related. This sense remains unarticulated in the generality in which it is held, and is expressed only in specific accounts of particular instances. I have called such a sense an explanatory model, for it functions as a model or schema of how explanations of particular phenomena in a domain are to be structured.[24] In behavioral endocrinology, for example, behavioral patterns of various sorts are attributed to hormonal exposures at critical periods of organismic development. There is no explicit general theory but rather a number of studies linking different behaviors to different hormone levels. Each of these, however, acquires significance on account of its similarity to the others. It is as though researchers are working with a general picture of a class of systems behaving in similar fashion, without ever articulating a general theory that can be evaluated as true or false. Such a theory, as a picture, is nevertheless a crucial element in the research, determining the way researchers look at and think about the systems under study, the questions they ask, and the experiments they design. Explanatory models, too, then, are scientific content that might merit both the designation "theory" and scrutiny as possibly deserving the honorific "knowledge."

Other philosophers of science have identified a number of other theo-

---

[24] Longino 1990.

retical contexts in which nonpropositional content is crucial to expressing the knowledge produced in those contexts. A Philosophy of Science Association symposium in 1990 focused on its role in biology. Michael Ruse argued that Sewall Wright's diagrams of adaptive landscapes were an essential part of Wright's "shifting balance" theory of evolution, so essential that "the science would not have been done without them."[25] James Griesemer argued that material models (whether three-dimensional structures or two-dimensional diagrams) play multiple roles in knowledge construction—as stand-ins for the material phenomena under investigation, as statement generators, but also as obstacles to conceptual change.[26] William Wimsatt argued that pictures offer in many cases "the most natural, economical, and inferentially fruitful representations of data."[27] Giere, too, stresses the role of visual, nonlinguistic representations in the expression and acceptance of scientific theories.[28] Nonpropositional expression of ideas must be accommodated in our conception of theories.

Two issues are mingled in the preceding discussion. One is whether there are modes of attributing success to content that can serve as alternatives to truth. Another is whether scientific theories, or scientific content generally, are or ought to be thought of as models. To the extent that any scientific content is nonlinguistic, its success must be evaluable in some dimension other than that of (linguistic) truth. Conversely, if there are ways of attributing success that do not require a propositional or linguistic notion of truth, then one obstacle to thinking of theories as models, or as containing nonpropositional content, is eliminated. Is there an alternative to true or false as the appropriate dimension of success? We already have a number of alternative expressions for designating representational success. Isomorphism, homomorphism, and truth, as well as approximation, fit, and similarity, are all species of representational or denotative success. As a more general, a more encompassing notion, I propose "conformation," a term I have already used in the preceding paragraphs to express success of content. This term conveys in a less tendentious and less problematic way than does "true," what the relation between some content—a representation—and the object of that content might be. It can apply to laws and to statistical claims that are not literally true, but that capture the relations in which we are interested. It can apply to linguistic and nonlinguistic entities. And it is open to sociologists' understandings of success in a way that most understandings of

[25] Ruse 1991, 73.
[26] Griesemer 1991.
[27] Wimsatt 1991, 112.
[28] Giere 1999, esp. 118–46.

truth are not. Finally, as a relation between content and object, it can be used to express the respect in which content qualifies as knowledge rather than opinion, for it treats success as at least in part a relation between content and some object or set of objects distinct from that content. "Conformation," thus, can serve as a general term for epistemological success of content.

What does conformation amount to? How can the notion enable users to avoid the problems identified for true or false? One good answer to this concern is found in considerations of maps.[29] A map is a representation of some particular terrain: elements of the map correspond to elements of the terrain—for example, colors to altitudes, dots to towns, lines to roads. What elements of the terrain are represented in a map depends on its purposes: a map for an economic geographer represents type of resource or of economic activity in given regions of the terrain; one for a hiker has altitudes, slopes, and distances; one for a political geographer has national boundaries and successions of them, or forms of governance. One of the criteria of adequacy of a map is that it preserve in the representation the relative dimensions of the relations of interest between the elements of interest as they are in the terrain. If distance is a relation of interest and A, B, and C elements of interests and the distance from A to B is twice that from A to C, the mapping conventions, or the idiom of the map, should enable the representation of this ratio, but if relative quantity of biomass is of interest, then that is what the idiom of the map should be able to express. There is a great deal of conventionality regarding the idioms of representation in mapping, but once the conventions are fixed, specifying, say, colors to represent types of vegetation rather than economic activity, then the features of the terrain itself (within the limits of the representational idiom and the purposes the representation is designed to serve) determine the adequacy or inadequacy of the map.

Maps teach us that there can be degrees of fit, degrees of conformation. How much conformation is required and of what to what depends on the purposes of the map. Once these are specified, conformity or failure of conformity depends on the terrain. The map with the best fit is not the one with the greatest possible resolution. Because that would duplicate the terrain being mapped, it would be useless. A map must be a partial representation; otherwise it fails to be a map. The best map is the one that best enables its users to accomplish their goals, whether that be

---

[29] See also Ronald Giere's discussions (1999) of maps. Giere uses his discussion to articulate his perspectival realism, but we are both emphatic about using a very general notion, such as representation, to refer to the content of scientific knowledge, as well as about the inappropriateness of "true" for many forms of that content.

distributing aid or police services, planning irrigation systems, or getting across a mountain range. Even if getting across a mountain range is the goal, different maps will be suited to different journeys. One may make the quickest routes salient; another may make the most scenic routes salient. Which is better depends on how and why one wishes to cross the range. Each map constitutes knowledge in specified respects of the terrain of which it is a map. Each is a product of complex knowledge-productive practices. Are maps a good model for other products of knowledge-productive practices—that is, for scientific knowledge?

Maps fit or conform to their objects to a certain degree and in certain respects. I am proposing to treat conformation as a general term for a family of epistemological success concepts including truth, but also isomorphism, homomorphism, similarity, fit, alignment, and other such notions. Classical truth is a limiting concept in a category of evaluation that in general admits of degree and requires the specification of respects. Truth is where degree and respects fall away. This approach avoids the crudity of a binary evaluation, and hence avoids one of the problems attributed to true or false. Iso- and homomorphism can be achieved in many ways. Many different representations will be isomorphic (or, mutatis mutandis, homomorphic) to a given natural process just because different combinations of elements of that process will constitute the set conformation with which is required. Alternative isomorphic or homomorphic representations must, therefore, be assessed not just with regard to their isomorphism but also with respect to the assessors' interests in that process. Idealizations like laws are not, strictly speaking, true because there is not a particular situation that they accurately and precisely represent, but they conform to the range of phenomena over which they are idealizations in the way a map conforms to its terrain. Like maps, they are useful just because they do not represent any particular situation, but rather make salient a feature common to a family of similar situations, and in particular because they make salient a feature in which the law's users are interested. Conformation permits sorting representations along a continuum or several continua, rather than dividing them into two exclusive classes, irrespective of how well they suit our purposes, as does the true-false binary.

Conformation is also more suitable than true or false for expressing the ways in which complex content, such as a theory or model, is successful representation. Complex content may contain, like the theory of optics, or the statistical representation of the population of a large city, some content that is conventional, some that is, strictly speaking, false but fits its object like a map fits its terrain, and some that is, given a set of conventions, strictly speaking, true. Similarly, content may be complex in virtue of being partially propositional and partly visual or material. We often want to say of a whole complex—for example, the theory of optics, the theory of special relativity, or the synthetic theory of evolution—that it constitutes knowledge. It conforms, even though its components conform in different respects and to different degrees. Its components are not all, strictly speaking, true, but as long as the whole conforms to its object in this sense, it constitutes knowledge.

The second issue embedded in the preceding discussion of models is whether scientific theories are best understood as models instead of as sets of propositions. What counts as a model in this discussion is a pretty heterogeneous assemblage: sets of equations, specifications of structure, visual representations, mental maps, diagrams, static three-dimensional objects like the wire and plastic models of the DNA molecule, or four-dimensional models that incorporate change or motion. Different philosophers stress different kinds of models in their presentations. Maps, as discussed previously, are a kind of model, and the same issues of appraisal that apply to maps apply with even greater force to models in general. Elements of any portion of the world stand in many relations to many other elements. Like a map, a model selects among those relations, presenting the results of that selection as a coherent, interrelated set. Like maps, many models can be isomorphic to some portion of the world as long as elements in the models stand in the same relations to each other as some set of elements in that portion of the world do to each other. The choice of a model, therefore, is not just a function of its isomorphism (or the isomorphism of a subset of its elements) with a portion of the world, but also a function of the relations it picks out being ones in which the users of the model are interested. It must represent the world in a way that facilitates the interactions its users seek to have with the modeled domain. Finally, like maps, models must be sorted into grades of adequacy in multiple categories, rather than into a single binary category.

In earlier publications I invoked these features of models as reasons to embrace the view that theories are, or are correctly analyzed as, models.[30] This strikes me now as too restrictive. I think that we ought instead to see models as one kind of representation in science, and a form in which theories are often presented.[31] Seeing how theories are like models can help us to understand aspects of scientific knowledge. But rather than deny that theories can be propositional, it may be more fruitful to transfer some of the attractive aspects of models to propositional presentations of theories. We may, for example, think of propositions as conforming to their intended objects just in case there is sufficient alignment between the elements of the proposition and elements of the object that we can successfully carry out our projects with respect to the object.

Treating scientific knowledge as (representational) content evaluable in regards to its conformation with its intended object makes it possible to incorporate both the sociologist's and the philosopher's sense of success. The sociologist treats knowledge as what is accepted in a community as knowledge. The sign of such acceptance is use. Theories and models are not treated as knowledge in a scientific community and the society that supports it unless they conform sufficiently to enable their users to interact successfully with the domain of which they are theories and models. This is why the philosopher balks at the idea that success could consist solely in acceptance. The distressing picture this conjures up is concluding that group differences in IQ are heritable because, if this were true, it would justify cutting off funding to Headstart, or limiting the study of cancer to genetic rather than environmental factors because genetic factors are easier to address or because the genetic approach is more compatible with the interests of contemporary industry.[32] Success can not just be a matter of the user *wanting* the theory to be correct or wanting to be able to act as if the supposed consequences of the theory are true. If they are not, reality will eventually bite back. To suppose that success has nothing to do with the interests of the users is just as fruitless, however. The idiom of representation must be such as to enable successful interaction with that which is represented. The choice of idiom, and of the degrees to and respects in which it must fit the objects of representation, is a social choice, a matter of goals collectively endorsed in the community conducting inquiry. In this sense the community determines what will count as knowledge. We rate the adequacy of theories and models by their power to enable us to pursue our endeavors successfully with respect to the domains of which they are representations.

The sociologist or cultural analyst is sometimes read as though she or he were advocating a view that the success of any individual representation is a matter of negotiation and that objects are constructed by constructing representations and persuading others to accept them. But Latour, for example, in talking of the construction of TRF or of the anthrax bacillus is talking about substances that can be moved from place to place and that have material effects. What the disputes are about is how to characterize these substances. Construction is not fabrication from whole cloth. Latour resists the claim that the anthrax bacillus as

---

[32] This is the picture that prompts critics of the sociologist to point out that we can not set gravity to zero just because we do not wish to fall when we step off the cliff. Such a criticism misses the point. After all, if wishing that something were so were all there were to it, there would be no point in the expense of science. The sociologist would have a much bigger explanatory problem.

manipulated in Pasteur's laboratory existed in the field with its laboratory properties waiting to be discovered. But there is no doubt that the bacillus whose virulence can be controlled in the laboratory is a real object.[33] Even Foucauldian objects are independent of particular representations. Representations within a discourse can succeed or fail to pick out aspects of the objects of inquiry propelled to attention or constituted by that discourse. A Foucauldian discourse does not create an object or a domain of objects out of nothing but foregrounds certain aspects of objects and processes or of sets of objects and processes in relation to some set of interests regarding aspects of experience in which those elements participate.[34] While the observation of a given phenomenon may be social and the conclusion that a given measurement correctly represents the phenomenon may also be achieved socially, what is being concluded is that the phenomenon is (or is not) represented in the respect and to the degree selected in the chosen idiom. This is not a matter of choice. If there is no conformation, no fit, we will be lost—in the mountains and in the laboratory.

Some philosophers might reply to all this that truth is as flexible a concept as conformation, that we can speak of degrees of truth and distinguish between useful truths and useless truths. They might even argue that we can speak of visual representations in terms of their truth or falsity. Other philosophers might balk at the introduction of a new term, when true is the accepted way of indicating epistemological success of content. These philosophers might advocate a deflationary analysis of truth and propose that gradation and utility can be predicated of the representations instead of their evaluations. I have no quarrel with such approaches as long as the role of degrees and respects (and hence of

[33] Latour underlines this point (1999, esp. 145–73).

[34] Some readers of Foucault seem to think that a discourse brings its objects into existence in the way a work of fiction brings its objects into existence. It is true that once a fictional world has been created, there are true and false assertions that can be made about its objects. This is one reason writers talk about discovering facts about their characters, and why literature instructors can mark a paper down if a student locates Don Quixote in the wrong century or wrong part of Spain. But the discourses Foucault is trying to understand require that there be real things corresponding in some sense to the objects of inquiry. What he emphasizes is the partiality and interest relativity of any discourse. A discourse specifies what sentences can be true or false and how that will be determined, but then it is the objects, or features of reality independent of the sentence, that determine for any qualifying sentence that it is true or false, not the other way round. The relation of power and knowledge requires that objects are what they are independently of what we say about them. Specifying what it is they are, however, is saying something about them, and what is said is always part of a discursive regime and cannot be understood or evaluated as a context-free entity. The looping effects of socially constructed categories noted by Hacking (1995) are productive of social phenomena, but those are no less real than nonsocial phenomena.

social interactions) in determining what counts as scientific knowledge is preserved. It is, however, the difficulty in making such alternative analyses stick that motivates my alternative proposal that there is a family of success terms or relations including but not limited to true or false in the general success category of conformation. What particular kind of success within the general category is required depends on features of the content (whether it is a singular statement, an abstract physical principle, a statistical claim, a diagram, a schema, an equation, etc.)

The purpose of this section has been to give an account of scientific knowledge in the sense of content in a way that remains open to elements of both the sociologists' and the philosophers' concepts. The success that has been the focus of discussion is success of content that warrants the designation "knowledge." This is distinct from the success of science, so often invoked in discussions of scientific realism. The success of science consists in successful prediction and interaction with natural phenomena and the consequent enhancement of human capacities as a consequence of scientific inquiry: the ability to send vehicles to the moon and to other planets, to manipulate seed stocks, to communicate almost instantaneously across vast distances. The scientific realist argues that only the literal truth of the theories that have made these feats possible can explain the success of activities that utilize them. The instrumentalist argues that the success of science requires only the empirical adequacy of the theories used in the performance of activities utilizing them. Conformation does not express the success of science, but the success of content that purports to be knowledge. The debate between the scientific realists and antirealists is partly a debate about the aims of science. Van Fraassen, speaking for antirealism, says science aims only at empirical adequacy and is successful when it achieves it. Realists think the point of science is to provide insight into the structure of the universe. Instrumentalists think the point of science is to enable successful prediction and control of natural processes. This difference can be expressed in the rubric of conformation. For the scientific realist the degree of conformation required is conformation of theoretical content of a theory with actual underlying structures and processes. For the instrumentalist or antirealist with respect to theories, only the observational content must conform to observable phenomena.[35]

---

[35] It's worth remembering here that the instrumentalist or the antirealist with respect to scientific theories is not (or not necessarily) an idealist. The instrumentalist must assume the reality of whatever she or he holds the observational content of a theory to be true of or hold for. Thus, metaphysical issues of realism are not avoided by any solution to the debates about scientific realism. See Rediehs 1998. The scientific realist and antirealist can be understood to differ as to how far scientific knowledge extends. This point is pursued further in the following chapter.

CONCLUSION

In the previous chapter, I distinguished three different senses of knowledge that are conflated in debates between the empirically oriented sociologists and the conceptually oriented philosophers. We can call these modalities of knowledge. "Knowledge" can mean knowledge-productive practices; a state ascribed to one who satisfies certain conditions (e.g., standing in an appropriate set of relations with representations and their objects); or a content, what is known, expressed in some medium or other. The respective concerns of the sociologists and their philosophical opponents bear on these different modalities in different ways. Part of the communicative impasse between the two camps is a function of criticizing views or responding to criticism of views relevant to one modality in terms relevant to another. In this chapter, I have offered alternative accounts of the elements to which knowledge is ascribed that involve contextuality of knowledge-productive practices or justification, interdependence of the agents said to know, and plurality, through the notion of conformation, of content. These accounts move the distinctions valued by the philosophers into the empirical domain investigated by the sociologists. Freed from the dichotomy that plagues the views discussed in the first section, these accounts show that the rational and the social are in some ways bound together and in others open to one another. The social is not a corrupting but a validating element in knowledge.

It is important to realize that the sociality thesis does not deny the importance of individuals in the construction of knowledge. *Of course*, Galileo and Newton and Darwin and Einstein were individuals of extraordinary intellect, but what made their brilliant ideas *knowledge* were the processes of critical reception. Comparing the fate of their ideas with those of a thinker of arguably equal intellectual power, Freud, demonstrates this. The (justificatory) activities of knowledge construction as distinct from belief formation (a generative process) are the activities of individuals in interaction, of individuals in certain relations (of criticism and response) with others. The cognitive abilities of individuals are both necessary and sufficient for the generation of ideas, but idea or belief generation is not the same as knowledge production, which involves processes of validation as well as of generation. The account of cognitive agency as involving interdependence means that individuals know to the extent they interact critically with others in cognitive communities. The context-bound character of validation and the characterization of cognitive agents as interdependent does not deny the importance of individual agents in the construction of knowledge. It does mean that attributing knowledge to them is attributing to them some relation to their cognitive communities, as well as to the objects and content of knowledge. Like other grounds of knowledge, the social is also a source of error. Thus, to say that the social aspect of cognitive practices is part of the ground of the distinction between knowledge and opinion is not yet to show how this is so. This is the task of the next chapter.

CHAPTER SIX

Socializing Knowledge

THE ANALYSIS continues by offering definitions of "knowledge" in each of the modalities distinguished in the previous chapter. These definitions incorporate norms applicable to social interaction as well as philosophically conventional epistemic norms. I offer three arguments for this socialized (not *sociologized*) account of knowledge: the socialized account overcomes the difficulties posed by the underdetermination problem without simply denying its existence or employing covert metaphysical principles; meets the challenges posed by the sociologizers and the rationalizers to one another; and, unlike other accounts, is neutral with respect to the question of pluralism or monism.

UNDERDETERMINATION AND CONTEXT

It is tempting to think that scientific knowledge is like ordinary knowledge except better.[1] But scientists are not (or not just) better observers and more careful reasoners than the rest of us, they also observe and reason differently and to different ends. The purpose of scientific inquiry is not only to describe and catalog, or even explain, that which is present to everyday experience, but to facilitate prediction, intervention, control, or other forms of action on and among the objects in nature. Description and classification are in service to these more overarching purposes, which move the focus of inquiry away from what is present to us to the principles, processes, and mechanisms that produce or underlie what is present to us. This involves making visible (e.g., via dissection or vision-enhancing instruments) what is invisible; in other cases it involves postulating, and devising indirect methods of investigating, processes and mechanisms beyond the range of human sensory capacities—too long or too short in duration, too big or too small to be perceived, outside of the frequency ranges to which human senses are open. In most cases these activities take place in and on idealized situations, whether in the laboratory or in thought experiments, so as to be able carefully to examine one aspect of a process rather than be stymied by attempting to render its full

---

[1] Kitcher (1993) seems to advance this position.

complexity. This way of experiment is arguably what most distinguishes modern Western science from other modes of knowledge or inquiry.

The concern with processes and mechanisms that facilitate human intervention in the natural world is manifest in the kind of science first fully developed in the modern period—mechanics—and in the close ties that have developed between Western productive capacities and scientific knowledge. In spite of this concern with what underlies experienced processes, establishing theories, in the sense of large-scale systematic accounts of a range of related phenomena, is not at the center of most scientists' work. Rather they presuppose theories and defend them when challenged, but as a distraction from their central mission, which is to answer (in light of general theoretical frameworks) specific, carefully articulated questions addressed to the idealized situation of the physical or mental laboratory or to some carefully circumscribed portion of the natural world. The practice of understanding natural phenomena by reference to underlying causal processes gives rise to the logical problem of underdetermination.

The representation of the general structure of inquiry as shaped by a theoretical framework both obscures and makes visible the underdetermination that is the condition of empirical research that seeks access to underlying states and processes. It obscures it by making questions asked in a real setting the salient feature of inquiry. Philosophical and sociological scholars of science who focus on the details of particular scientific investigations move issues of large-scale justification to the periphery of concern as they show how knowledge is produced within a framework both they and the scientists whose work they study hold constant. Thus, the issue of justification as traditionally understood, and for which underdetermination is a clear challenge, is displaced from the center of attention. But, at the same time, this representation makes underdetermination visible by referring, even if parenthetically, to the theoretical framework within which questions are formulated. The dependence on such frameworks, necessary to engage in constructive reasoning about underlying processes, produces a gap. This gap between what is present to us and the processes that we suppose produce the world that is present to us, between our data and the theories, models, and hypotheses developed to explain the data, has been at the heart of philosophical reflection about scientific knowledge. Once the logical empiricists abandoned the notion that all meaningful theoretical statements could be fully translated into observational statements, the problem of characterizing the relation between observation and theory haunted philosophy of science. Russell Hanson, Thomas Kuhn, and Paul Feyerabend emphasized the ways in which theory influenced observation.[2] They introduced the notion of the

---

[2] Hanson 1958; Kuhn 1962; Feyerabend 1962.

"theory-ladenness" of observation—that is, that observation is not neutral, but is permeated by theoretical commitments. The meaning of scientific terms, too, was held to be theory-laden. This closes the gap between observation and theory, but at the price, as many philosophers protested, of circularity. Philosophical discussion of theory-ladenness seems to have stabilized in agreement that observation reports both depend on and imply theoretical commitments, but that as long as the theory that loads the observation or description of data is not the theory for which the data are invoked as evidence, circularity is avoided.[3]

Underdetermination, however, persists. As long as the content of theoretical statements does not consist of generalizations of data or the content of observational statements is not identified with theoretical claims, then there is a gap between hypotheses and data, and the choice of hypothesis is not fully determined by the data. Nor do hypotheses specify the data that will confirm them. Data alone are consistent with different and conflicting hypotheses and require supplementation. This problem is distinct from the traditional problem of justifying induction, which concerns the relation between a generalization and its instances. Pierre Duhem, the first philosopher of science to raise the underdetermination problem, emphasized assumptions about instruments, for example, that a microscope has a given power of resolution, or that a telescope is transmitting light from the heavens and not producing images internally, or not systematically distorting the light it receives.[4]

But the content of background assumptions also includes substantive (empirical or metaphysical) claims that link the events observed as data with postulated processes and structures. For example, that two kinds of event are systematically correlated is evidence that they have a common cause or that one causes the other in light of some highly general, even metaphysical, assumptions about causality. The correlation, for example, of exposure to or secretion of a particular hormone with a physiological or behavioral event is evidence that the hormone causes the physiological or behavioral phenomenon in light of an assumption that hormones have a causal or regulative status in the processes in which they are found rather than being epiphenomenal to or effects of those processes. Such an assumption has both empirical and metaphysical dimensions. Assumptions of this kind establish the evidential relevance of data to hypotheses. They provide a model of the domain being investigated that enables particular investigations to proceed. Some philosophers have proposed principles, such as simplicity or explanatory power, as closing the gap

[3] See in this connection Hesse 1980, 63–110.
[4] Duhem 1954.

between hypotheses or theories and their evidence.[5] There are well-known difficulties in interpreting any of these proposed principles, as well as in applying them.[6] So, while individuals or even research communities may rely on them in the selection of hypotheses, their epistemic status is the same as that of more substantive assumptions.

Underdetermination has sometimes been called the Duhemian problem and, as such, has been expressed as the in-principle possibility of constructing multiple empirically equivalent, mutually inconsistent theories for any given body of evidence. Quine enlisted a version of Duhem's arguments in his attack on the logical empiricist version of the distinction between observation and theory, and in support of his views concerning the revisability of *any* statement in a network of beliefs. In the absence of equally developed empirically equivalent theories, this possibility seems, as Hacking puts it, fanciful.[7] But this is only one way of understanding underdetermination. The underdetermination problem, as I understand it, does not depend on wholistic views about meaning, or on a metaphysical or semantic view about observation and theory. It is an epistemological problem: the consequence of the gap between evidence and hypotheses produced by our postulation of different entities and processes in our explanations of phenomena than occur in our descriptions of those phenomena.

The background assumptions that fill that gap, then, include substantive and methodological hypotheses that, from one point of view, form the framework or proximate intellectual context within which inquiry is pursued and, from another, structure the domain within which inquiry is pursued. These hypotheses are most often not articulated but presumed by the scientists relying on them. They facilitate the reasoning between what is known and what is hypothesized. From a traditional perspective this raises major problems for justification: if the justification of hypotheses requires assumptions, then how are these assumptions in turn justified? And how is it possible to screen out biasing factors such as individual idiosyncrasies, wishful thinking, values, social prejudices, ideologies, tacit metaphysics? In some cases evidence for assumptions can be offered, but the same problem of underdetermination besets this evidential reasoning as well. Even if scientists are not concerned in their daily practice with directly justifying the assumptions that structure their reasoning, philosophers concerned with the nature of scientific knowledge must be.

---

[5] See, among others, Kuhn 1962, 1977; McMullin 1983; Quine and Ullian 1970.
[6] See van Fraassen 1989; Longino 1996.
[7] Hacking 1999.

The logical problem of underdetermination shows that empirical reasoning takes place against a background of assumptions that are neither self-evident nor logically true.[8] The identification of good reasons is similarly context-dependent, whether this is accomplished by the scientist in action or by the philosopher in reflection. As we saw in chapter 1, some sociologists of science have used versions of the underdetermination problem to argue that epistemological concerns with truth and good reasons are irrelevant to the understanding of scientific inquiry. The point, however, should not be that observation and logic as classically understood are irrelevant but that they are insufficient. The sociologists' empirical investigations show that they are explanatorily insufficient. The underdetermination argument of philosophers shows that they are epistemically insufficient. Rather than spelling doom for the epistemological concerns of the philosopher, the logical problem of underdetermination together with the studies of laboratory and research practices changes the ground on which philosophical concerns operate. This new ground or problem situation is constituted by treating agents or subjects of knowledge as located in particular and complex interrelationships and acknowledging that purely logical constraints cannot compel them to accept a particular theory. That network of relationships—among other individuals, social systems, natural objects, and natural processes—is not an obstacle to knowledge, but can be understood as a rich pool of varied resources, constraints, and incentives to help close the gap left by logic.[9] The philosophical concern with justification is not irrelevant, but must be somewhat reconfigured in order to be made relevant to scientific inquiry.

SOCIAL NORMS FOR SOCIAL KNOWLEDGE

Elsewhere I have argued that an individualist bias in philosophy stands in the way of solutions to problems, such as underdetermination, confronting the possibility of scientific knowledge.[10] Some see the solution afforded by a social account of knowledge as worse than the problem. I claim, in contrast, that this judgment is a result of accepting a false dichotomy between the rational or cognitive and the social and that scientific knowledge is produced by cognitive processes that are fundamen-

---

[8] For a reaffirmation of the problem of underdetermination against a variety of recent attempts to defuse it, see Potter 1996. For another recent discussion, see Hempel 1988.

[9] I am grateful to C. K. Waters for his helpful suggestions regarding this formulation. It puts philosophical concerns into relationship with actor-network theory rather than seeing them as antagonists.

[10] Longino 1990.

tally social. An adequate normative theory of knowledge must then be a normative theory of social knowledge, a theory whose norms apply to social practices and processes of cognition.

Critical discursive interactions are social processes of knowledge production. They determine what gets to remain in the public pool of information that counts as knowledge. Thus, a normative account of knowledge must rest on norms governing such interactions. Criticism must be epistemologically effective—by helping a community avoid falsehood and by helping to bring its accepted content into alignment with its cognitive goals and its cognitive standards. Effective critical interactions transform the subjective into the objective, not by canonizing one subjectivity over others, but by assuring that what is ratified as knowledge has survived criticism from multiple points of view.[11] I reiterate, with some modifications, the criteria I take to be necessary to assure the effectiveness of discursive interactions.

1. *Venues.* There must be publicly recognized forums for the criticism of evidence, of methods, and of assumptions and reasoning. This means that criticism of research ought to be articulated in the same standard and public venues in which "original research" is presented: journals, conferences, and so on. In addition, critical activities should be given the same weight or nearly the same weight as is given to "original research": effective criticism that advances understanding being as valued as original research that opens up new domains for understanding; pedestrian, routine, or uninformed criticism being valued comparably with pedestrian, routine, or incompetent "original research." As Mill argued, criticism not only spurs evaluation and reevaluation of hypotheses, but also leads to better appreciation of their grounds and of their conequences. Readers may wonder whether the availability of venues is not so trivial a requirement as not to be worth mentioning. On the contrary, a complex set of processes in the institutions of contemporary science in the industrial and post-industrial world works against satisfaction of this requirement. The limitations of space, the relation of scientific research to production and commerce whose consequence is privatization of information and ideas, and an understanding of research as the generation of positive results, all contribute to the marginalization of critical discourse.

2. *Uptake.* There must be uptake of criticism. The community must not merely tolerate dissent, but its beliefs and theories must change over time in response to the critical discourse taking place

[11] The transformation in question is one of status, not one of kind. For additional discussion of subjectivity and objectivity, see Longino 1990, 1994; Lloyd 1995a, 1995b.

within it. This standard does not require that individuals or research groups capitulate to criticism, but that community members pay attention to and participate in the critical discussion taking place and that the assumptions that govern their group activities remain logically sensitive to it. The change may comprise the acceptance of different beliefs, the modification of beliefs, the development of new data, reasons, and arguments. Uptake is what makes criticism part of a constructive and justificatory practice. Uptake cuts both ways: not only must the community be responsive, but the claims of advocates of a line of criticism must take account of those responses.

3. *Public Standards.* There must be publicly recognized standards by reference to which theories, hypotheses, and observational practices are evaluated and by appeal to which criticism is made relevant to the goals of the inquiring community. First, in order for criticism to be relevant to a position, it must appeal to something accepted by those who hold the position criticized. Similarly, alternative theories must be perceived to have some bearing on the concerns of a scientific community in order to obtain a hearing. Participants in a dialogue must share some referring terms, some principles of inference, and some values or aims to be served by the shared activity of discursive interaction.[12] Thus, shared elements are necessary for the identification of points of agreement, points of disagreement, and what would count as resolving the former or destabilizing the former. Second, relevance to the concerns of a community is not a function of the whim of individuals but rather of public standards or criteria to which members of the community are or feel themselves bound. The point is not so much that individuals spontaneously act out their allegiance to these standards as that they acknowledge their relevance to the evaluation of cognitive practices in their community of inquiry. A community's standards are themselves subordinated to its overall cognitive aims, which will be implicit in its practices even if not fully explicit.

The point of requiring standards that are public is that by explicitly or implicitly professing adherence to those standards individuals and communities adopt criteria of adequacy by which they may be nonarbitrarily evaluated. The satisfaction of goals of inquiry is not ascertained privately, but by evaluation with respect to shared values

---

[12] For intracommunity criticism, this condition satisfied by definition, because communities are partially constituted by such shared discursive elements. For intercommunity criticism, effort is required to identify commonalities and produce agreement or disagreement. This effort is subject to all the vicissitudes of cross-cultural communication and translation.

and standards. This evaluation may be performed by anyone, not just by members of the community sharing all standards.

Finally, standards are not a static set but may themselves be criticized and transformed, in reference to other standards, goals, or values held temporarily constant. Indeed, as in the case of observation and the assumptions underlying justificatory reasoning, the presupposition of reliance on such standards is that they have survived similar critical scrutiny. There is no particular act of adopting or establishing standards. Rather they come to operate as such in the same ways that content is accepted as knowledge: by being let stand through multiple acts of microcognition and microcriticism.[13]

4. *Tempered Equality*. Finally, communities must be characterized by equality of intellectual authority. Put this way, the criterion is too crude.[14] The experience of most people reading this passage is that, even when we limit our consideration to adults, members of our communities differ in intellectual capacity. The difficulty is that some may differ because of innate endowment: some of us are better at certain kinds of things than others. And some may differ because of schooling and other opportunities. So, equality must be qualified or tempered. Specification of the kind of tempering to which equality must submit requires specifying the role and purpose of this criterion.

A diversity of perspectives is necessary for vigorous and epistemically effective critical discourse. The social position or economic power of an individual or group in a community ought not determine who or what perspectives are taken seriously in that community. Where consensus exists, it must be the result not just of the exercise of political or economic power, or of the exclusion of dissenting perspectives, but a result of critical dialogue in which all relevant perspectives are represented.[15] While this criterion has obvious affinities with Jürgen Habermas's account of truth, it is not offered as a criterion of truth, but as a criterion distinguishing legitimate from illegitimate consensus. The requirement of (tempered) equality of intellectual authority implies both that the persuasive

---

[13] For the role of *letting stand* in collective belief, see Gilbert 1987.

[14] C. K. Waters has persuaded me that equality *simpliciter* is too crude. He proposes "appropriate distribution of intellectual authority" as a more sensitive criterion. I have instead opted for "tempered equality," borrowing from the title of one of his papers, but not at his suggestion.

[15] Here is where this criterion, as an epistemological criterion, differs from equality as a moral or political criterion. The latter would require only that different perspectives have an equal chance of being included, whereas epistemic effectiveness requires that all (relevant) perspectives be included.

effects of reasoning and argument be secured by unforced assent to the substantive and logical principles used in them, rather than by properties, such as social or economic power, of those who are propounding them; and that every member of the community be regarded as capable of contributing to its constructive and critical dialogue.[16]

The point of the requirement is to ensure the exposure of hypotheses to the broadest range of criticism. An example of the consequences of this condition is the kind of judgment it supports of exclusionary practices. The exclusion of women and members of certain racial minorities from scientific education and the scientific professions constitutes not only a social injustice but a cognitive failing. Similarly, the automatic devaluation in Europe and North America of science from elsewhere constitutes a cognitive failing. Feminist scholars have demonstrated how assumptions about sex and gender structure a number of research programs in biological, behavioral, and other sciences.[17] Historians and sociologists of racist practices and ideologies have documented the role of racial assumptions in the sciences.[18] The long-standing devaluation of women's voices and of those of members of racial minorities means that such assumptions were for a long time protected from critical scrutiny. Even if the absence of women and members of ethnic minorities was self-chosen, rather than imposed, it would constitute a flaw, as their absence reduces the critical resources of the community. Thus a community must not only treat its acknowledged members as equally capable of providing persuasive and decisive reasons and must do more than be open to the expression of multiple points of view; it must also take active steps to ensure that alternative points of view are developed enough to be a source of criticism and new perspectives. Not only must potentially dissenting voices not be discounted; they must be cultivated.

Equality is, nevertheless, tempered in several respects. While the criterion imposes duties of inclusion and attention, it does not require that each individual, no matter what their past record or

[16] There can be mixed cases. The substantive principles may include socially, economically, or otherwise valenced content. And there may be occasions when dialogue selects several possibilities, community selection among which is effected by mimicry of the most powerful. In such cases, delegation to a subgroup should be regarded as a practice or standard that must survive criticism in conditions characterized by the four criteria.

[17] Cf. Keller 1985, 1992; Bleier 1984; Hubbard 1990; Jordanova 1993; Haraway 1989, 1991, among others.

[18] Cf. Lewontin, Rose, and Kamin 1984; Proctor 1988; Gould 1981; Paul 1995, among others.

state of training, should be granted equal authority on every matter. The public standards mentioned in the preceding condition are intended partly to protect inquiry from such cacophany, for their obligations cut two ways. Subscription to them does impose obligations on members of a knowledge-productive community to attend to criticism that is relevant to their cognitive and practical aims. But it also limits the sorts of criticisms to which a community must attend to those which affect the satisfaction of its goals. The point of the present condition is that such criticism may originate from an indeterminate number of points of view, none of which may be excluded from the community's interactions without cognitive impairment. Nevertheless, the advocates of a point of view, and through them the point of view itself, may lose or even forfeit intellectual authority if their discursive interactions do not satisfy the second condition of uptake. That is, reiterating the same old complaint no matter what response is offered eventually disqualifies one as a member of a discursive community of equals.

The foregoing remarks are both gestures toward spelling out how equality must be tempered and indications of the sorts of questions that must yet be addressed. For example, in determining what counts as inappropriate exclusion of dissenting perspectives, does it matter what kind of issue is involved? Are the duties of inclusion different when the question is, Should we be trying to learn about such and such, for example, atomic fission? than when it is, Is atomic fission a controllable or uncontrollable process? What is the range of matters to which the criterion of tempered equality applies? Does it extend, for example, to whether and how to use nonhuman animals in experimentation? Furthermore, the condition speaks of intellectual authority, not cognitive authority.[19] It is compatible with according greater cognitive authority on some matters to those one regards as having acquired more knowledge concerning those matters than others. What bearing should greater cognitive authority have on the attribution of intellectual authority, understood as the capacity to participate in critical discussion and thus to contribute to critical understanding? The tempered equality condition also raises complex questions of community membership. It requires both that scientific communities be inclusive of relevant subgroups within the

---

[19] In this distinction, cognitive authority has to do with the amount of knowledge one has, and is thus fairly domain-specific. One can be cognitively authoritative with respect to matters in astrophysics but ignorant of cell biology. Intellectual authority is less a matter of having knowledge than of having cognitive or intellectual skills of observation, synthesis, or analysis, which enable one to make cogent comments about matters concerning which one knows less than another.

society supporting those communities and that communities attend to criticism originating from "outsiders." It makes us ask who constitutes the "we" for any given group, and what the criteria are for providing an answer. Are "we" those actively engaged in producing knowledge of a certain kind for a certain aim, as members of a laboratory group are, or should "we" encompass also all those potentially affected by that knowledge? Do our educational practices exclude certain perspectives or discourage criticism? The social approach to scientific knowledge places such questions at the center of philosophy of science. While some of them will be broached in later chapters, they require far more discussion than is possible in this book.

The features I have enumerated are features of an idealized epistemic community. In practice, then, they are criteria of knowledge-productive capacity that take the critical interactions within communities and institutions as their domain of application. As such they constitute norms applying to the social practices and processes of cognition described in the previous chapter. Satisfaction of these norms assures that theories and hypotheses accepted in the community will not incorporate the idiosyncratic biases (heuristic or social) of an individual or subgroup. We might call them conditions of effective or transformative criticism. Insofar as a community satisfies these conditions, that is, insofar as a community maintains means of disseminating and responding to criticism, and is constituted of members who hold themselves answerable individually and collectively to a set of standards and reach consensus as a result of discursive interactions including all relevant perspectives and uninhibited by political or economic power, it will qualify as a knowledge productive community. Because the norms represent ideals that can be partially satisfied, this qualification is a matter of degree. Communities may be more or less dependable and effective as producers of knowledge.

Whereas the previous chapter offers accounts of the senses or modes of knowledge which made salient their social aspects, this chapter offers norms of (discursive) interaction that apply to these social aspects. These norms enable us to distinguish those social interactions which are productive of knowledge from those which are not. I have argued that cognitive practices are social and that the located character of empirical subjects and the underdetermination problem together mean that scientific justification must be social. To the degree that cognitive processes and practices are social, they are subject to evaluation according to those norms, as well as according to the basic empiricist norms of (experiential) evidence and (valid) reasoning.

Socializing knowledge and epistemology in this way has consequences. First, knowledge does not have to be regarded as a fixed content but can be seen as constantly changing. The content changes not just by expanding, but by replacement as cognitive criteria and aims themselves change as a consequence of the application of knowledge to the solution of practical problems. Knowledge can be understood as dynamic, producing the conditions of its own eventual surpassing. Second, even though a community may operate with effective structures that block the spread of idiosyncratic assumptions, those assumptions that are shared by all members of a community will not only be shielded from criticism, but, because they persist in the face of effective structures, may even be reinforced. One obvious solution is to require interaction across communities, or at least to require openness to criticism both from within and from outside the community. Here, of course, availability is a strong constraint. Other communities that might be able to demonstrate the non-self-evidence of shared assumptions or to provide new critical perspectives may be too distant—spatially or temporally—for contact.[20] Background assumptions, and public standards generally, then, are only provisionally legitimated; no matter how thorough their scrutiny given the critical resources available at any given time, it is possible that scrutiny at a later time will prompt reassessment and rejection. Such reassessment may be the consequence not only of interaction with new communities but also of changes in values or other assumptions within a community. Thus, the changes in a community's knowledge can have multiple sources: new data generated within research, new values, reassessment of basic assumptions.

DEFINING *KNOWLEDGE*

The analysis of the previous section can be integrated with that of the previous chapter to generate definitions of knowledge in the three senses distinguished. To do so it is useful to summarize the proposal of the preceding section as follows:

> Some content A is *epistemically acceptable* in community C at time *t* if A is or is supported by data *d* evident to C at *t* in light of reasoning and background assumptions which have survived critical scrutiny from as many perspectives as are available to C at *t*, and C is characterized by venues for criticism, uptake of criticism, public standards, and tempered equality of intellectual authority.

[20] Rick Creath (personal comment) asks whether this might imply a role for history of science and of philosophy. Certainly, contact among different cultures and traditions has facilitated mutual critical interaction in this century; there's no reason specialists in reconstructing the thought of another time should not generate further bases for critical interactions.

The notion of "epistemic acceptability" (akin to justifiability) incorporates both the traditional empiricist norm of justification by empirical data and the social norms applying to those discursive interactions constitutive of reasoning.[21] The analysis it makes possible differs from traditional philosophical views, but it also differs from the sociological view by introducing norms both of success and of procedure. The concept of epistemic acceptability and that of conformation discussed in the previous chapter can be brought together to provide definitions of knowledge in each of the senses of knowledge distinguished in the prior chapter. One can think of these definitions as applying only to scientific knowledge, if one takes the restrictive view of the arguments for sociality, or as applicable to knowledge generally, if one takes the unrestricted view of those arguments.

Knowledge as Content

A given content, A, accepted by members of C counts as *knowledge* for C if A conforms to its intended object(s) (sufficiently to enable members of C to carry out their projects with respect to that/those object(s)) and A is epistemically acceptable in C.

The content may be embodied and expressed in many ways. It may be embodied in internal (mental) representations (however these are understood) as well as in representations in books, journals, and other media of content storage. It may be propositional in form, but also visual or kinesthetic, as in diagrams and other images, three-dimensional models, instruments, and the products of visualizing instruments, such as electron micrographs or PET scans. Knowledge is social in two ways: the status of epistemic acceptability is acquired through social interactions concerning the content carried out in contexts characterized by the conditions of effective criticism; and the projects or goals of C with respect to a given

---

[21] The wording of this definition permits the acceptance of conflicting data as long as they satisfy the conditions of being stabilized via critical scrutiny. Furthermore, epistemic acceptability of A requires not that A *be accepted* as supported by *d* in light of reasoning and assumptions, but that A *be* supported—that is, the support is indexed to background assumptions of the community, but the judgment that, relative to those assumptions, A is supported by *d*, is not. The definition, thus, presumes some minimal logic that is not context-specific. By a minimal logic I mean one that takes only the principle of noncontradiction as basic. There are stronger and weaker versions of less minimal logics, depending, for example, on whether the law of excluded middle is included.

It is conceivable that C and a community C' might disagree as to whether *d* supports A in light of a set of background assumptions (whose acceptance in C satisfies the conditions of effective criticism). In this case, critical discussion between (members of) C and C' is required to determine whether this is a function of background assumptions operative but not yet articulated in those communities or of their embracing different logics.

set of objects or processes will be determined in the same way. Conformation is a matter of being in one or another of the semantic relations included in the family. We find out whether some content A conforms by carrying out experiments, making predictions, and the like—that is, by finding out whether accepting A enables us to carry out our projects in the domain A is about.

Knowledge-Productive Practices

Processes and practices of content construction and acceptance, such as those comprised in the categories of observation and reasoning, are *knowledge-productive practices* in C, if, when engaged in by members of C, they tend to result in the production or adoption of epistemically acceptable content that conforms to its (intended) objects sufficiently to enable members of C to carry out their projects with respect to those objects.

Processes and practices that repeatedly fail to result in content that conforms sufficiently will be rejected by a community whose interest is in accounts of natural and social processes that enable dependably successful interaction with those processes. And if a community does not reject them, then this is grounds for saying that, in engaging in those practices, they are seeking something other than knowledge.

Knowledge as Attribute (or Relation)

Philosophy of science has traditionally been concerned with analysis of the practice and content senses of knowledge just defined, and not with knowledge as an attribute or relation of some individual or collective of individuals. One reason for this disjuncture is that the content of knowledge in the attributive sense is usually something that can be expressed in a single statement or small number of them. It is the sort of thing one tests in an examination. Someone can be said to know that the boiling point of water is 212 degrees Fahrenheit or that the pressure and volume of a gas at constant temperature are inversely related. But, in a scientific context, we are less interested in this kind of knowledge than in knowledge of how these parts of an account relate to other parts of an account. When ascribing knowledge to others in science, it is a different kind of knowledge than singular propositional knowledge that is usually at issue. One attributes knowledge of a theory or model, as in "She really knows gauge theory, she's the one for your team" or sometimes of an organism or kind of system, as in "She really knows *C. elegans*" or "She really knows symbiosis." The diehard may insist that all this amounts to lots of singular propositional knowledge. But it is more than knowledge that p for many p_i that is involved here. What is important, and what is valued, in this individual's knowledge is her appreciation of the relationships between all the components of her knowledge. What we value in knowing *qua* scientific knowing is less knowing that something is the case than understanding it.[22] Nevertheless, a definition of the ascriptive or relational sense can be given that follows the traditional pattern but incorporates the kinds of norms of success and procedure invoked here. The version I provide utilizes the notion of responding to criticism.

S *knows* that p if

i. s accepts p,

ii. p (or p conforms to its intended object sufficiently . . .)

iii. S's response to contextually appropriate criticism of p or of S's accepting p is or would be epistemically acceptable in C (i.e., S's response does or would satisfy standards adopted by C, and would itself be so evaluated by the relevant subgroup of C, in situations characterized by the conditions of effective criticism).

These definitions do relativize the various concepts of knowledge to communities, but those communities must themselves satisfy certain conditions in order that the cognitive activities occurring within them qualify as knowledge or as knowledge-producing. This relativization is not equivalent to traditional relativism, which (1) relativizes knowledge and epistemic acceptability not just to individuals, but to individuals' opinions at any single moment, and, consequently, (2) treats all beliefs as epistemologically equivalent. It constitutes instead a contextualization of knowledge. From a perspective of monism and individualism, contextualism is difficult to distinguish from relativism, but from a nondichotomizing perspective that accepts plurality and provisionality as features of the knowledge of empirical subjects, contextuality *is* the nonrelativist position.

Both the notions of conformation and the norms of epistemic acceptability distinguish these definitions from their dichotomizing counterparts, whether sociological or philosophical. Conformation introduces an element of constraint by and responsiveness to the world, but not so tight as to exclude nonreconcilable alternative accounts. The norms of effective criticism introduce constraints on procedure but locate the grounds of these constraints in certain kinds of social interactions. The challenge of the sociologist was that philosophical epistemology was concerned with idealized knowers and hence irrelevant to empirical knowers, who are socially, historically, and geographically located. The challenge

---

[22] This may be one of the reasons why twentieth-century analytic epistemology and philosophy of science have seemed to have little mutual relevance.

of the philosopher was that sociological attention to empirical knowers obliterated the distinction between knowledge and opinion, between sound and unsound science. These challenges are two sides of the same dichotomizing coin. Disable the dichotomies, and both can be met. The challenge of the sociologist is met by showing that the epistemological concerns of philosophers can be articulated for the empirical subjects that the sociologist studies without idealizing the process beyond recognition. The challenge of the philosopher is met by showing that norms *can* be articulated for social processes. Satisfaction of these norms does not mean that knowledge is purged of the social (as required by the philosophical accounts discussed in chapter 3) but rather that social processes and practices can be distinguished as to their success in producing knowledge. So, it is possible to distinguish between epistemically good and bad science, without denying that good science is or can be significantly affected by a variety of social factors.

The dichotomizers each propose one kind of principle as either explanatory or justificatory or both. Philosophical dichotomizers propose logic and a basic empiricism. Sociological dichotomizers propose social interaction. The former operate as norms, the latter as causal explanation. What each proposes is necessary, but neither is sufficient either as explanation or as justification. Logic and observation alone underdetermine, social interaction alone (where it determines at all) overdetermines. Both logic and observational evidence *and* social interactions are required. Reasoning, sensory experience, and social interaction are involved in the generation and justification of scientific content, and the satisfaction of the norms appropriate to those processes and practices is necessary for the ascription of knowledge. While norms of each kind fail sufficiently to constrain what can count as epistemically acceptable, in concert they are quite binding. This account, therefore, does not dismiss the work done by philosophers of science concerned with elaborating principles of reasoning or of evidence. Indeed, it presupposes basic empiricism and logical norms, while remaining neutral with respect to ongoing philosophical debates (e.g., the status of Bayesianism, multivalued logics). Instead, it proposes to add to those norms traditionally studied by philosophers (and about whose precise nature there is ongoing disagreement) those that (ought to) govern the social interactions also partially constitutive of scientific knowledge. Thus can underdetermination be countenanced without collapsing into relativism.[23] Not only is the dichotomy between the rational and the social dissolved, but the (post-

[23] Duhem, as is well known, proposed the good judgment of scientists ("le bon sens") as filling the underdetermination gap. It is possible to read the social analysis I have offered as an explication of "good judgment," although it goes far beyond gap-filling "good judgment."

or nondichotomous) definitions constitute elements of an account of knowledge that can withstand the skeptical challenge to philosophy from the social and cultural analysts of science.

KNOWLEDGE, PLURALISM, AND PROVISIONALITY

I suggested guidelines in chapter 4 that an account of knowledge might observe in order to avoid dependence on the truth of a metaphysical position or to foreclose possibilities that may be in nature. How does the social account of knowledge and inquiry I am advocating satisfy those guidelines? I restate them here, presenting them in reverse order.

    1. *A suitable humility requires a modest epistemology. An epistemology—as a theory of human knowledge—ought not to promise complete knowledge (or trade in other absolutes, like certainty) but ought to give sense to the distinctions and normative judgments that are a part of epistemic discourse.*

The epistemological approach I've outlined does not trade in absolutes but it does, through the notion of criticism and the criteria for epistemically effective criticism, preserve the meaningfulness of distinctions like that between justified and unjustified belief or between knowledge and opinion.

    2. *A satisfactory epistemology should be open to theoretical plurality or theoretical unity being the final result of inquiry.*

The approach I advocate requires pluralism for the conduct of inquiry, but a characteristic of a process need not be a characteristic of its product. This approach does not preclude the possibility of some single all-encompassing theory being the final result of inquiry nor does it preclude the possibility of multiple accounts. It is logically possible that all social and material cognitive interactions should come to an end in a single unified story, but also possible that they should end with a multiplicity of partially overlapping, but noncongruent, accounts.

    3. *The issue of theoretical pluralism ought not be decided by one's choice of epistemology.*

The kind of social epistemology I advocate does not commit itself to any metaphysics of nature. It is an approach compatible with pluralism or monism as views about the final outcome of inquiry. Of course, particular communities may be committed to metaphysical assumptions, but these are not the same as a general social epistemology being so committed. Similarly, as we have seen, philosophers may use metaphysical assumptions implicitly in their development of a general epistemology. This is, I have argued, a flaw in such accounts, because it requires an argument for the metaphysics as part of the support of the epistemology.

4. *The plurality of representations in biology (or any other science) may be a function of how the world is or of human intellectual equipment for and interests in understanding the world. Our epistemology cannot dictate which.*

The epistemological approach advocated here is neutral as to whether plurality results from human intellectual capacity and interests or from features of the world we seek to understand. As several later instances will show, some cases of plurality in biology are best understood as a function of diverse human cognitive interests, others as a function of how the world is. I take it to be a virtue of the approach to knowledge developed here that none of these substantive questions concerning pluralism is preempted by the approach but remains to be decided by other forms of analysis or by time.

The account of knowledge I have offered is neither metaphysically antirealist nor epistemologically relativist. It does not, however, suppose that there is a single way nature is that writes itself into our representations provided we get our methodology just right. It is not committed to monism. Our modes of representation will pick out aspects of nature and natural processes with greater or lesser degrees of success. Nature may be so complex that it is impossible for any single account of a given process to represent fully all the factors that make a difference to the precise course of the process. On the other hand, it may be possible that, in the long run, a unified complete representation of nature will emerge from the processes of inquiry. On the account developed here, we do not have to wait that long to claim knowledge.

One of the difficulties in discussions of realism in philosophy of science is that metaphysical realism is often conflated with scientific realism.[24] The problem of realism in the philosophy of science has traditionally centered on the distinction between observables and nonobservables. An antirealist like Bas van Fraassen holds that empiricism does not license an inference from the truth of statements about observable entities and processes to the truth of statements about nonobservable entities, states, and processes; and that science aims not at truth but at empirical adequacy. A realist like Jarret Leplin or Richard Boyd holds that the success of science can only be explained by the literal truth of scientific theories. These positions are not the metaphysical positions of realism or idealism but are rather positions about the semantics of theories, the aims of science, and what one's epistemological theory does and does not license. Thus, one can be a realist in the sense of holding that

[24] See Rediehs 1998.

there is a world independently of our thinking that there is one, without being a scientific realist in the sense of holding that the success of our best theories consists in the world having exactly the features attributed to it by those theories. Whether the success of science demands that the world have the features attributed to it by successful theories depends on the aims of science. But there is not a single aim of science. There are multiple aims. A community of scientific realists will hold that one of the aims must be the true representation of the structure(s) of nature. A community of scientific antirealists or of pragmatists will hold that empirically adequate or useful content is a sufficient aim.[25]

A different but analogous distinction to the observable-nonobservable distinction is in play in debates between pluralists and monists. This is a distinction between the simplified systems that we construct for investigation and the natural systems they stand for. Monists hold that science aims at a unified picture of the natural world, and that the ultimate success of science will consist in the production of that picture. This assumes that the simplified systems constructed for investigation each fully captures the causal processes of a given natural system and that all models or theories of such systems can be integrated into a single coherent theory or conjunction of theories. In practice, the systems constructed for investigation by particular theoretical approaches both diverge from one another as those approaches become more empirically successful and overlap one another in their application to the natural world. Pluralists hold that the complexity of the natural world is such that a single unified picture of the world is not possible. Although monism seems more congenial to realism, both pluralists and monists are realists. Indeed pluralism only has the bite it has in the context of realism. Various kinds of realism have been proposed to accommodate pluralism: minimal realism,[26] tempered realism,[27] promiscuous realism,[28] relational realism,[29] perspectival realism.[30] What these realisms have in common is a resistance to treating the susceptibility of our singular world to multiple adequate representations as grounds for metaphysical idealism or for epistemological skepticism.

There seem to be at least two choices one can make about the use of the term "knowledge" in a dynamic and social epistemology of this sort.

---

[25] To the extent that each may be a source of methodological criticism, the arguments of the previous section suggest one might want to have representatives of both perspectives in one's scientific community.

[26] Longino 1990.

[27] Waters 1991.

[28] Dupré 1993.

[29] Rediehs 1998.

[30] Giere 1999.

If one wants to count a community's acceptable theories as knowledge, one can treat knowledge as provisional, partial, and context-dependent. But those uneasy with the instability this permits may propose to disqualify the provisional and the context-dependent as objects of knowledge. This might eliminate theories and models as objects of knowledge, leaving as knowable only the observational data that support them. This criterion is even more draconian than it seems, however. While the observed or measured character of data warrants a different level of doxastic confidence, there are still important senses in which the data, too, are provisional and partial. Different theoretical frameworks can make different data, different descriptions of data, or different aspects or measurements of the data salient. Different statements about observation will be meaningful and relevant in different theoretical contexts. Some descriptions of celestial bodies, while salient to sixteenth-century astronomers and twentieth-century navigators, are of no interest to twentieth-century astronomers. The measurements of contemporary astronomers may prove to be as useless to astronomers of the twenty-fifth century as the earlier measurements are to the former. Systems of measurement change, criteria of good measurement change, the kinds of relationships among data that are important change, the kinds of data that are important change. So if, as on the first alternative, we deny that the provisional counts as knowledge, then little or nothing remains as knowledge. Because we cannot predict which of our beliefs will persist and which wither into disuse, almost nothing we count as knowledge can be ascribed permanence or certainty. The temptations to legislate provisionality away and the untoward consequences of doing so suggest that our concept of knowledge contains elements that are brought into tension with each other when confronted with science and its history. This tension necessitates decisions of a semantic nature that will utilize some aspects of the concept at the expense of others.

CONCLUSION

The socialized account of knowledge integrates, rather than dichotomizes, the rationality and sociality that are equally aspects of knowledge. The central normative notions are epistemic acceptability and conformation (of content to its intended object to a degree sufficient to enable the realization of projects with respect to that object). These involve both traditional evidential norms and the community norms of effective critical interaction (criticism, for short). Epistemic acceptability for a community C is defined in terms of experiential evidence (data), logic, and the satisfaction by C of the conditions of effective criticism. Conformation is a general semantic notion of which truth is a special case. Given that conformation can be achieved in many different ways, it requires anchoring. The anchoring is provided by the community's projects with respect to the intended object of the representation. These projects (and judgments regarding the degree of conformation necessary) must be (or must be such as would be) endorsed by C in contexts satisfying the norms of effective criticism. Sociality and contextuality are pervasive in the account of knowledge. Plurality, provisionality, and partiality will be features of knowledge of any degree of complexity in the short term and possibly, but not necessarily, in the long term as well. On the account I am offering it is not necessary to wait for the ever receding long term correctly to claim or ascribe knowledge. While I see this as an advantage of the account, others may be less persuaded. In the next chapter I take up a series of questions and objections that have been raised against the kind of analysis I am offering here.

CHAPTER SEVEN

Clarifications and Responses

THE SOCIAL account of scientific knowledge thus far raises several kinds of question or objection, including the role of individuals and the relation of cognitive individuals to cognitive communities. Another kind of objection charges that the distinctions that it is the job of epistemology to clarify just get obliterated in the social account, at least in the kind of social account offered here. A third question concerns the relation of the account proposed here to alternative approaches to social (or socially sensitive) epistemology. The distinctions and redefinitions of the previous chapters offer ways of addressing these issues.

INDIVIDUALS WITHOUT INDIVIDUALISM

The role claimed for critical interaction in knowledge has required the articulation of norms directed at community structures and processes rather than at individuals. One of these, public standards, stipulates that what holds a community together must be public. Adherence to some set of standards as regulative of cognitive endeavours constitutes a cognitive community out of a set of individuals. These standards define a set of cognitive goals, and of practical ends to which the cognitive are related. In addition, they specify criteria for satisfying these goals, including methodological procedures, tolerable error limits, as well as substantive assumptions about the domains under investigation that must be preserved in any model or theory of them. All of these elements of a set of standards can change, and there can be subsets and nested sets corresponding to subcommunities within a broader community. These standards, which probably encompass everything discussed as methodology by philosophers of science and more, are not well viewed as rules individuals follow in constructing their contributions to the whole. Rather, they are better understood as touchstones of critical interaction—principles to which community members profess (literally or behaviorally) allegiance, and which therefore ground their critical discursive interactions.

A cognitive community is any group bound by some set of common goals and shared public standards regulating critical (knowledge-productive) discourse and the stabilization of representations as knowledge. Given that every group organized for some purpose, whether for governance or self-governance (from nation to village), mutual protection, production of goods, exchange of goods, provision of services, the expression of religious devotion, the appreciation of beauty, or the advancement of learning, must base its activities in representations of its universe of action, every group or society is among other things a cognitive community. Some communities are more narrowly focused on knowledge production, whereas others use knowledge as a tool or instrument for the satisfaction of practical ends. I am assuming here that even those groups least actively engaged in the production of knowledge required for the realization of their ends nevertheless adhere to a set of standards determining what will count as knowledge for them. They simply trust that those on whom they depend have satisfied those standards. (If the knowledge providers fail to do so, this eventually becomes apparent in the frustration of action based on that purported knowledge.)

This picture of public standards and cognitive communities raises several questions. How are individual and community related, that is, how are individual agents or subjects of knowledge related to the cognitive communities of which they are members? Are individuals subsumed by communities, so that only the community and not the individual can be said to know? Do individuals enjoy some degree of autonomy within a cognitive community?

Social epistemologists and sociologists of knowledge have offered various models of the relation of individual knowers and their communities. The analyses of some writers imply that individuals are subsumed by their communities, that individuals know only what their communities know and know in virtue of their membership in their communities. Versions of the Strong Programme, which focus on shared content, seem susceptible to this wholist interpretation. Philosopher Lynn Hankinson Nelson makes it explicit: "I know only what we know for some we."[1] She means at least that an individual cannot know anything her community cannot know. She may also mean that an individual cannot know anything her community does not already know. Nelson is reworking Quine's doctrines about meaning and knowledge into a form of feminist empiricism, just as Bloor reworks Quine's views to provide part of an argument for the Strong Programme. Nelson wants to extend Quine's rejection of the distinction between analytic and synthetic truths to the distinction between factual and normative discourse: there is no firm distinction between descriptive and evaluative concepts; they enter equally into the transformation of sensory stimulation into experience. Because individuals experience the world through socially shared categories, they have knowledge of that world. Conversely, they can have no knowledge

[1] Nelson 1993.

that is not shaped by those socially shared categories and, thus, no knowledge their community does not also have. Nelson and Bloor treat the processes of knowledge production as identical to the processes of belief formation. Thus, in their frameworks, it seems that individuals also cannot have any beliefs that their communities do not have. Not only do they not have cognitive autonomy; they do not have doxastic autonomy, either. This seems too restrictive. As Heidi Grasswick points out, it is difficult to see how there can be change or growth of knowledge in this view.[2] It is also difficult to see how there could be critical interaction within a community, or between communities.

Michel Foucault's proclamation of the death of the subject and identification of epistemes (or the subject positions they privilege) as the controlling factors in the generation of knowledge seems another denial of the autonomy of the individual. To me, however, the death or elimination of the subject seems to refer not to individuals or to human subjectivity but to the idealized Subject of modern epistemology. This is the transcendent ego capable of the view from nowhere, the unconditioned (or universally conditioned) Subject that generates universally and eternally valid, complete knowledge of the world. Doing away with *that* Subject, however, does not settle anything about embodied, socially located, and culturally conditioned subjects or about their relation to knowing, knowledge, and knowledge production. To deny that the individual human subject has the capacity for that kind of knowledge is not to deny that human subjects can know. For the problem with that kind of knowledge is not that it is too difficult for humans to achieve, but that its very possibility is a philosophical illusion.

Sometimes the death of the Subject—and the affirmation of contextually privileged subject *positions* as the producers of knowledge—is read as though individual subjectivity were entirely conditioned by the episteme of its particular context. This is to read the episteme as akin to Kantian conditions of understanding, but local rather than universal. But individuals are affected to varying degrees by the basic assumptions and the rules for producing knowledge in effect in their particular contexts. And we know from simple experience and exchange with others that our individual subjectivities are alike in some ways but unlike in others. Thus, these readings of Foucault are also unsatisfactory in the account of individuals they make possible.

There are two features of the account developed in the previous chapters that permit forms of individual differentiation without falling into individualism. One is the disambiguation of knowledge into its multiple senses; the other is the emphasis on the interactive aspect of sociality,

[2] Grasswick 1996.

rather than on the sharing aspect of sociality that characterizes Nelson, the Strong Programme, and many of their followers. I use these features to dispel some misconceptions about the communication of knowledge, which can put us in position to dissolve the puzzle about the relation of individual and community.

SOCIALITY

There have been two major proposals regarding the form of sociality in cognitive communities. One holds that members are bound together by common concepts, categories, and theories, so that they experience and interpret the world in the same way. This is the view of Nelson, writing as a philosopher, and of Bloor and the Strong Programme, writing as sociologists of science. It is also a way to read Foucault's elimination of the subject in favor of discourse. Here, "social" means "shared." The other understands sociality not as sharing but as interaction. This is the view of Latour and of Knorr-Cetina, writing as social scientists.

By "social," I have meant "interactive." Certainly, some assumptions and values are shared in any community, but genuine interaction requires diversity among the members. What identifies a given community as a community is a not a set of shared substantive beliefs, but a set of public standards to which community members appeal in critical discursive interactions. These standards may include substantive content, but they also include criteria of evidence and reasoning, methods of investigating. Such standards do not function as elements in the causal process of transforming sensory stimulation into representations. They are not proposed as features for which neurophysiological correlates or equivalents must be found. They are, instead, regulative elements of critical discourse. They come into existence in the course of the elaboration of such a discourse and are themselves subject to the same kind of critique they regulate. They may be internalized by individuals, but this is a consequence of their status in community interactions and not the other way around. Shared standards permit diversity of beliefs, but unity in their methods of evaluation.[3]

TESTIMONY AND THE MODALITIES OF KNOWLEDGE

I have argued that the knowledge-productive practices of the sciences are social. Knowledge production is the activity of a community whose

[3] The requirement of standards is not a requirement of universal standards but of standards accepted by all those engaging in a common inquiry or dialogic interaction. Standards are also discussed at greater length in chapter 8.

members interact with each other as well as with members of other communities, in relation to sets of shared standards and common sensory experiences. I would argue that the same holds for less specialized communities, the difference being that the interactions are more often presupposed, are not institutionalized, and are perhaps governed by less exacting standards. Producing knowledge, however, is not the same as knowing. The one is engaging in the variety of activities—designing experiments and the instruments with which to perform them, conducting field studies and field trials, debating the interpretation of data—involved in knowledge production in a particular context. The other is being in a certain relation to some content and the state of affairs purportedly represented by that content.

Both knowledge production and knowing involve agents or subjects. Knowledge as content, though it has to have been produced by some agent(s) in some context, can be materially detached from particular agents or subjects. It exists in representations. This kind of knowledge is commonable—that is, it can be stored and transmitted from one person to another.[4] Books, journals, newspapers, lectures, radio broadcasts, posters, conversations are means of transmitting knowledge. Of course, the content has to have been knowledge to start with, but its being transmitted does not degrade its quality as knowledge. The receiver of a transmission that p, knows that p upon receipt just as much as does the producer of the knowledge that p.[5] To deny this is to confuse the dynamic process of knowledge production with the static relation of knowing. It would also make science impossible. Even though we can, since Kuhn (and with a further assist from Canguilhem via Foucault), recognize that there are traditions in science with beginnings and ends, these traditions are not evanescent, but can persist for centuries (and there can be nested traditions and overlapping traditions). Within a given tradition, there is progress, what Kuhn called normal science: the accumulation of data, of phenomena, of generalizations, within an intepretive framework (paradigm); the refinement and proliferation of theoretical models; reliable recipes for intervention; an increasing range of action in the world. Such progress demands that knowledge be transmissible—that the knower of p need not be identical with the producer(s) of knowledge that p. If it were a requirement of the concept of knowing that the knower have produced or participated in the production of what she knows, we would all have to start from the beginning in order to know

---

[4] See Welbourne 1981.

[5] Welbourne (1981) lists several conditions in order that a communication count as a transmission of knowledge.

anything, rather than being able, as we are, to build on the achievements of others.[6]

This is a point at which the disambiguating of "knowledge" is particularly helpful, and the failure to do so productive of difficulties. It makes sense to think of knowledge as the outcome or product of knowledge production, as something that accumulates through a community's continued engagement in a set of practices guided by a given set of standards. But the elements of knowledge in this sense (though detachable from particular individuals) cannot be detached from the contexts in which they are produced for insertion into a context-free matrix like that of the traditional "S knows that p" without generating puzzles or imposing conditions too strenuous to be met. Descartes, for example, developed an ideal of knowledge as knowing that involved being able to hold an entire system of knowledge in mental view, in particular being able for any element to perceive or perform its derivation from foundational, clear, and distinct ideas. Locke, rejecting the rationalism in this picture, nevertheless imposed a similar requirement on knowing—that the knower have had direct experience of the sensory grounds of the proposition known.

Subsequent philosophers have embraced this absolutist concept of justification. It seems plausible when one is talking of objects of knowledge within the range of fairly immediate experience and, hence, the kind of belief that is caused by sensory interaction with those objects. It is less plausible when one is talking of more remote objects. Our practices of journalism and of education show that we do not subscribe to this restrictive and individualist concept.

For example, I had no direct experience of the war in the former Yugoslavia, and I could not list the exact sources of my beliefs about it, but it would be foolish to claim that I have no basis for thinking that the international community failed the noncombatants of that region.[7] If I learned this from appropriate sources, there seems no reason why I should be able to reconstruct an argument that includes among its premises reports of my experience of the war in order that my belief be called knowledge. Furthermore, it is not even clear that I should be able to reconstruct how I came to have this knowledge by, say, naming the authors of the news reports I have read and providing evidence of their trustworthiness. I am a member of a community for whom the war was, however distant, a matter of ongoing concern and conversation. Our

---

[6] This point is stressed in Downes's (1993) argument that scientific theories have an embodied existence in books, journal articles, etc.

[7] Kaplan (1994) makes a similar point about "common knowledge," those things "we all know," without knowing how we came to know them—that Canada is in North America, or that salted water comes to a boil more quickly than unsalted water.

beliefs or knowledge about the war were sustained by repeated encounters with news reports, reports of news reports, and so on. Some of what we believe may not be true, because our sources have reported innaccurately, or we may distort accurate reports in memory or retelling. This is the kind of thing revealed in challenges or objections. All that is required in order for me to know that p, when p, is to be able to respond to the degree required by the standards applicable in the context in which the question has arisen.

Consider, too, the practices of education. Students are expected to learn, on the authority of their teachers, all variety of material. At the end of a given period of instruction, if they pass their exams, they are said to know or to have acquired knowledge of a number of fields. They are held to different standards appropriate to their age and state of previous education, and what it is reasonable to expect them to learn in a given period about a given subject depends on what they have already learned about it. Thus, a student in a high school biology classroom, will not be required to know the nucleic acid sequence of any genes, in order to be said to know genetics. If an aspiring applicant to graduate study in biology shows no more knowledge than the high school student, however, her chances of admission are quite slim. What is important here, is that, at whatever level of instruction, students are expected to know at the end of a course what their instructors have attempted to teach them.

Both education and journalism are practices of knowledge dissemination and reception. To be sure, not everything transmitted in such a practice is knowledge. There are innaccuracies, ideas that have failed the tests of critical discursive interaction or that have not been subject to them. The recipient need not personally sift through each transmission to determine what is or is not true in it in order to receive as knowledge what already is knowledge. That there is chaff amongst the wheat does not diminish the status of the wheat as wheat, although it does mean that there is less of it per unit of volume. Although we (attempt to) teach our students to think critically about what they read and hear, we do not expect them to perform new experiments and calculations to confirm what they hear in their physics and biology lectures. We want them to read original texts, but do not require that they do archival research before accepting what we say in our lectures about the lives and thought of Descartes or Hume. Nor do we need independently to confirm what we read in the newspapers in order to receive knowledge from them, even though we know (a second-order knowledge) that not everything reported in the paper is reported correctly. The idea that we ourselves need to reconfirm what we receive as knowledge in order to be said to know it is another expression of individualism. Understanding ourselves as interdependent in the production of knowledge not only frees us from the burden of producing the truth on our own; it also frees us from this burden with respect to its transmission. Because we are members of communities, we can rely on the further discursive interactions we will have to assist us in sorting out what, of the purported knowledge transmitted to us, is genuine knowledge. In some cases, when it really matters, we will seek out such interactions; in others we can be more opportunistic.

Knowing, then, does not require that one have produced or even participated in the generation of representations or the critical interactions that confer the status of knowledge on content. It requires, rather, that one be appropriately related to the practices of knowledge production and dissemination in one's cognitive community. In chapter 6's language, someone knows that p if her response to criticism does or would satisfy standards adopted in her community in situations characterized by the conditions of effective criticism and the assessment of her response also does or would satisfy those conditions. She need not have inferred p from what she takes to be a reason for p on her own, nor need the reasons she currently accepts be the same as those which originally led her to accept p. She needs only to be able to respond to challenges by producing justificatory reasons. This is one way in which knowers need not be identical to knowledge producers.[8]

John Hardwig has described a quite different, but increasingly common scenario in the sciences.[9] He draws our attention to a feature of contemporary physics: the design and implementation of experiments requiring many participants distributed across many laboratories. None of the participants has direct experience of all of the elements of the experiment. Instead each participant or subset of participants contributes their data or calculations to the whole, producing a very complex network of results produced in different laboratories linked together by chains of reasoning engaged in by yet other participants. All of the participants, says Hardwig, are linked by trust, because they cannot verify for themselves that the results contributed by the others are accurate, correctly reported, and so on. The final result is a paper of under four pages with one hundred authors. Hardwig asks who of these hundred authors can be said to know the whole (story). The two answers he offers, each presented as equally, but differently, unpalatable, are that the group as a whole (but no single individual) knows or that it is possible to know vicariously. Talk of the group or the community, but no individual member, knowing smacks of superorganisms and transcendent entities

---

[8] There is some sense in which all members are participants in all knowledge-productive practices in their community. For knowledge-receptive practices are necessary for the sustenance of knowledge-productive practices. This suggests the need for a distinction between direct and indirect participation.

[9] Hardwig 1985.

and Hardwig shrinks from that solution. But vicarious knowledge, knowing without possessing the evidence for the truth of what one knows, requires "dramatic changes in our analysis of what knowledge must be."[10]

Hardwig's puzzlement can be dissipated if we invoke the distinction between knowledge production and knowing. The group as a whole, as individuals in interaction with each other, has produced the knowledge, rather as all the assembly line workers who touched it (and the designers, engineers, etc.) have produced the tractor that finally rolls off the line. We must presume the occurrence of critical interactions at various stages and then critical discussion of the whole experiment once the paper is published. Once the knowledge has been produced in this way, however, it is commonable. Not only does or can each member of the team know, but we can know, too, as long as we are in appropriate relation to the production and dissemination of the knowledge. Here again, then, is a case in which knower and producer are distinct. The producer is the community—no one individual or subset of individuals produced the final result; they all did. Once the knowledge is produced, each member can know the result. But mere participation in the process does not constitute knowing; it is necessary to familiarize oneself with the whole result, by reading and comprehending its final write-up. This one can do without having had the capability of producing any of its parts. Thus, those team members and other physicists or physics-literate individuals who do the work of understanding the paper can be said to know the magnitude of the charm cross section of particles obtained by exposing hydrogen in SLAC's bubble chamber to a 20 GeV laser beam, providing they can respond to contextually appropriate objections. While Hardwig presents us with a striking example of the epistemic dependence of scientists on one another, it is a common, not an anomalous feature of scientific inquiry. The reliance on the published results of others, on statistical methodologies developed by others, in the conduct of research are more mundane examples and subject to the same kind of analysis.

AUTONOMY AND COMMUNITY

So far I have argued that knowers and producers of knowledge need not be identical. We are still not completely in a position to address the question with which this section began: namely what degree of autonomy do individuals enjoy with respect to their cognitive communities? Two pieces remain: underlining the distinction between knowledge and doxastic states like belief and attending to the possibility of membership in multiple communities. First of all, knowledge, as I have discussed it,

---

[10] Ibid., 349.

emerges as the outcome of discursive interactions among individuals with different points of view. Points of view are constituted of attitudes, opinions, evaluative categories, social location, and spatiotemporal orientation. Some of this mixture may constitute knowledge, some "mere" belief. Individuals can come to have beliefs, or to be committed to representations, that have not passed the test of discursive interaction. They may well have reason to think they are true or like enough to put into play in critical discourse. This is sufficient for the generation of cogent criticism. It is not necessary to criticize a proposal from a position of knowing that something else is the case, merely from the position of having some reason to think so. Individuals have doxastic autonomy in the sense that what they believe is not constrained by the beliefs of their community, although their belief in any given instance may be the result of particular interactions. The community constraint is exercised on justification or epistemic acceptability, and, hence, on the attribution of knowledge: an individual is said to know if she or he can respond to contextually appropriate objections. The content may be quite novel; it is the standards that are shared.

Furthermore, most of us have specialized relations to particular parts or aspects of the natural and constructed world—from babies to assembly lines to ancient texts to elementary particles. Thus, we belong to specialized cognitive communities nested within our common community. Some cognitive communities are also productive communities, or are focused on action in some way; others are organized specifically to produce knowledge about a particular portion or aspect of the world. These are scholarly and scientific communities. As I have suggested, some communities are knowledge producers, whereas others are knowledge users. There will be some shared standards and some distinctive ones linking and separating subcommunities with encompassing communities. Standards developed in a subcommunity can be used to refine or reinterpret standards in the encompassing community. And, as a subcommunity develops a somewhat complete and coherent set of standards, it may split off to some degree from the original encompassing community, as natural philosophers in the sixteenth and seventeenth centuries split off from a larger intellectual community, and psychologists in the nineteenth and twentieth centuries split off from philosophy.

Individuals in a complex society participate in the interactions of different communities, observing different standards. The members of scholarly and scientific communities are members of the lay public with respect to the knowledge production in communities other than their own. Some individuals may be members of more than one specialized community, may be, for example, members both of a philosophical community with standards oriented to conceptual analysis and of a scientific community with standards oriented to empirical inquiry. Individuals may be members of communities whose standards are in even greater tension with each other, for example, members of a scientific subcommunity and members of a social group (identified by race, gender, or social class) suspicious of knowledge produced by more socially privileged communities.

Membership in multiple communities may be a source of internal conflict, but it is also an epistemological resource. It permits an individual to compare standards and to assess (purported) knowledge produced and accepted in one community in reference to standards proper to another. It confers on individuals the ability to see things from more than one point of view or at least to understand that there could be more than one point of view about a given matter. As indicated in an earlier chapter, criticism must be articulated in relation to the standards observed in a community in order to be relevant and hence effective in that community. Nevertheless, if a person can generate a criticism of a hypothesis or assumption being entertained in one of her communities from the point of view of another (and make it relevant to the concerns of the first), she thereby introduces another test the hypothesis or assumption must pass. Furthermore, she can develop criticism of standards by exploiting the inevitable tensions within any given set. This, too, may be facilitated by her appreciation of standards operative in others of the communities in which she participates.[11]

Individuals, then, have a significant degree of autonomy in this system. First, knowers need not be knowledge producers—or, more precisely, because we are all knowledge producers to some extent, the knower that p need not have participated in the production of knowledge that p. Second, knowledge and belief or commitment to a representation are distinct. Knowledge requires actual or anticipated social interaction. Belief and commitment occur against a background of shared linguistic and representational practices, but are individual as well as community-wide. The constructive and critical practices essential for knowledge production need not be based in knowledge but only in belief. Indeed, they need not require commitment but merely the ability to articulate an alternative point of view on the part of one engaging in criticism. Third, individuals can belong to more than one cognitive community, each of which as a consequence enables a critical perspective on the beliefs and standards of the others.

The positions I have developed concerning recent debates about the relative roles of individual and community are based primarily on the

---

[11] This requires a degree of psychological flexibility that will, of course, vary among individuals.

distinction in modalities of knowledge. Richard Foley has offered a more general argument for the reasonableness of relying on (the authority of) others, which nevertheless accords autonomy to individual agents.[12] Foley's point is that, while it is the case that each individual is in the end responsible for what she or he believes, this does not license "epistemological egoism." "Epistemological egoism" is the view that, in the end, one is one's own epistemic fundamental authority and cannot grant such authority to others. Thus, another's believing p can never serve as a prima facie reason for my believing p. Foley contends, on the contrary, that another's believing p can so serve—that is, that a sufficient reason for my believing that p is that another does. "If I grant fundamental authority to myself, then I must in consistency grant it to others. I must do so because it is reasonable for me to think that my intellectual faculties and my intellectual environment are broadly similar to theirs."[13] Like all prima facie reasons, this type, too, has its defeaters. If I have a belief in conflict with p, or if I think there is indecisive evidence for p, then another's belief that p does not count as a reason for me. So, another's belief is most strongly a reason for me when I have no opinion on the matter (or when my opinion accords with that of the other). Foley's argument recognizes that each individual is responsible for her or his judgments—indeed, cannot help but be—and is in this sense autonomous, while at the same time is dependent on her or his community or communities for the standards of reasonableness, of evidence, and for the assumptions on the basis of which such standards are applied. I would add that what makes any of this knowledge, as distinct from individually or personally reasonable, however, is that it has passed through critical scrutiny in a context characterized by the four conditions of effective criticism. Hence, an additional defeater would be that the community to which my informant is responsive fails to satisfy one or more of those conditions.

CREATIONISTS AND FORTUNE-TELLERS

The philosopher may still have residual worries. I consider two objections intended to show that the socialized account will include as knowledge what most "enlightened" persons would reject. One is that, in spite of intentions to guard against them, it permits egregiously unworthy claims, such as those of the so-called scientific creationist, to count as science. A related objection is that it licenses any rule whatsoever to

---

[12] Foley 1994.
[13] Ibid., 63.

count as a knowledge-productive practice. If these objections could stick, they would defeat my claim that the account does not fall into strong, anything-goes relativism.

Wrongheaded Content

Some critics, skeptical of the social account's capacity to capture the distinction between knowledge and opinion, worry that it permits the creationist to claim that she knows that the universe was created six thousand years ago.[14] This possibility must be treated carefully. The creationist who is troublesome is not the creationist who believes, as a matter of religious faith not impinging on science, in the creation of the universe by a being that intended to do so. This creationist may be puzzling but does not threaten the account.[15] The troublesome creationist is the one who claims that her creationist belief is as warranted epistemically as any current scientific (e.g., evolutionary) alternative. Can an account that accepts variation in standards and that is open to plural accounts draw a line that keeps troublesome creationism on the other side of the epistemically acceptable? Two features of the account are treated as grounds for skepticism on this point. One is the role of goal attainment in the specification of success. The other is the role of the community in determining what counts as sufficient warrant or justification, that is, epistemic acceptability.

GOALS

If the success norm were purely pragmatic, if, for example, it required only that accepting p would enable one to achieve one's goals (or the goals of one's community), then it would warrant skepticism. What is counterintuitive about such purely pragmatic accounts of success (or truth) and what warrants the suspicion that they admit egregiously wrongheaded content as knowledge, is that, in general, beliefs that have no real-world correlates would be admitted as instances of knowledge (provided the other clauses were met). In the case of the creationist, the goal is, presumably, salvation. The skeptic is worried that the creationist's belief counts as knowledge as long as acceptance that the universe was created by a divine being about six thousand years ago enables the cre-

---

[14] This objection has been raised by many philosophers. My response is directed specifically to its articulation in Kitcher 1991.

[15] If this creationist were to claim knowledge, then there might be issues of a community's treating scriptural revelation as a knowledge-productive practice. A general form of this objection is treated in the next section.

ationist to achieve his or her goal: salvation.[16] Even if a being had instead created the universe billions of years ago by, say, initiating the Big Bang, she might reward the hapless twentieth-century creationist with salvation just for believing the fantastic against so many odds. This would make the creationist's belief effective in the ways required, but, *ex hypothesi*, this belief fails to be knowledge. Part of what is counterintuitive in the situation is that the creationist's acceptance is effective, rather than any relation between the content of what is accepted and elements, structures, and processes represented by that content. One way of describing the difference between the creationist's and the scientist's approach to such questions as the origin of the universe and the origin of life is that the creationist holds beliefs about a domain (the origin of the physical universe) in order to achieve goals that do not involve action in that domain, salvation in the hereafter, whereas the scientist is interested in achieving goals that involve action within the domain about which she seeks knowledge. This difference is expressed in the conformity portion of the success clause, which makes success more than merely pragmatic. Thus, if the content of the creationist's belief does not conform to that which it is about, that content does not count as knowledge. But, of course, we do not know, independently of the methods the creationist is calling into question, that the content does not conform. The focus of the objection then shifts to the norm of epistemic acceptability.

EPISTEMIC ACCEPTABILITY

How is the norm of epistemic acceptability thought to ratify wrong-headed beliefs? A society will validate processes of inquiry that result in it or its members having beliefs that satisfy the success clause. But the inclusion of the norms of effective criticism in the account of epistemic acceptability or warrant is important. It means that there must be critical exchanges in which the full variety of perspectives are represented and that they are treated as equally capable of generating significant challenges to theories. For the creationist belief to be ratified by this norm, all participants to the dialogue would have to share an overriding commitment to the goal of salvation or to the intermediate goal of fostering awe of the almighty. This, however, is to limit the included perspectives by content, not by past performance, and hence is in violation of the norm of epistemic acceptability.

The skeptic thinks the creationist claims cannot be criticized without

---

[16] Of course, this presupposes that salvation is an attainable goal. If attainability is a condition on the kinds of goals admitted into the account, then it is not obvious that the creationist is as foolhardy as most of her opponents suppose. One can develop a more complicated formula that expresses how the anticreationist perceives the situation. For discussion, see Longino (1994).

the adoption of methodological norms that are not forced on individuals (or groups) simply by virtue of their commitment to a practice of open criticism and discussion, that is, the skeptic thinks such a practice is insufficient to rule out wrongheaded or obviously false beliefs. But this is not at all obvious. A practice of genuinely open criticism and discussion requires an openness to all perspectives: no claim or belief can be held immune to criticism. The creationist counterexample is often presented as though the anti- or noncreationist is the only party on whom the norms are binding. This is not the case. Creationism must withstand critical scrutiny and challenge from any perspective that can make a connection to some standards of the creationist community to count as knowledge. Second, the supposition that additional methodological norms would be required presupposes an insulation of cognitive goals from practical and social goals that we have no good reason to assume. A commitment to salvation that ratified procedures of inquiry warranting creationist beliefs about the relatively recent origin of the universe would be in conflict with other goals of an inquiring community, and could be shown to be in such conflict if the community were indeed open.[17] Thus, even if a first-order challenge—evidence—were rebuffed, the creationist would still have to meet a second-order challenge to the standards that permit dogmatism. Of course, the creationists, like anyone else, can continue to believe whatever they want, but, if their knowledge-productive practices fail to conform to the norms of effective critical interaction, then the outcomes of these practices do not qualify as knowledge on our account.[18] And that is all that needs to be shown.[19]

Wrongheaded Rules

The second skeptical objection claims that intuitively wrongheaded standards will be permitted by treating the community as determinative of

---

[17] For example, all the technologies and theories involved in identifying geological eras and the relative age of objects found in different geological formations as well as those involved in astrophysical methods of estimating the age of the universe would have to be abandoned, not just the claims about age.

[18] For a similar approach to wrongheaded belief, but using the example of astrology (another philosopher's miscreant), see Thagard 1978.

[19] In particular, I do not have to show that the creationist is compelled to accept my account of knowledge. The creationist can reject the account, but (to the extent that I have correctly articulated the normative dimensions of the concept) this amounts to giving up the claim that she *knows* in any shared sense of "know," that is, in any sense that makes a claim on our practices or credence. Of course, the creationist can open up a third-order challenge (to the concept of knowledge being employed), but all sides must agree to some standards that will regulate debate on that question.

standards.[20] Does this account permit the adoption of a rule to believe the tea leaves? Let us suppose there is a method of interpreting the tea leaves (ratified by a tea-leaf reading community). There are two possibilities to be considered. Either following the rule has the outcome that one accepts content that conforms sufficiently to its intended object(s) to enable members to pursue their aims successfully with respect to those objects, or following the rule does not have this outcome. If it does, then one is in a position to respond to contextually appropriate objections by pointing to its success. If it does not, then it is not clear what response its user might offer to a criticism.

The skeptic says: does one not have to consult the tea leaves to know whether the rule is successful? If the tea leaves say yes, then, if one is following the rule, one believes the rule is successful. One difficulty with this kind of counterexample is that it presupposes a disembodied cognitive subject—a subject that does not need to eat, to cross streets, and the like and that has no independent means of assessing the value of the rule. One can imagine consulting tea leaves through an infinite regress of justification when belief does not matter to survival, when all that matters is conformity to the intended object, and any independent way of ascertaining conformity is subject to the rule of the tea leaves. Embodied subjects, however, have checks other than abstract rules: physical, sensory experience. Community standards regulate the justificatory role such experience plays in the formation of belief. Hunger pangs are not banished on the say-so of tea leaves or comparable prognostications. A community that endorsed the rule—believe the tea leaves—would either have access to some extraordinary tea leaves, or would find itself frustrated in the attempt to realize its goals. This frustration would lead it to revise its rule or its goals. Because revising its goals to make physical experience irrelevant to belief is a self-defeating option for a community of embodied subjects, we must assume that no community would long entertain the rule: believe what the tea leaves say. Thus, it does not seem to me that the account permits the adoption by communities of intuitively wrongheaded standards.

Some wrongheaded standards are ruled out by the philosophically conventional norms that this account incorporates. Thus, counterinductive rules, like "The more regularly E has occurred in the past, the less likely it is to occur in the future" or "If all previous instances of X have been Y, the next instance of X will be not-Y," or self-defeating rules, like "Always accept Dutch book odds," or contradictory rules, like "If p, believe not-p," are not countenanced by the social approach. But other rules

---

[20] I am indebted to Paul Boghossian for this formulation of the wrongheaded rules objection.

seem wrongheaded to us not because they violate basic logical or empirical principles, but because, like "Believe the tea leaves," they have not
been successful in achieving the presumed ends of reasoning practices:
acceptance of content that can guide our interactions with the objects of
that content. But this is a matter of experience with the rule. It is conceivable, if, to almost everyone likely to be reading this book, highly
improbable, that "Believe the tea leaves" might be a dependable rule for
someone—that following the rule could lead to better results for that
person than following any other. It is also possible that interaction with
advocates of alternative perspectives might bring that person to abandon
the tea leaf rule for a different rule ("Trust your senses about x, y, and z")
with better results.[21] Similarly, a rule like "Don't believe whatever Xs
[Christians, blue-eyed persons, red-haired persons, etc.] say" seems not
only as wrongheaded as "Believe the tea-leaves" but contradicts the
openness required by the tempered equality requirement. But there are
circumstances (slavery, oppression) in which it might be an acceptable or
reasonable rule (for those oppressed or enslaved by those in whom dis-
trust is recommended).

Thus, although the social approach does not offer a single standard of
justification, it does have a mechanism for ruling out the endorsement of
epistemic standards whose adoption, like "Believe what is false" or
"Believe what you feel" would undermine the chance for a community
and its members to attain their goals. Critical discursive interaction can
undermine such wrongheaded rules when logic and data, in cases of
underdetermination, cannot.

But is critical interaction enough? Consider cases of self-sustaining
systems of belief, which appear irrational by the standards accepted in
late twentieth-century industrial societies, but nevertheless serve, or
served, pragmatic ends. The persecution of witches in pre- and early
modern Europe is an example.[22] According to anthropologist Marvin
Harris, the witch-hunts served the purpose of maintaining the power
structures of European societies: rather than blaming those in power for
their problems, ordinary folk blamed those of their neighbors whom they
suspected of being witches.[23] There were well-defined rules for determining whether someone was a witch. If guiding one's belief acceptance by
those rules served pragmatic ends, does this system not pass muster in
the social approach? This sort of example resembles the creationism
example, in that it involves the construction of a system of belief that

---

[21] But the conversion could go the other way, as well. One assumption of this discussion
is that the rule's value is assessed by reference to the sense experiences of its users subsequent to its use.
[22] I am grateful to Brian Huss for bringing this example to my attention.
[23] Harris 1974.

mimics but is insulated from ordinary empirical inquiry and the objects of which (an intended creation of the universe six thousand years ago, witches) we believe to be nonexistent. Were the rules of witch detection subject to critical scrutiny responsive to the standards observed in other activities (e.g., planting and harvesting), it's unlikely they would survive for long. What a witch is would have to be determined and some reasons given for thinking that the detection rules correctly picked out individuals matching that description.[24]

On the social account, communities determine the standards by which they evaluate beliefs; different communities may adopt different standards, and single communities may countenance different standards for different contexts. But those standards are themselves subject to critical scrutiny. Two things are supposed in the claim that critical interaction eventually results in the weeding out of wrongheaded standards. One is that the conditions of critical discursive interaction are satisfied. The other is that any community of embodied agents will have among its cognitive interests an interest in accurate description of its physical environment. The standards developed to secure that interest will always be available as a resource for those engaging in critical interaction with (or in) that community.

I am not averse to saying that regard for logic and for the evidence of sensory experience are universal features of knowledge constructive communities, even partially constitutive of such communities. But because the particular forms of logic and of experience may vary, this is not to say very much.[25] My claim is not that logic and experience are subsumed by the success condition, but that the terms of the success condition for embodied subjects are such as to require adherence to some logical standards and some standard of sensory evidence. Thus, they do not license counterlogical or countersensory rules.

RELIABILISM AND REFLEXIVITY

Another kind of worry is that the socialization of knowledge is unnecessary: that the features of scientific inquiry that prompt it can be accommodated in methodologically individualist epistemologies. Both reliabilism and norms of reflexivity have been proposed as candidates. If there are simpler alternatives, why introduce the complexities of the

---

[24] A stickler might also point out that the pragmatic benefit of this system was limited to the ruling elite. The folk who applied the identification rules to turn in their neighbors were not benefited by the system of witch persecution.

[25] For a formal argument regarding variation in logics, see Chakraborty and Basu 1999; Basu, Chatterjee, and Chakraborty, n.d.; for a relevant empirical study, see Hamill 1990.

social account? One answer is that if the cognitive practices of the sciences are social, this must be reflected in accounts of scientific knowledge. But the other answer is that neither reliabilism nor a norm of reflexivity offer what the social account offers.

Reliabilism

Alvin Goldman is one of the foremost expositors of reliabilism.[26] His reliabilism is a view about justification and it is attached to what he calls a "veritist" success norm.[27] A reliabilist view of justification or epistemic acceptability holds that someone, S's, belief that p is justifiable (or epistemically acceptable) if the belief that p was produced by a cognitively reliable process R and there is not a further cognitively reliable process R_r such that had R_r been employed as well as R, it would have resulted in S's not believing p.[28] Here, the reference to a community and its satisfaction of norms of critical interaction is eliminated, and any inadequacies in the traditional notions of empirical support are avoided by substituting the reliabilist criterion. Is not the objection to "Believe the tea leaves" that it is an unreliable process (or, if a rule, an unreliable one)? But that is not the objection made to the rule in the previous section. Maybe it is and maybe it is not reliable. It is at least logically possible that some individual might get consistently right answers by consulting the tea leaves, in which case the rule would be reliable, and that individual would be able to respond to criticisms of her or his use of the rule by pointing to its success. And as long as this is logically possible, the reliability or unreliability of the rule cannot be affirmed a priori.

One of the problems with reliabilism is that it requires that the epistemologist be able to identify the cognitively reliable processes. But, as John Pollock has argued, once the reliabilist accepts that our ordinary cognitive processes are reliable in some circumstances but not in others, she or he faces the task of specifying the circumstances in which a given process is cognitively reliable (or those in which it is not).[29] It is not helpful to characterize a rule or process as reliable in the circumstances in which it is reliable, without saying something about how its reliability is ascertained. But, then, the method of ascertainment becomes more basic epistemologically than reliability. The judgment that a rule or process is reliable presupposes we have a way (independently of the process) of determining that the outcome hoped for from the process is obtained.

[26] See Goldman 1979, 1986, 1987.
[27] Goldman 1986.
[28] Goldman 1979.
[29] Pollock 1984.

Reliabilism is of little use in the scientific contexts that involve the adoption of frameworks of inquiry, background assumptions, experimental strategies, instruments, and the like, where precisely what we are determining is that these are reliable. Of course, in the end we want processes and practices that are reliable, but our judgment that they are reliable is secured through the material and discursive interactions discussed earlier; not by the epistemologist, but by the community that employs them.

There are two ways to think about the relation between reliabilism and the social account. One can say that reliabilism subsumes the social account—that critical interaction under the conditions specified is one among other reliable processes. Or one can say that critical interaction under the conditions specified is what determines whether a process is reliable. The former begs the questions both what the other processes are and how their reliability is determined. The second takes advantage of the multilevel practice of critical interaction. Criticism plays a role in determining the epistemic acceptability of particular content but also in determining the validity of cognitive standards and of cognitive goals. Reliabilism, while formally correct, is also empty without a method of determining reliability. Critical interaction provides a determinant that is not just a higher-order version of the property in question and stops the otherwise infinite regress. The social account, therefore, cannot be replaced by reliabilism. Instead, it completes a set of which reliability is one element, just as it completes a set consisting of philosophically traditional epistemic norms.

Reflexivity

Philosophers as diverse as Sandra Harding and Deborah Mayo have proposed norms of reflexivity as the appropriate response to underdetermination, the multitude of methodologies, and the vulnerability of inquiry to contextual factors.[30] There are two senses of "reflexivity." One of these refers to the attribute of self-applicability. This is the sense meant by Steve Woolgar in his advocacy of irony for social studies of science.[31] The social account is reflexive in this sense, in that the norms validating any particular content are applicable to themselves. The norms by which a specific content is deemed epistemically acceptable are themselves held to the same criteria of epistemic acceptability. The other sense of "reflexivity" invoked in epistemological discussions refers to a kind of self-examination. Harding recommends examination of one's own

[30] Harding 1991; Mayo 1991.
[31] Woolgar 1983.

(or one's own culture's) values and presuppositions. Mayo recommends what she calls "metascience," the examination of one's experimental and statistical methodologies and acknowledgment especially of the specific uncertainties associated with them. Reflexivity in this sense is an outcome of the critical practices of a community, because they are directed to identifying the epistemic strengths and weaknesses of content and practices. The social account builds reflexivity in, but does not leave it up to individual self-examination (which is often blind to the deepest assumptions). Awareness of values and presuppositions is imposed on inquirers through interactions with those who do not share them. The uncertainties endemic to particular methodologies are ascertained in the same way any other empirical hypothesis is assessed. Furthermore, in requiring uptake (i.e., change that reflects the critical discussion taking place), the social account is stronger than a norm requiring merely self-awareness.

ALTERNATIVE APPROACHES IN SOCIAL EPISTEMOLOGY

How does this account differ from those advanced by other philosophers advocating a stronger social epistemology than that sanctioned by Goldman or Kitcher? Miriam Solomon, Joseph Rouse, and Steve Fuller have all taken on board some portion of the sociologists' claims and have developed approaches that do not rely on the rational-social dichotomy. Even so, their approaches also do not attend to its inhibiting influence on the discussion of both rationality and sociality. Hence their approaches perpetuate to different degrees and in different respects some of the ossification in the views they reject.

Solomon's Social Empiricism

Miriam Solomon has proposed a view she terms "social empiricism."[32] Using both empirical work by cognitive psychologists and case studies in twentieth-century science, she proposes that while individual scientists are irrational or just not rational, the community to which they belong can be termed rational if belief ultimately converges on an empirically successful theory. The relevance of the work of the cognitive psychologists is that it offers classifications of some of the variety of factors that can influence the belief-forming processes of individuals. The case studies reveal these processes at work.

In developing this view Solomon relied first on one case study and later on two. The first provided her with the descriptive parts of her

[32] Solomon 1992, 1994a, 1994b.

view. Adding another enabled comparisons that ground the normative aspects of the view. The saga of plate tectonics in twentieth-century geology shows that individual scientists committed and arguing for or against the thesis were influenced as much by factors such as the salience and availability to them of certain kinds of data as distinct from other kinds, peer pressure and the urge to conform, prior investment in a view, and so on, as much as by whatever evidence they possessed. There was not a set of generally accepted facts about whose explanation there was disagreement. And the general acceptance of plate tectonics in the 1960s was not a matter of hitherto prejudiced members of the community throwing off their cognitive blinders. Rather, according to Solomon, the persistence of individuals in the same old patterns that earlier produced discord eventually resulted in a collective accord regarding the adequacy of the theory. Not only was collective accord achieved but it was accord on the correct or empirically successful theory.[33] This characterization of the end of debate differs from the characterization Kitcher offers in two ways. First, the rationality of the group is independent of the rationality of its members. Second, whereas Kitcher sees bias as whatever deflects from the pursuit of truth, Solomon sees biases as productive and enabling. Thus, where Kitcher and other philosophers take their task to be defending individuals (and the profession or community to which they belong) from the charge of irrationality allegedly leveled at them by sociologists of science, Solomon sees no such need. The rationality of science lies elsewhere.[34]

Where Hull, Goldman, and Kitcher treat bias as, at best, a kind of self-interested motivation that certain things be true rather than others and hence as a blemish or obstruction to proper cognitive procedure, Solomon treats bias as a clinical rather than as a normative concept. Bias, for her, is anything focusing attention or inclining belief, and is a feature of any doxastic situation. Social, psychological, instrumental biases are equally included in the mix of factors affecting belief change. The sociologists' work is to be incorporated into a multivariate theory of scientific change, not rebutted.[35] Solomon, then, is among those philosophers, like Giere (1988), who think that the sociologists' work can simply be

---

[33] Again, see Grandy 2000 for a differently emphasized account of this episode.

[34] The emphasis Solomon places on community processes as opposed to individual ones in the development of scientific knowledge has formal-structural similarities to the view developed as critical contextual empiricism in Longino 1990. There and elsewhere I argue that scientific knowledge is the outcome of community processes and interactions, rather than a collection of outcomes produced by individual scientists each adding their bit to a whole. But Solomon is, at least ostensibly, concerned with characterizing scientific rationality, where I have been concerned with knowledge and objectivity.

[35] Solomon 1995.

incorporated into a more complete account of inquiry. Because Solomon sees biases as productive, inducing scientists to pursue research in certain directions, the lesson is not the need to eliminate bias. The key normative issue instead, is, in addition to empirical success, the distribution of bias. But there are problems with both her interpretation of sociological claims and with the normative account she proposes to extract from her description of scientific change. I focus on the latter.

In spite of her resolute naturalism, Solomon is nevertheless working with normative concepts. In declaring that individual belief change is not and need not be rational, for example, she is working with a concept of rationality by reference to which individual (and social) behavior is evaluated.[36] What is the concept of rationality that she assumes or advances? And what are her norms, norms for? Although in some expressions of social empiricism it seems that individual rationality, as certain rules of procedure that individuals violate, is procedural, the concept of rationality that applies to communities is best described as consequentialist because it references outcomes. Scientific decision making is rational "when empirical successes are produced and maintained [by that decision-making (HL)]. . . . Empirical successes are engagements with the world which include experimental, observational, predictive, and some technological successes."[37] As long as theories have different empirical successes, it is rational that scientists adopt different theories. Agreement on a theory is rational when a theory has all the empirical success, no matter what the reasons or causes of individual assent. This is one bit of prescription. The final bit of prescription is the requirement that biases be well distributed. What counts as a good distribution, which awaits a theory of weights and interactions, lies in the future. But it is not clear why one could not give the same kind of consequentialist account as is given of rationality: bias is well distributed in a community if the community does not agree on a theory until and unless it has all the empirical successes. That Solomon feels another kind of account is called for suggests a procedural view of distribution.[38] Moreover, given a consequentialist account of rational scientific decision making, it is not clear why

---

[36] It is not clear whether Solomon attributes irrationality to individuals in relation to some technical, philosophical, sense of "rationality" (e.g., epistemically pure, or conforming to Bayesian principles) or attributes it in a nontechnical sense of acting against one's interests without (moral, long-term pragmatic) reason.

[37] Solomon 1994b, 226.

[38] A consequentialist view would mean that we could not use the distribution of bias as a criterion in determining whether to trust a community's consensus position. How would we determine that a theory has all the empirical successes without independently knowing that biases (which would generate results for inclusion) are well distributed? Solomon (forthcoming) holds that in an epistemically balanced state of dissensus, biases (now termed nonepistemic decision vectors) should be equally distributed among contesting theories.

individuals, even if biased, can't be rational as long as their decision making produces some successes, or the success that matters to them. Thus the claim that they are not rational, or need not be rational, must be made in reference to some ideal of procedure rather than in reference to outcome.

Solomon's work offers two candidates for a definition of rationality in social empiricism, one in terms of outcome, the other in terms of procedure—success and distribution of bias. A community seeking empirical success will strive for a good distribution of bias as a means of achieving that success. Why is rationality a property of the community rather than of the individual? Individuals may achieve some successes, but their locatedness means that they are not sensitive to all the phenomena for which a theory must account. But if "all" means "all possible" how do we ever know that a theory has all the successes (as distinct from the successes available and evident in the aggregate to a particular collection of differently biased individuals)? One answer could be: consensus in a community characterized by a good distribution of biases guarantees that all relevant results are accounted for and thus that the consensus has formed around the theory with all the empirical successes. If so, there must be a way to specify a good distribution apart from that distribution which has as outcome a or the theory with all the empirical success. This brings us back to the procedural sense of rationality, but then there must be some way both of specifying the procedure independently of outcome *and* of connecting the procedure to the desired outcome—that is, some demonstration, conceptual or empirical, that links well-distributed biases to success. Without independent specifications of procedure and outcome, social empiricism collapses into tautology.

In the definition of epistemic concepts given in chapter 6, procedure and outcome are independently specified. The procedural dimension of epistemic acceptability is specified independently of outcome and vice versa. This captures the intuition that one can believe truly without being justified, and one can be justified in believing something that is nevertheless false. The practices of knowledge production are evaluated with respect to logical, empirical, and social norms. The outcome of those practices is successful if it achieves the desired degree of conformation to the object of inquiry.

Rouse's Practices

Both Joseph Rouse and Steve Fuller are concerned with questions of cognitive authority and the claims of authority made on behalf of science.[39] The directions they propose for philosophy of science are, however,

---

[39] Rouse 1996; Fuller 1988.

quite different. Rouse has argued that we should put scientific *practices* rather than scientific representations (theories, models) at the center of our philosophical accounts.

Rouse thinks that both the philosophers and the sociologists have (mis)identified the central philosophical question about science. They have seen it as a question about legitimation: the legitimation of empirical science as against metaphysics, politics, or religion. The philosopher seeks to explain why science is an epistemologically superior method of belief formation relative to these other intellectual pursuits. The sociologist wants to explain how this explanation perpetuates a myth and to explain instead how the sciences have attained authoritative status—how they manage to perpetuate the myth of epistemological superiority. Both the philosophers and the sociologists treat science as in need of legitimation. According to Rouse, the legitimation problem arises in part because of a mistaken focus on representation (representationalism) and in part because of an interest in the legitimation (or delegitimation) of science considered as a whole. Philosophers assume incorrectly that scientific content *qua* representation is both immaterial (e.g., propositional) and ahistorical. The legitimation project further assumes that the beliefs and desires of individual epistemic subjects constitute a coherent unity. These assumptions, according to Rouse, allow for the detachment of representational content from the contexts of its production and use, and the consequent neglect by philosophers of important questions such as those about the concentration of knowing subjects in wealthy societies, the effects of social stratification within those societies on science, and the role of emotional dynamics in the production of knowledge. Rouse proposes that science studies focus on scientific practices rather than on representational content and that the focus of inquiry shift from the legitimacy to the significance of those practices. A practice, for Rouse, is a pattern of activity in response to a situation.[40] It exists only through being constantly reproduced, an achievement requiring coordination among multiple participants and things and maintenance of that coordination over time. The analytic shift to practice enables us to treat scientific knowledge as dynamic and as dependent on the coordination of skills, models, concepts, and statements by spatially and temporally dispersed communities.

The shift Rouse recommends does indeed open up a broader range of scientific activity for philosophical scrutiny. His illumination of the transformative and regulative effects of integrating scientific results and practices into social practices in his earlier book is a fine example of the kind of analysis the shift he recommends makes possible.[41] To reject represen-

[40] Rouse 1996, 26.
[41] See Rouse 1987.

tation along with representationalism is, however, to court some of the same dangers the move is designed to avoid. It presupposes that a philosophical interest in representation must perforce treat representations (models, theories) in an ahistorical, decontextualized fashion. It also forecloses on the possibility of rethinking epistemological concepts afforded by nonhyperbolic readings of the sociological work. That is, it leaves the dichotomy between cognitive reason and the social untouched. Finally, if one focuses on practices within research programs, as, for example, Latour and Woolgar did, the political questions to which Rouse thinks we should attend remain unadressed. Thus, the substitution of practice for representation runs the same risks of marginalizing important questions as are run by the legitimation project.

Fuller's Panglossian Epistemology

Steve Fuller takes a different set of lessons from the sociological work. Fuller keeps scientific representations as the subject matter of his social epistemology but is concerned with their circulation in scientific communities, rather than with the conditions of their production. Like Rouse, he treats the normative aspirations of traditional philosophy of science to be its undoing. But whereas Rouse interprets the normative project as about the legitimation of science *tout court*, and hence to be abandoned, Fuller seems to think that we need not to abandon the normative project, but rather to reread it as a question about the ascription and distribution of cognitive authority. He, too, draws attention to the gap between the normative accounts of philosophers of science and the empirical accounts of the sociologists of science. Fuller partially accepts the sociologists' claim that the normative accounts fail to get a purchase on actual practices, but takes this as a challenge to relocate the normative interests of philosophers. Fuller offers several ways to understand the failure of normative accounts—either as descriptively inadequate or as normatively incomplete. Opting for the second alternative, he proposes his version of social epistemology not only as the solution but as the culmination and true agenda of both classical epistemology and the new sociology of science.

Classical epistemology, he claims, was really about the allocation of cognitive authority. In philosophy of science this is expressed as an inquiry into the structural relations between scientific disciplines, particularly into the possibility of intertheoretic reduction.[42] Sociology of science, on the other hand, he represents as having been concerned initially about the distribution of power implicit in the allocation of cognitive

---

[42] Fuller 1988, 5–6.

authority. "New-wave" sociologists (Knorr-Cetina, Latour) have broken the tight connection between knowledge and social interests assumed in the older-wave sociology. Nevertheless, they confuse, according to Fuller, the context-dependence and open-endedness of science, especially the fact that "no one can predict how [his or her] results will be used by others," with the claim that "any scientist is free to tailor other knowledge claims to [his or her] specific research situation."[43]

Setting aside the issue of the correctness of Fuller's interpretations, I wish to comment only on two central elements of Fuller's constructive program: epistemological Panglossianism and epistemological materialism. The first of these, named for Voltaire's Dr. Pangloss, is the treatment of every case of knowledge production as if it were the best case.[44] Scientific practices are not evaluated against some independently articulated standard or relative to some independently identifiable goal. Instead the Panglossian epistemologist, assuming that the various parts of the knowledge-productive process function optimally to achieve some end, inquires into what that end could and could not be. To facilitate the Panglossian's work, Fuller proposes a reconception of knowledge in economic terms, what I am calling epistemological materialism. Knowledge production should be seen as an economic process, which means for Fuller that the quantity of knowledge is a constant. Knowledge is identified with its material embodiments: books, articles. It is this material whose quantity is constant.[45] The task of normative (social) epistemology is then how to redistribute knowledge more equitably (through that material).[46] This in turn, requires knowing how credibility is redistributed by changes in the microstructure of knowledge and how knowledge is "translated" at the macrolevel to produce changes of content in a constant material quantity. For Fuller, the social epistemologist who masters these skills will be in a position to regulate the production of knowledge by regulating the (rhetorical, technological, administrative) means of its communication.[47]

---

[43] Ibid., 14.

[44] Ibid., 26.

[45] Fuller must have in mind a measure slightly more complicated than mere quantity of material embodiments and some notion of live as opposed to dead knowledge. He does not, however, provide this measure or a conservation principle that would have constancy as its outcome. (One can see that there are limits to what any individual can actively know, that is, have available in mind, so that at some point new items must replace, rather than augment, old. But material embodiments are technologies to overcome that limitation.)

[46] Cf. Fuller 1988, 251–75.

[47] Fuller includes as an appendix to his book a curriculum for the social epistemologist–knowledge policy analyst and planner. This curriculum includes "transideological policy-making," that is, the skills of simultaneously insulating knowledge from and accommodating it to political pressures; "prognostics and diagnostics" in knowledge policy, that is, the skills of determining the "categories and procedures for charting the development of

One difficulty with this proposal is that "knowledge" is either treated as an undefined primitive or is identified with the products of scientific practice. If it is treated as an undefined primitive, then it is not at all clear that the normative social epistemology Fuller devises for "knowledge" has anything to do with garden-variety knowledge that has been the concern of most epistemology (e.g., my knowledge [or not] that there is a red barn on the hill). It also leaves unanswered the question in virtue of what feature the Panglossian epistemologist identifies a given process as a *knowledge*-productive practice. If on the other hand, "knowledge" is defined as the products of scientific practices, then it rules out of order the question, Is this product knowledge? But one could be a Panglossian about scientific practices and assume that they function optimally to achieve their ends, without supposing that that end is knowledge as conventionally understood.[48] Fuller might respond that having knowledge is just having credibility, that there is nothing more to belief change than the redistribution of credibility, and that credibility is an ascriptive, not a categorical, status. I believe, on the contrary, that our interest in epistemology (and social epistemology) stems from an antecedent conception of knowledge that makes it something worth having. The value of credibility is parasitic on this (normative) conception of knowledge. Fuller's social epistemologist assumes this value in studying the circulation of knowledge and credibility in society. What makes Fuller's social epistemology social is his interest in the operation of knowledge in society. This kind of social epistemology does not address the dichotomy between the cognitive and the social and leaves certain fundamental assumptions about knowledge incorporated into that dichotomy untouched. I have argued for a different kind of social epistemology— one that integrates the normative ("prenanalytic") understanding of knowledge with the social character of its production, or at least with the social character of the production of scientific knowledge. This is an epistemology within which it is possible to ask, of any given product, whether it constitutes knowledge, a question that Fuller's account seems to render meaningless.

Summary

All three of these philosophers try to incorporate what they take to be the important points from the sociologists into new approaches in philos-

---

knowledge" and of identifying at what stage in this development any given instance of knowledge production is; "administration of knowledge policy," which involves the "design and implementation of norms for effective knowledge growth" (Fuller 1988, 291–93).

[48] One might interpret Panglossianism as the view that there can be a variety of cognitive goals, but Fuller does not seem partial to the pluralism this interpretation entails.

ophy of science. Although they agree that taking this work seriously opens up new questions for philosophy, their neglect of the rational-social dichotomy that structures both philosophical and sociological thought leads them to abandon traditional epistemology. I have argued that in order to appreciate the sociologists' contributions, the rational-social dichotomy and its constitutive binaries must be addressed and taken apart. The consequence is not an abandonment of traditional epistemological questions, but their rearticulation for empirical subjects. This rearticulation does not reject traditional epistemological concepts, but localizes and contextualizes justification and epistemic acceptability, emphasizes the interdependence of cognitive agents, and is open to unresolvable plurality of content.

CONCLUSION: *KNOWLEDGE* AND EPISTEMOLOGY

The localizing of such status as justification and acceptability may leave one puzzling about what epistemology might then consist in. One of the puzzles, of course, is what happens to the prescriptive or normative aspect of epistemology if justification is context-dependent. One solution to this puzzle is to distinguish between local and general epistemology. General or philosophical epistemology becomes an interpretive inquiry, an exploration of the meaning of concepts like knowledge, truth, justification. Normative epistemology, understood as prescriptions for belief acceptance, would then be the set of public standards endorsed in a community whose authoritative reach extends only to those who intend, through membership in that community, to be bound by its strictures. The relation of local and general epistemology is more complex than this division indicates. For example, the status of the conditions of objectivity or transformative criticism advanced in chapter 6 is problematic. Whose conditions are these, and what is the ground of their normative claim? If we say that they are a community's conditions, then it is an empirical question whether they form part of a community's standards, or of a community's epistemology, and they have no general claim. But if they are general, then their proposal as normative contravenes the view that normative epistemology is local.[49] I think it is best to treat them as an explication of "objectivity," or a partial explication of "knowledge," and thus as the result of an interpretive exercise in general or philosophical epistemology. As norms they can be understood not as categorical but as hypothetical imperatives: "if you wish to be objective, then do X." Indeed, following Kaplan,[50] it makes sense to treat them not as directions

---

[49] I am grateful to Robert Audi for presenting me with this dilemma.
[50] Cf. discussion in chapter 5.

but as grounds for criticism of claims to knowledge, grounds derived from a shared sense of what knowledge is. The argument I have offered for these conditions depends on an analysis of the relation between cognitive aspirations and cognitive resources and on an intuitive distinction between knowledge and opinion that I take to be shared. To the extent the intuition is shared and correctly articulated in the conditions, the analysis specifies in normative terms the meaning of a normative concept. Those who reject the conditions have a different concept of knowledge, or perhaps, a concept of something else. So, there is a sense in which even the general conditions are local, just less local than particular norms adopted in particular communities in conformity with the general conditions.

It is satisfaction of these hypothetical norms that gives even Western scientific communities whatever claim they have to our doxastic allegiance. For the only non-question-begging response to challenge must be: "We are open to criticism, we do change in response to it, and while we may not have included all possible perspectives in the discursive interactions that underwrite our methodological procedures, we've included as many as we have encountered (or more than others have)." It does not follow, however, that the standards and warranting procedures could not change further in response to new sorts of criticisms. (Indeed, if feminist, environmentalist, and other critics of the sciences are successful, the standards and the knowledge they legitimate will change.) The point is that there is nothing further, that appeal to standards or methodological norms beyond those ratified by the discursive interactions of an inquiring community is an appeal to transcendent principles that inevitably turn out to be local.

CHAPTER EIGHT

Pluralism and Local Epistemologies

IN CHAPTER 4, I urged that a satisfactory epistemology for science should not foreclose the choice of pluralism versus monism. There are at least two forms of epistemic plurality. One form results from the diversity of cultural and ideological perspectives that influence the conduct of scientific research. The second is a feature of contemporary science conducted within the cultural framework of Western industrialized societies. The former is a complex phenomenon encompassing both relations between approaches within Western science and relations between Western science and science practiced in non-Western cultural contexts. This dimension of plurality warrants a separate study and is not addressed in this volume.[1] The second form of plurality has been attracting the attention of an increasing number of philosophers of science.

Although there are numerous philosophers who continue to see unification as a central aim of scientific inquiry, many philosophers of science are now embracing forms of pluralism.[2] Patrick Suppes argued, in the context of what he called probabilistic metaphysics, for a pluralistic understanding of scientific knowledge. The multiplication of subdisciplines with their own specialized vocabularies, he argued, spelled doom for the radical unification envisioned by Oppenheim and Putnam.[3] John Dupré has argued, drawing partly on biology, for the radical disunity of science and an accompanying metaphysics he calls promiscuous realism.[4] Nancy Cartwright has argued that not even physics displays the kind of unity presupposed as an ideal.[5] Nevertheless, contemporary biology has stimulated most contemporary pluralist thinking.

The biological sciences have been the sites of fierce debate over both theory and method at least since Darwin. Whereas earlier in this century these debates were quite general—mechanicism versus vitalism, for example—current debates tend to be conducted within or about particular subfields. Evolutionary theory is the site of debates over the units and

---

[1] For some beginnings, see Keller 1983, 1992; Levins and Lewontin 1985; Longino 1996; all of which address diversity within Western science. See Hess 1995; Nader 1996; Needham 1954; and Raina 1996, for work that addresses intercultural scientific diversity.

[2] Kitcher 1993.

[3] Suppes 1984.

[4] Dupré 1993.

[5] Cartwright 1995.

levels of selection. Behavioral biology is not only the site of debates about nature versus nurture, but also encompasses multiple biological approaches—genetic, biochemical and physiological, neurological—which may or may not be reconcilable in an integrated theory. In cell biology, scientists debate about the extent of the regulative role of DNA. In ecology, too, researchers debate both conclusions and the methodologies used to reach them. Although these disagreements involve both substantive and methodological issues, usually one aspect is the focus of debate in any given instance. Controversy and debate are highly noticeable indicators of plurality. Sometimes, however, potentially conflicting theories or methods either do not give rise to debates or else give rise to debates that do not fully engage the researchers themselves or engage only some members of the relevant fields. This suggests that whether different theories and methods are drawn into debate depends on factors other than the difference, even, incompatibility, between them. Furthermore, the practical conduct of inquiry does not wait upon the resolution of these debates nor does it require consensus on a single theory or method. This is what Suppes was pointing to in his brief for pluralism.

PLURALITY, STANDARDS, AND COGNITIVE AIMS: EXAMPLES FROM TWENTIETH-CENTURY BIOLOGY

Goals and standards are one way to distinguish cognitive or investigative communities from one another. While a goal of knowledge is indeed common to all cognitive communities, as so stated it is insufficiently specific to generate inquiry. As Richard Popkin is reputed to have teased scientists, if all one wants is knowledge or truth, why not count the number of bottle caps one can lay down between Los Angeles and San Diego or between Minneapolis and St. Louis? One wants knowledge (and truths) about particular things or sets of things. To articulate what those are is already to become committed to some (admittedly sketchy) account of them.[6] To want to know what causes cancer is to be committed to the existence of cancer and of a cause or causes of it. To want to know the structure of matter is to be committed to the existence of matter and to the assumption that it has a structure. Minimal though these assumptions may seem, they are nevertheless assumptions that guide inquiry and play a role in the interpretation of data.

The role of assumptions in inquiry means that epistemological analysis of scientific theory and inquiry must include analysis of the social and

---

[6] See Longino 1990, chap. 5 for further discussion.

intellectual context in which inquiry is pursued and theories and hypotheses are evaluated. The intellectual context is constituted of background assumptions and investigative resources—instruments, samples, experimental protocols. The social context is the set of institutions and interactions in and through which assumptions and resources circulate as well as the larger social environment in which institutions and interactions are embedded. The analysis of effective criticism outlined in previous chapters states (the kinds of) conditions such institutions and interactions should meet. Meeting these conditions, however, does not permit detaching justification or acceptability from the context within which justification is achieved. Thus, attention to both the social and the intellectual context is important for appreciating the scope and limits of any given claim. The following examples illustrate the emergence and immanence of locally normative epistemologies from and in their particular contexts of research. Plurality is evidenced in substantive claims, in methodologies, or in both.

Experiment and Measurement in Ecology

As the discipline of ecology has turned to experimental methods, differences have arisen both regarding the proper kind of experimentation to conduct and regarding the merits of experiment at all, in contrast to noninterventive field observation.[7] One recent debate concerned worldwide drops in amphibian populations. A research group in Oregon conducted an experiment with paired sets of frog eggs, one set exposed to and the other set protected from ultraviolet (UV) radiation. The protected eggs developed into tadpoles at a much greater rate than the exposed ones, from which the researchers concluded that increased UV radiation was the culprit in the observed decline of amphibians. Dissenters claimed that there was no investigation into whether UV radiation had increased over the time amphibian mortality was on the rise and that only a long-term observation of an ecosystem and its inhabitants could ascertain the cause of mortality in the field as opposed to in the laboratory. Even among experimentally oriented ecologists, there are differences as to the relative value of ecosystem experimentation (e.g., seeding patches of ocean with iron) and experimentation with model systems like the paired sets of frog eggs in the laboratory or even more complicated but still constructed and controlled systems. Ecosystem experimentation which manipulates variables in actual environments is more

---

[7] For a general account, see Roush 1995; for advocacy of ecosystem experimentation, see Carpenter, Chisholm, and Krebs 1995; for model systems, see Lawton 1995.

realistic, but model systems, while both deliberately and unintentionally simplified, offer better opportunities for identifying and controlling possible causal factors. Given that different (and different levels of) elements are present in the two kinds of experimental regime, even when one is intended to be a model of the other, studies of the effects of introducing the same agent will yield different quantitative results in the different approaches. Advocates of the ecosystem approach applaud its value for evaluating and predicting the effects of environmental change. Advocates of the model approach stress the replicability and control of relevant parameters that the approach offers.

Field or Laboratory in the Study of Speciation

David Magnus has analyzed the role of different methodological-epistemological values in a case that prefigures the current debate among ecologists: the early-twentieth-century debate between advocates of Hugo deVries's mutation theory of speciation and advocates of David Starr Jordan's isolation theory.[8] This debate was not just about theories of speciation but about evidence and method in biology. Mutationists were experimentalists, whereas isolationists were naturalists, and their disagreements focused largely on the probative character of the kinds of data proper to each kind of study. Experimentalists derogated the field study methods of the naturalists in favor of the experimental control possible in the laboratory. The results of field study were compatible with many hypotheses and not capable of picking out the real causes. Naturalists did not deny the value of experiment but assigned it an auxiliary role to that of field study. The results of laboratory experiment were of necessity confined in their validity to the species experimented on, some of which, as laboratory creations, might not reflect anything occurring in nature, the rest of which, as only a small sample of nature's variety, did not license generalizations about processes in the wild. Magnus understands these debates as reflecting conflicting epistemological values. The naturalists' emphasis on the need for variety of data expressed a Whewellian requirement for consilience of inductions, "the convergence of different lines of evidence in support of a theoretical view."[9] Experimentalists, on the other hand, favored the use of control groups characteristic of laboratory research. Embracing epistemological and natural parsimony, they were of the view that, as the natural world was characterized

[8] Magnus 2000a.
[9] Ibid., 115.

by parsimony of mechanism, they could "replace a variety of lines of evidence with one privileged line."[10]

Magnus concludes his discussion by noting that the theoretical views of the naturalists were crucial to the development of the evolutionary synthesis in which, ironically, their epistemological views were eclipsed. However, later debates in the synthesis period to be discussed shortly, and the debates among contemporary ecologists, show that these conflicting epistemological views have remained in play, even if under different guise. Because these are debates about how to weigh different kinds of evidence the conflict between the epistemological values cannot itself be resolved evidentially. Their contrary pull ensures that the preeminence of one is only temporary. This epistemological excess does not mean that the decision in favor of one or the other is arbitrary, but that the judgment in any particular case rests on a complex of factors and is neither retrospectively captured nor evaluable by a single epistemic rule. Plurality, thus, characterizes the epistemological as well as the substantive aspects of this domain of inquiry.

Standards of Adequacy in Electron Microscopy

Historian of science Nicholas Rasmussen's work on electron microscopy offers another example of difference in approach related to differences in methodological assumptions.[11] In the 1950s two groups of researchers, one in Sweden and one in New York, using electron microscopes to study mitochondria disagreed about the internal structure of these organelles. Mitochondria look like elongated ovals. The New York group argued that perceived transverse ridges inside the mitochondrial walls were partial—that is, did not extend all the way across the interior space—thus leaving a free channel through the length of the interior. The Swedish group argued that at least some of the transverse structures were platelike membranes extending across the whole diameter of the mitochondrion, thus blocking any free channel. The groups also disagreed about the relation of these internal structures to the external or surrounding membrane.[12] These disagreements over structure were a function of disagreements over how to interpret and evaluate the electron micrographic evidence. Each group had micrographs that supported its theory of structure. But the micrographs yielded different images of the mitochondria. These differences were a result of the use of different fixating and other sample preparation techniques. There were two

[10] Ibid.
[11] Rasmussen 1995.
[12] Ibid., 396.

related issues involved in the debates as to which set of images was the superior set: one is what the *real* structure of mitochondria is; the second is which representation of the structure to adopt. One group argued that the micrographs should be assessed by criteria internal to micrography such as degree of resolution of the image. The other group argued that consistency with data from other sources (fractionation biochemistry, in this case) was at least equally, and perhaps more, relevant to determining which of the conflicting images was the best representation of mitochondrial structure. Here, too, there was not a higher-level epistemological principle that could settle the conflict. Both lines of argument represented epistemologically respectable positions.

Multiple Causes to One End in Behavioral Biology

Philosopher of biology Sandra Mitchell has examined the variety of explanations of the division of labor in social insect colonies.[13] There are both evolutionary and ontogenic explanations, and among the ontogenic, or self-organization, explanations there is a variety of causal models of the division of labor. One appeals to genetic diversity among the individual colony members, which results in different response thresholds to a given stimulus, which results in turn in a division of labor. Another proposes that all colony members are born with an identical work algorithm, but that the nest architecture varies the stimulus received, thus evoking different behaviors from different individuals. While some would see this as a matter of incompatible explanations requiring resolution through choice of one, Mitchell argues that these models do not need to be seen as incompatible in that sense. They are idealizations and as such map onto an ideal world rather than the real world. In applying them in the actual world, we might say that each applies but in different circumstances. Some species accomplish the division of labor in one way and others in a different way. Thus, there cannot be a single model of division of labor in social insects. Nature produces the same ends with different means. Natural complexity, according to Mitchell, stands in the way of a unified science and requires pluralism.

Model Organisms in Developmental Biology

Biologist Jessica Bolker describes a situation combining features of the previous three examples.[14] Her concern is the model-system approach in

---

[13] Mitchell 1995.

[14] Bolker 1995. I am indebted to Kevin Lattery for bringing this article to my attention.

PLURALISM AND LOCAL EPISTEMOLOGIES **181**

developmental biology. "Model system" means something slightly different in the context of developmental biology than it does in ecology. In developmental biology, certain species of organism have come to be used as standard experimental models for the purpose of conducting research. These are organisms for which standard strains have been developed or characterized, enabling communication about a uniform subject among research groups focused on different aspects of the organism's development, or on the development of certain traits, such as the capacity for photosynthesis. Bolker argues that the exigencies of experimentation impose constraints on the choice of organisms to serve as model systems. In particular, organisms are preferred that have a rapid rate of development and a short generation time. Smaller organisms, which can be more easily accommodated in laboratories, are preferred to larger ones. And organisms whose embryogenesis is uniform, hence strongly canalized and insensitive to environmental perturbation, offer better models from which to generalize. But the evolutionary pressures that resulted in these traits may have produced adaptations that make the model species unrepresentative of their taxa. For example, maternal effects may be stronger in quickly developing than in slowly developing species, and short cell cycles in such species may impose constraints on the length of genes. Species that are smaller in size than larger species of their taxa may also have undergone simplifications or outright loss of structures and may have evolved morphological novelties.

Bolker cites several consequences of reliance on these more experimentally convenient organisms. Researchers may overgeneralize, extending what is true for *E. coli*, or the guinea pig, to the elephant (to paraphrase Monod). Once a theoretical model of the development of a trait or process has been articulated based on one or a few such model organisms, contrary information from other species may be ignored and existing knowledge of alternate developmental pathways may be lost. Reliance on only a few model species will fail fully to represent the variety in nature and the reliance of developmental and evolutionary studies may be inverted. These consequences, we might say, follow from a resistance to pluralism.

Kevin Lattery points out that the phenomenon Bolker describes extends throughout biological research.[15] Citing Hans Krebs, he notes that different organisms are differentially suited for research on particular organic systems, and processes, as blue-green algae are ideal for studying photosynthesis, and pigeon breast muscle was crucial to studying oxidative metabolism. Lattery goes on to note that not only are preferred model systems in general likely to be unrepresentative of their

[15] Lattery 1999.

taxa, but the conditions of biological experimentation also denature their subjects in various ways, either by producing lineages found only in laboratories, like the oncomouse, or by isolating tissues and cell lines so that their interactions with elements of their biological context do not interfere with research. Each experimental system provides partial knowledge of the natural system it models.

Causal Assumptions in Selection Theory

C. K. Waters implicitly endorses a stronger form of pluralism in his analysis of the units of selection controversy.[16] Biologists and philosophers of biology have argued whether selection acts on genes, genotypes, individual organisms, or groups of organisms. Waters claims that the parties to these debates who are also realists have made two unexamined assumptions:

> **1.** For any selection process there is a uniquely correct description of the operative selection forces and the level at which each impinges.
> **2.** Population level causes must enhance the probability of their effects in at least one context and not decrease it in any other.

The first assumption fuels debates among theorists committed to analysis of selection at different levels. The second is used by opponents of genic selectionism to discredit that view. Waters analyzes cases and arguments offered by Williams, Dawkins, and Sober and Lewontin, with the aim of showing that different selection theorists parse the domain and its environment in different ways. This parsing, for which no claims of unique correctness can be claimed, supports the identification of different levels as the level at which selection forces are acting. A similar analysis emphasizing the heterogeneity of real environments supports Waters's contention that *all* selection forces are context-sensitive. If they are all context-sensitive, then they will not act in the same way in all contexts, and principle 2 must be abandoned. Rather than see the levels-of-selection debate as a controversy requiring a unique solution, he advocates instead what he calls tempered realism, which transforms the above two assumptions as follows:

> **1A (TR)** Accounts that differ as to the level on which selection is operating can nevertheless accurately represent the same causal network in different ways.
> **2A (TR)** Population level forces can increase the chances of their effects in some contexts and decrease them in others.

[16] Waters 1991.

1A (TR) effectively says that the selective forces and units selected can be differently but equally correctly represented by different theories of the same process. And the principle of causation (2) used by proponents of one level of selection to eliminate forces at a competing level of selection has to be abandoned and genic selection theories tolerated when the parsing of domain and environment requires it. Waters's argument is that a situation of controversy that seems to require a unique solution is better seen as a situation in which multiple accounts can be correct. Tempered realism is pluralism in all but name.

Multiple Approaches in Neurophysiology

Studies of the role of the brain in behavior offer another illustration. In earlier work, I analyzed two approaches to the biological study of behavior: one originating in neuroendocrinology and another in brain physiology and development.[17] These approaches were characterized by different questions, vastly different experimental and investigative strategies, and different models of brain structure and function. They could also be seen as conforming to different epistemological values: simplicity and unity of scope in one case; adequacy to a preferred set of observations in the other. They came into conflict because they supported different conceptions of human action and behavior when extrapolated from their laboratory contexts to these more general questions.[18] Looking at them solely within the laboratory context, however, they could be understood as addressing different questions arising in different contexts of inquiry. The neuroendocrinological community was interested in discovering the causal capacities of hormones and, as part of that effort, conducted experiments in animal models that varied the exposure of organisms to various hormones and measured behavioral outcomes in those organisms. Neurophysiologists and neuroanatomists focused on brain cortex were engaged in articulating a model of brain development, structure, and function that could eventually account for high-level cognitive performance characteristic of humans. While these models conflict when extrapolated to human behavior, they each nevertheless provide (partial) knowledge of brain and neural processes, accounts that conform to their different domains sufficiently to support further research in those domains.

---

[17] For a fuller account, see Longino 1990, chap. 6, 7, and 8.

[18] See, for example, Ehrhardt and Meyer-Bahlburg 1981 for the neuroendocrinological approach and Bleier 1984 and Fausto-Sterling 1985 for the other approach.

LOCAL EPISTEMOLOGY

Different features of these cases illustrate different aspects of the pluralist thesis, which holds that a plurality of adequate and epistemically acceptable explanations or theories can be generated by a variety of different factors in any situation of inquiry. The assumptions which partially constitute the intellectual context of a given approach or inquiry are of at least two kinds: substantive and methodological. Substantive assumptions concern the way the world one is investigating is. They may be compositional or processual. An example of the former is the assumption that the material world is constituted of particles that at the most fundamental level are indivisible. A processual assumption that had a following recently is the assumption that all biological development is controlled by genes. The assumptions in the units of selection debate discussed by Waters are substantive assumptions about the uniqueness of levels at which selection operates and, indeed, about the nature of causality itself.

Methodological assumptions have to do with the means we have of developing and acquiring knowledge. They can range from general philosophical views like the commitment to some form of empiricism to quite particular views about the kinds of data appropriate for kinds of question: field observation versus experiment, for example. The ecology debates revolve around such methodological issues and each approach is shaped in part by its commitment to a particular methodological strategy. Similarly, the choice of model system in developmental biology expresses assumptions of a methodological character. Additional choices involve those between performing experiments on animal models versus clinical human studies, in vivo versus in vitro studies, and so on. Other methodological assumptions concern how much data of a certain type should be required, what kinds of data are relevant, and what mix of kinds of data from different kinds of study techniques should be required. They include assumptions about what various kinds of investigative instruments and experimental protocols can produce and about the reliability of those instruments and protocols. The range of methodologies obviously depends in part on the availability of investigative resources, but these are not sufficient to limit methodologies to one.

In addition to such clearly substantive or clearly methodological assumptions, others concern what we might call the form of knowledge and are both methodological and substantive. These include such properties of theories or models as simplicity and unification, which are sometimes treated as epistemic virtues by philosophers. To treat them as such is to treat them as markers of truth. The insistence on ascribing the division of labor in social insect colonies to either genetics or an environmental feature like nest architecture is (in part) expressive of a commitment to unification. Such a commitment constrains the form of acceptable knowledge of (insect) behavior, requiring explanatory models involving a single causal principle that can be incorporated (as consequence) into a more comprehensive theory.

Philosophers who have treated virtues such as simplicity and unification as epistemic have often been seeking a solution to underdetermination arguments that does not involve substantive assumptions, especially substantive assumptions that can be shown to have sociopolitical dimensions.[19] This is a false hope on several scores. The theoretical virtue of simplicity itself involves substantive assumptions—that is, the assumption that the world is simple.[20] So does the theoretical virtue of unification, which presumes the world to be sufficiently uniform as to be explained by the same basic theoretical principles. And as van Fraassen has argued, the virtues advanced as epistemic virtues are generally not all maximally satisfiable by any single theory or model; hence an additional virtue of balance among these virtues must be introduced.[21] But then what counts as the right balance? Furthermore, virtues like simplicity can be shown to carry the sociopolitical dimensions their invocation was intended to avoid.[22] And, finally, there are communities preferring alternative values to those so often cited as the scientific values. Feminist and environmentalist research communities endorse such values as ontological heterogeneity, as against the uniformity implied by simplicity. Larry Laudan has documented how the values of research communities have changed in response to tensions within the reticular triad of theory, methodology, and axiology.[23] The so-called epistemic virtues, then, are really, at best, standards around which a cognitive community can coalesce, standards that its members adopt as theirs, but not standards that hold universally.

The one standard that is common to any scientific community is empirical adequacy, that is, truth of the observationally determinable portion of theories or models. Claiming universality for this standard is not claiming as much as might initially appear. Given the partiality of models and theories, a model may be empirically adequate without thereby containing an element corresponding to each observable aspect of the entire domain modeled. The model cannot have observational ele-

[19] For advocacy of the epistemic virtues, see Quine and Ullian 1970; Churchland 1985; McMullin 1983.
[20] Simplicity can mean many things. Whatever meaning one assigns to it, treating simplicity as a sign of the truth of a theory assumes that the world is simple in whatever sense is required. See Longino 1997.
[21] Van Fraassen 1989.
[22] See Longino 1996.
[23] Laudan 1984b.

ments that are inconsistent with aspects that are observed or observable with the observational apparatus of the model's approach, but there may be observed or observable aspects of the gross domain that are not within its representational repertoire. Whether this is a deficiency of the model depends on what our interest in constructing it is. Moreover, any approach has to set standards of precision and accuracy that determine what empirical adequacy really requires in particular contexts of measurement. The permissible error bars may be much larger for studies in a natural setting in ecological experimentation than they are for trials in a controlled laboratory setting.

Second, and relatedly, the point of requiring empirical adequacy is that it is necessary for the purposes for which we engage in scientific inquiry—to understand the world around us, that is, the world we experience, and to interact with it successfully. We cannot interact successfully without a model whose observational elements correspond to some extent to the phenomena in the world with which we wish to interact or with which we must interact in order to engage in the interactions we desire. And whether our interactions are successful depends on our particular aims with respect to the portion of the world with which we interact. Someone's leaping off a bluff and falling to the ground will count as successful or unsuccessful depending on whether their aim was flight or reaching the next level down. So, of course, as long as a community has interests in interacting with the world, empirical adequacy will figure among its cognitive standards. But sharing the standard of empirical adequacy does not mean that scientific communities will come to consensus regarding a single or single set of theories, or that they will interpret or weigh empirical adequacy in the same way, as long as their other values or standards, the standards that among other things determine the range of application of empirical adequacy, differ. Thus, in Rasmussen's example from electron microscopy, another value—portability or standardization—outweighed the most natural way of reading empirical adequacy.

Given such an array, one can understand investigative, or scientific, communities as constituted around selections of substantive and methodological assumptions. These selections are a function of both the aims of research and inherited tradition. To call them selections does not mean that they are deliberately picked out from a possible assortment but that they represent a subset of possible alternatives, reliance on which can be defended by reference to the goals of the particular research community and which have survived or been let stand through critical scrutiny. All of these—substantive assumptions, methodological assumptions, aims and goals, and the arguments linking assumptions and practices to aims and goals—are subject to critical scrutiny, debate and defense, and all of them may bear complicated relations to social, political, and aesthetic values of a community's cultures.

Such a set of methodological choices, commitments, or standards can be called a community's epistemology. Characterization of such an epistemology would include a specification of a number of elements in addition to specific methods relied on to produce answers to questions and standards of necessity and sufficiency of various kinds of data. A full characterization would include a specification of the kind of knowledge sought: causal or processual (e.g., how x works); compositional (e.g., what y is made of); distributive (e.g., what is the frequency of occurrence of z in contexts $c_1 \ldots c_n$; descriptive (e.g., the number of species in an ecosystem, the boiling point of s). Causal questions may, furthermore, be either mechanical or historical. The specification of kind of knowledge sought might also include formal characteristics (e.g., how general the knowledge is that is sought). This much of an epistemology is what was referred to earlier as an approach: the application of an epistemology to a particular domain. A complete characterization of a local epistemology would also provide some account of why the methods used are thought adequate in relation to the kind of knowledge sought. Such an account will typically involve reference to substantive assumptions and cognitive values but there may also be pragmatic and professional reasons to choose particular methods or standards of evidence. Such reasons may include the availability of necessary instruments, the unavailability of alternative procedures; they may involve issues of communicability and standardization, acceptance within related communities, and so on.

If methodological rules and procedures are not claimed to be self-evident and context-independent, then their rationale, as stated earlier, must lie in the aims and goals of the inquiring community (or in its traditions). Identifying these features of a local epistemology, particularly the assumptions and values that link methods to kinds of knowledge sought, is a matter not just of picking out the methods and standards that link data to hypotheses in research articles but of reconstructing them from an analysis of the context of inquiry: correspondence; accounts of controversy and of interventions in controversy; study of institutional settings, priorities, and constraints. Because individuals may have a variety of motives for engaging in community activities, the values and priorities that organize an approach cannot be identified simply from individuals' values and interests, but must be shown to be both commonly or institutionally endorsed and effective. A local epistemology is a dynamic complex of beliefs, norms, goals, and practices. These elements can change as a community encounters external and internal challenges. External challenges can include interaction with other communities; internal challenges are generated when social goals and values change or when the application of particular norms and practices in concrete situations yields results that are in tension with other elements. Scientific inquiry produces not only answers to questions, but those answers themselves open up new issues for investigation, new landscapes of ignorance. This dynamic aspect of inquiry means that its epistemology must accommodate its dynamism.

On the account of epistemic acceptability offered here, that a theory is acceptable in a community C at one time does not imply that C will not come to abandon it at some later time. Furthermore, there's no requirement that members of C reject background assumptions simply because they are shown to be contingent or lacking firm support. Unless background assumptions are shown, through critical discourse, to be in conflict with values, goals, or other assumptions of C, there is no obligation to abandon them—only to acknowledge their contingency and thus to withdraw excessive confidence. On the other hand, there is an obligation to seek out criticism, so insulation from criticism is no guarantor of epistemic acceptability.[24] Background assumptions are, along with values and aims of inquiry, the public standards that regulate the discursive and material interactions of a community. The point here is that they are both provisional and subordinated to the overall goal of inquiry for a community. The *kind* of knowledge a community seeks, the *purposes* for which it seeks it—that is, the uses to which knowledge will be put— guide the development of the community's standards.

Local epistemologies enable us to think of situations characterized by a plurality of theories and models in a pluralist framework, rather than as a sign of the immaturity of a given field of research.[25] An approach to inquiry is characterized by a kind of question and a set of investigative tools used to develop answers to the question(s). Question and tools together often presuppose a theoretical claim or, at the very least, a model of the portion of the world being investigated.[26] Different approaches to a phenomenon and, thus, different local epistemologies can be generated by differences in methodological assumptions, principles, or strategies, by differences in goals, or by differences in substantive assumptions, such as basic characterizations of the domain under investigation. On the pluralist view, approaches informed by different theoretical assumptions and generated by different kinds of question produce

---

[24] As my earlier remarks on tempered equality suggest, this is not a simple and straightforward matter. The complexity of the task does not diminish the obligation.

[25] This is not to say that a situation characterized by plurality is never an instance of immature science, as Kuhn seemed to think, but that plurality is not in itself evidence of such immaturity.

[26] This presupposition of a model encompasses what I (1990) described as the presupposition of an object of inquiry or of explanatory model.

different knowledge about a given phenomenon. Debates about the theoretical claims arise under particular social or institutional conditions, but are not forced on practitioners of different approaches merely because of difference in theoretical content. Meeting criticism can involve showing how the claim is vindicated by aspects of the community's knowledge-productive practices, showing how those practices satisfy certain goals, and then perhaps defending these goals, or modifying the claim or aspects of the practice—for example, by moderating or qualifying its scope or altering aspects of the research process itself. The debates between approaches can be understood as critical interaction that advances all of them rather than as a duel requiring a single victor.

REVISITING SETTLED CASES

The examples adduced at the beginning of the chapter involved conflictual or unresolved issues. One might use Bruno Latour's image of notion of the Janus face to argue that the conflict and irresolution simply show that in these cases plurality is to be expected.[27] Prior to community consensus concerning an experiment, hypothesis, or theory, it is fragile and, as Latour puts it, dependent on the actions of scientists. After consensus, the constructive role of scientists disappears, and the result or theory is seen as inevitable, an expression of nature. As Latour also says, it has been black-boxed. It is no longer disputed but has become itself the basis for additional experiments, for further theorizing. Its origins and even its justification no longer matter. Plurality and the operation of social processes are to be expected in ongoing, unstabilized science. But stabilization and black-boxing are not just the elimination of the traces of the social; they are also the elimination of plurality. Demonstrating the social processes that have cemented a particular achievement is often taken as a piece of debunking, as an intended demonstration that agreement was premature or misguided or contraindicated by the evidence. Such a response is a function of the dichotomy discussed in previous chapters.

The evolutionary synthesis and the discovery of the double-helical structure of DNA, both triumphs of twentieth-century biology, lend themselves to a slightly different analysis. They both involve the resolution of debates and the formation of consensus against certain hypotheses or explanatory strategies and in favor of others. If understood from a perspective of monism or unificationism, however, they invite epistemological finger-shaking. A pluralist approach enables both a more generous and a more adequate reading of both cases.

[27] Latour 1987.

The Evolutionary Synthesis

The years 1920 and 1947 are generally regarded as marking the opening and finale of the process of integrating Darwinian evolutionary theory and Mendelian genetics into a new "synthetic" theory of evolution. At the opening, a number of obstacles stood in the way of understanding the relation between genetic processes and evolutionary ones. These included intellectual obstacles such as the very different criteria for determining species characteristics (relevant to identification and differentiation) employed by taxonomists and speciation researchers and the methodological disagreements between experimentalists and naturalists as well as institutional obstacles such as the absence of venues for interaction among researchers of different specialties. Historically minded biologists have offered different views of what the synthesis, or resolution of those difficulties, amounted to, encouraging a new generation of historians of science to revisit the period. These historians emphasize a number of points, which cohere with a social and pluralist approach to the episode.

John Beatty takes note of Stephen J. Gould's protests against what Gould terms "the hardening of the synthesis."[28] Gould, a champion of punctuated equilibrium in the account of speciation, means by "hardening" that the biological community shifted from accepting a variety of mechanisms of evolutionary change to treating natural selection as the sole or primary mechanism, a view often referred to as "panselectionism." Panselectionists and proponents of random drift disagreed about the evidential bearing of some central cases of speciation. Cases first analyzed as instances of random drift were later analyzed as instances of selection. Panselectionists treated these reversals as grounds for rejecting nonselectionist mechanisms. Proponents of random drift resisted the generalization from the small number of investigated cases (relative to the very large number of cases yet to be studied). Beatty takes a prescriptive turn, using the debate to ground distinctions between the pursuit and acceptance of a hypothesis and between individual and community judgments. Whereas individuals were certainly within their rights to accept panselectionism in light of the evidential situation, the community was not. It was still reasonable for individual researchers to pursue random drift (and other hypotheses) with respect to particular cases of speciation, and therefore the community as a whole should have remained open to the pursuit by some of its members of nonselectionist hypotheses. The resulting research would either strengthen the case for pan-

---

[28] Beatty 1985.

selectionism or provide reasons for continuing to entertain nonselection-ist mechanisms of evolution. The community, he says, should have remained pluralist.

C. K. Waters draws attention to Julian Huxley's rather eclectic under-standing of the mechanisms of evolution.[29] Huxley's book, *Evolution: The Modern Synthesis*, one of the core texts of the synthesis, abounds with section and chapter headings such as "The Multiformity of Evolution," "The Heterogeneity of Evolution," "The Factors of Evolution," and "Different Types of Speciation."[30] Under these headings, such topics as gradual versus discontinuous variation, saltational evolution, the role of natural selection versus other mechanisms of speciation, and the varied types of selection are discussed and attachment to one or the other of them attributed to whether the researcher in question is from paleontol-ogy, systematics, physiology, genetics, or some other discipline. Huxley attributes difference in theory to difference in approach. It also seems to be Huxley's view that the many kinds of selection can be antagonistic in their effects, that they may operate at the same time in the same organ-ism or population, but may not operate or interact in the same way in all instances.[31] In Huxley's view what seems to have been important about the synthesis was the elimination of Lamarckian and orthogenetic approaches to evolution. He was quite happy to admit multiple mecha-nisms and interacting causal systems as long as they did not involve such seemingly nonphysicalist principles as are at play in Lamarckism and orthogenesis.

William Provine has argued that this means that Huxley failed to pro-duce the synthesis he had claimed to produce.[32] Waters, drawing on Frederick Churchill's discussion of Huxley's work in embryology, sug-gests instead that the achievement of the synthesis for Huxley lies in the new found ability to pool *results*—the geneticists' laboratory findings and the naturalists' observations of species in the wild—from disparate fields without having to integrate the theories from those fields. The pooled results could be encompassed within a very general framework for under-standing selection that could accommodate a variety (a plurality) of theo-ries and mechanisms.

Different meanings of "synthesis" are at issue here. According to Joe Cain, this kind of ambiguity is what enabled the original group of syn-thesizers to work together.[33] Cain's interest is in the institutional develop-ments that facilitated and cemented the intellectual developments known

[29] Waters 1992.
[30] Huxley 1942.
[31] Ibid., 125.
[32] Provine 1992.
[33] Cain 1993, 1995.

as the evolutionary synthesis. Evolutionists from different fields, including genetics, systematics, paleontology, and ecology, succeeded in redefining what the problems of evolutionary thinking were and in creating an infrastructure—professional associations, journals, definitive texts—for addressing these problems. These institutional innovations provided an interdisciplinary context where specialists from distinct subfields could address one another and collaborate on solutions to evolutionary questions. However, Cain argues, there was no consensus regarding *what* the theory of evolution now consisted in, or regarding what the synthesis of genetics and Darwinian theory consisted in. Nor was there agreement regarding how to assess which were the most important contributions to the synthetic theory. Cain's view as historian echoes to some extent Huxley's as participant: participants' interpretation of these points depended on their subdisciplinary location.

Cain illustrates this point by describing different readings of George Gaylord Simpson's very well received *Tempo and Mode in Evolution* (1944), a book widely seen as reconciling paleontology and genetics. The character of this reconciliation was not understood in a uniform manner. Geneticists read it as affirming that (the new) paleontology was the deductive extension of principles of genetics to the fossil record, and that the importance, therefore, of independent paleontological findings was the confirmation they provided to genetics. Others read it as affirming paleontological principles and findings in a fashion that demonstrated the consistency of paleontology with genetics. Still others (paleontologists) read it as affirming distinctively paleontological contributions to the basic understanding of evolution, especially having to do with evolutionary rates, but concerning other aspects as well. These readings—deductive extension, consistency, independent but complementary principles—illustrate both the different conceptions of what "synthesis" might mean and of what the synthetic theory of evolution might consist in.

Cain suggests that a productive equivocation about "synthesis" enabled researchers from different fields to reorganize evolution studies around a set of common problems that treated mechanisms of divergence and isolation in populations as central processes of speciation and evolution without having to come to consensus regarding their explanation. They could be (like Huxley) unified against Lamarckism or other views like "aristogenesis," while still emphasizing different processes compatible with the overall view. Each of the fields could take something from the others while retaining centrality for its distinctive principles. Laboratory researchers could use some of the findings and strategies of the naturalists and vice-versa. This mutual dependence was both exploited and supported by the creation of a common infrastructure, including the Society for the Study of Evolution and the journal *Evolution*. The result is, in

Cain's view, better understood as coalition rather than as integration or unification. Evolution research was federalized rather than centralized.

This explanatory plurality continues today—both regarding the issues that divided the early synthesizers and regarding additional difference made possible by the new knowledge produced within the synthesis framework. I have already mentioned Waters's claims about the levels and forces of selection. Another example of plurality best understood within a pluralist spirit is developed in Carla Fehr's work on the evolution of sex.[34] Fehr argues that there are multiple explanations for the evolution of sex, depending on how one construes the phenomenonal domain. She demonstrates that two of these, the "Red Queen" explanation and the DNA Repair explanation, apply to the evolution of sex. These are irreconcilable explanations, but because the evolution of sex can be seen to be part of different, but overlapping, phenomenonal domains, they are each equally explanations of the evolution of sex.

The Double Helix and the Central Dogma

Consider now the other great achievement of twentieth-century biology, the identification of the double-helical structure of DNA. James Watson and Francis Crick were not working in a vacuum—neither an intellectual nor a social vacuum. The analysis of the double-helix was at its heart a collaborative effort. While no ethnographer was around the Cavendish Laboratory to record them, both Watson and Crick have themselves attested to the importance of their interactions with each other. Furthermore, DNA was by the early 1950s believed to be the medium of hereditary information, the constituent of chromosomes, although its structure and mechanism were a mystery. Many scientists were trying to unravel this mystery and Watson knew that solving it would open a new era in biological research and also bring instant fame to the researcher responsible. Robert Olby shows how the subdisciplinary approaches addressed from 1900 on to the problems of the structure and mechanism of the medium of transmission of genetic information focused and limited the perspectives of individual researchers and research communities.[35] This enabled them to solve parts of the puzzle, but no single approach had the tools to solve all of it.

Watson has described the competitive context in which he felt himself to be working.[36] Even though the competitive aspect may have been largely self-created, the variety of proposals regarding the structure that

[34] Fehr 2000, 2001.
[35] Olby 1974. See also Judson 1979.
[36] Watson 1968.

were being floated in the late 1940s and early 1950s constituted part of the intellectual context within which he and Crick conducted their exchanges. In addition, they were dependent on a half century of cytology, genetics, and biochemistry, then on the conceptual transformation resulting from the migration of physicists into biology, and, of course, crucially dependent on the crystallographic images produced by Rosalind Franklin. Thus, the work of producing a structural description of the DNA molecule was social, both collaborative and competitive. Thus far, the story is compatible with Kitcher's understanding of the sociality of scientific inquiry. The work of producing the structural description, however, would have gone unnoticed had the larger community of biologists and biochemists not been ready for it, were DNA not already thought to be the molecule carrying genetic information, were the puzzle of replication of genetic information not uppermost on biologists' minds. The salience of these functional problems led first to the immediate and almost unanimous acceptance of the double-helical structure. Acceptance of the structural description and refocusing research on the functional problems that that description now made solvable changed the face of biology. In particular, it accelerated the development of the new subfield of molecular biology, which not only attained identity as its own discipline, but which has, by now, permeated all other biological subfields. This refocusing was guided by what Francis Crick dubbed the Central Dogma: DNA makes RNA, RNA makes protein (and proteins make the rest).

The dogmatic part of the Central Dogma concerned the route of causation and of transfer of information, which, according to the Dogma, extended in one direction from DNA through proteins. DNA is the source of information to the rest of the organism, while remaining itself unaffected by changes in its cellular and organismic environment. This conception of DNA seems consistent with the by-then entrenched notion of gametic, or germ plasm, independence of somatic change, but the Central Dogma extended to DNA in somatic cells as well as in gametic cells. As Francis Crick expressed it, "once 'information' has passed into protein it *cannot get out again.* In more detail, the transfer of information from nucleic acid to nucleic acid, or from nucleic acid to protein may be possible, but transfer from protein to protein, or from protein to nucleic acid is impossible."[37]

Compelling and fruitful as the Central Dogma was during the period following 1953, it was not uniformly accepted. Researchers as different from each other as Barry Commoner and Barbara McClintock resisted both the idea that the chromosomal material was causally insulated from

[37] Quoted in Olby 1974, 432. The dogma was also given vivid expression in Monod 1971.

the rest of the organism and the idea that it was a stable and unchanging origin of biological processes. McClintock had argued from the mid-1930s that this material, now known as DNA and RNA, was rearranged in response to signals from the cellular environment, which itself responded to changes in the organic and extraorganic environment. Embryologists and later developmental biologists also resisted the DNA bandwagon. The story of the marginalization and later vindication of these researchers has been told by historians such as Jan Sapp[38] and Evelyn Fox Keller.[39] The point I wish to stress is that while the plurality of approaches to the problems of the structure and function of the medium of biological inheritance was reduced by announcement of the double helix, plurality was not thereby eliminated. Instead the base line of difference changed, and the differences in approach assumed different aspects centering around functional questions. Thus, where the subdisciplines in play pre-1953 were biophysical and experimental ones such as structural chemistry, colloidal biophysics, experimental cytology, and cytochemistry, as well as genetics and macromolecular chemistry, once the structural solution was accepted, the loci of dispute shifted to genetics, cytology, molecular biology, and developmental biology. Researchers have been divided most visibly regarding the self-sufficiency of DNA. More recently, philosophers of science looking carefully at contemporary biology have shown how multiple understandings of the concept of "gene" are operative in different contexts of research.[40]

I have given both of these cases a pluralist reading. Latour's image of the Janus face holds with respect to a single salient aspect of dispute and its resolution, but only if that aspect is detached from the full context in which it is embedded. Before 1953 a gene could be a segment of a single helix, a triple helix, the alpha helix of Pauling, a double helix with the bases on the outside, a double helix with the bases on the inside. After 1953 the gene is a segment of a double-helical macromolecule, with the bases on the inside and phosphate groups on the outside. The structure beautifully answers how DNA, and hence a gene, could duplicate itself, or at least answers part of the "how." Questions about how precisely genes contribute to phenotype can now be focused on this molecule so understood. But, despite there being some reasons to adopt the Central

[38] Sapp 1987.

[39] Keller 1983, 2000.

[40] Recent work suggests that there are multiple concepts of "gene" produced by the interaction of functional and structural aspects of the understanding of genes or that the concept of "gene" underspecifies what precisely will count as a gene. Plurality persists even at the molecular level. See Magnus 2000b, Waters 2000, and essays in Beurton, Falk, and Rheinberger 2000.

Dogma, these issues are by no means settled by what was demonstrable in the 1950s. The structure was black-boxed but not the processes.[41] Explaining what enabled the Dogma to prevail involves a complex of both technical and social-institutional issues.[42] The provisional settlement among a certain group of researchers initiated an extremely productive period of research, although it eventually fell victim to the complexities of biological processes. Even though the Central Dogma is no longer as hegemonic as it once was, researchers still differ in their understanding of gene function in intra- and extracellular processes depending largely on the approach of their subdisciplines. And they also differ in their understanding of gene structure, but the old differences have been replaced by new ones.

The history of the synthesis offers a similar story. One set of contesting views is replaced by another set when consensus is reached regarding what the evolutionary problems are and regarding which approaches to rule out. In both of these episodes the transformation goes through a period of relative constriction—the heyday of the Central Dogma and that of panselectionism—only to open out again to admit multiple emphases and multiple approaches. Rather than full closure, the picture both present is instead one of partial closure or stabilization propelling cycles of constriction and expansion. In both cases, too, foundations with energetic leaders—Warren Weaver at the Rockefeller and John Merriam at the Carnegie—directed funding support in ways that advanced the emergence of the new disciplinary or cross-disciplinary constellations. And in both cases, researchers were reacting (although in different ways) to the preeminence of physics in the postwar period and seeking comparable status for biology.[43] Thus a full understanding of the intellectual trajectories of both of these transitions requires sensitivity to the interaction of technical and institutional and affective issues involved. I hope I have said enough to show that social and pluralist approaches offer a

---

[41] Hacking's (1992b) account of stabilization in laboratory sciences also seems apt for this story. The structure was stabilized, but views of how it worked depended on from what perspective its working was examined.

[42] For example, the promotion first of the concept, and later of the field, of molecular biology by the Rockefeller Foundation and the director of its Natural Sciences Division, Warren Weaver, is widely regarded as having played a role in encouraging research organized thematically around the Central Dogma. And Keller (1992) has argued that an unconsciously drawn pair of parallels between nucleus and sperm and cytoplasm and egg, as well as the language of secrets, gave the Dogma an affective import that strengthened its hold on researchers.

[43] Smocovitis (1992) has argued a different line: that synthesis efforts were strongly motivated by the unity of science ideal promoted by the Vienna Circle and its intellectual allies. This thesis has recently been the subject of a heated exchange. See Cain 2000 and Smocovitis 2000.

fruitful perspective on both of these founding episodes in twentieth-century biology.

MODES OF PLURALITY

A monist or unificationist philosophy requires that all these examples of difference or dissension be ultimately resolved in favor of one account, or that models (or the domains to which they are to be applied) be restricted in their scope to eliminate conflict. How does the analysis of scientific knowledge and inquiry recommend we treat these examples? The ecology, speciation, and electron microscopy cases involve methodologies and assumptions regarding them. The social insects cases and the selection case, by contrast, involve substantive assumptions about the domain. The developmental biology case involves assumptions both methodological and substantive, as does the brain and behavior case. Some of these cases are characterized by debate, others by peaceful coexistence.

In the ecological case, one can understand the different experimental approaches as driven by different kinds of question—how elements in a natural system together respond to a particular kind of change or what effects a given change can produce on a restricted set of elements within a system. These different questions impose different evaluative standards on investigative strategies. In the first case, one wants to understand what changes can be expected by changing one parameter in a complex system. This does not require establishing how any particular element in the system responds to that change, but how the system as a whole changes. In the second, one may be establishing that a given element or substance can have a particular kind and quantity of effect on a specific element, process, or interaction. Such an effect can disappear in a complex system, either by being canceled by a subsequent process or by being swamped by other effects. It can also be magnified by subsequent processes and interactions. The ecosystem experiment and the model system experiment are designed to answer different kinds of question. That they assign different effects or different magnitudes of effect to the same substance is not a matter requiring resolution, but one requiring tolerance of ambiguity and uncertainty. Debate should be understood as an ongoing process of critical interaction that both prevents closure where it is inappropriate and helps to establish the limits of (relative) certainty. Further study of the contexts of inquiry is required to understand how proponents of these different experimental strategies would relate them to goals of research, the discipline of ecology, the current social and political concerns about the environment, and the multiple institutions within or under the sponsorship of which their research is conducted.

Unlike the ecology example, the dispute about the mitochondria images was resolved. Perhaps contrary to intuitive expectation, the New York group advocating the free channel succeeded in having its micrographs accepted as the standard, even though they were by micrographic standards inferior. Their image was fuzzy, but the discernible image cohered with data from biochemistry. This example is interesting because it demonstrates the displacement of a conventional value—greater detail, and hence, presumably, accuracy—by another, transmissibility and standardization of results across different disciplines. Here one might ask under what circumstances these different values take precedence and what the circumstances were in this case which resulted in assigning priority to standardization. Rather than assume that one party was right and one wrong, the historian or philosopher may be better served by instead studying the operation of the different epistemologies that underlay the conflicting positions about the proper representation of mitochondria. Because standardization means the stabilization of a representation and a consequent broadening of our ability to act on the object represented, pressures for action on environmental problems may produce similar dynamics in the ecological context. Rasmussen shows that resolution of conflict does not necessarily mean that a representation has been determined to be the closer to nature, but that it has been determined to be the more usable. Utility is a paradigmatically provisional and context-relative quality.

As a practicing biologist, Bolker is concerned to offer recommendations of practices that counter what she perceives to be the negative consequences of overreliance on model organisms. Her recommendations reflect a pluralist point of view. Bolker is not rejecting the model systems approach, but endorsing a plurality of approaches and their interaction. Specifically, she advocates more support and attention to developmental research in nonmodel systems; interaction between developmentalists working on model systems and comparative morphologists and developmentalists working on nonmodel systems; and acknowledgment of the limitations of the model-systems approach. These are also recommendations that would flow from application of the norms of community interaction outlined in chapter 6. Venues for and uptake of criticism from alternative perspectives and tempered equality of intellectual authority translate into support for and attention to developmental research in nonmodel systems and interaction between research communities pursuing different research agendas. Acknowledging the limitations of any single approach is an acknowledgment of the partiality of any given framework and of the consequent necessity of multiple approaches to the same phenomenon.

In her discussion of the social insect case study, Mitchell argues that nature's diversity and complexity mean that there are multiple accounts of the division of labor in social insect colonies. She does think, however that integration is ultimately possible: each causal story is a model that applies to a particular species or subspecies. For each species there is a model that uniquely fits. Her view seems to be that nature is complex in the sense of having multiple routes to the same end, but that for any causal process there is one correct account. Even though there is not one account of the division of labor applicable to all insect colonies, there is an integrated, comprehensive account of insect behavior in which nest architecture and genetic structure can be treated as distinct paths to a common end, each of which has a single correct account. This case supports a weak pluralism. It is weak in holding that for any causal process there is a uniquely correct causal story. On the other hand it is pluralist in holding that there is not a single causal process, and hence that the expression of a given form of insect behavior in different insect species cannot be explained by reference to a single causal principle.

Waters, by contrast, argues that the very same phenomenon can be approached in different ways that yield different representations and explanations, different tracings of causal pathways. His current view is that the complexity of nature is such that no single causal account can capture all of the forces acting on and in a single biological system.[44] In the selection case, this is a function of choosing one initial representation of the domain over others. This initial representation ("parsing") constrains what will be isolated as a causal factor. From the point of view of which of the accounts of selection most correctly represents nature, the choice is arbitrary. From the point of view of the further questions a research team may have, the choice may not be arbitrary. But there is no one correct way to represent the situation. Philosophers of biology in the grip of monism have joined evolutionary biologists in developing arguments supporting the unique role of one or the other level. Waters instead uses this example as a key element in his case for pluralism.[45]

In the case of multiple approaches in neurobiology, each must be understood in terms of the kind of knowledge sought and the adequacy of methods used to answer the questions characterizing the different approaches. The domain can be configured differently depending on the questions one is asking. What effect does exposure of the fetal organism to estrogens or androgens have on behavior b, or on capacity c? What effects do prenatal estrogens or androgens have on brain development? How does neuronal connectivity develop? Different instruments, experi-

[44] Waters, in conversation.
[45] The Fehr, Mitchell, and Waters discussions together raise intriguing philosophical questions about the identification and individuation of causal processes.

mental setups, and theoretical assumptions are available depending on which question one is asking. As a consequence, approaches driven by questions about the effects of specific substances produce different accounts of brain development and function than accounts driven by questions about neuronal connectivity. Like the debate about units and levels of selection, this is a debate whose import changes as it moves from the laboratory context to the social context. Different approaches to studying brain physiology and development are transformed into competing theories about the nature of human behavior.[46] Thus, the need for resolution may not be a function of the local epistemologies employed by the researchers, but of the epistemologies employed by the users and consumers of the research, both in other disciplines, like psychology or the social sciences, and in the general public.

CONCLUSION

These examples indicate that plurality of accounts or representations can arise in multiple ways: the variety of causal pathways to a similar end; focus and emphasis on one aspect of a complex causal process, whether as a function of explicit interest (what is the hormonal contribution to x?) or as a consequence of initial parsings of the domain under investigation; use of observational methodologies or experimental systems that of necessity show only that aspect of a process that they are designed to show or use of evaluation criteria that in a given context are satisfied by inconsistent representations. Finding a uniquely correct account would require identifying the uniquely correct starting point in each of these reservoirs of plurality. But this cannot be an epistemological project without arbitrarily closing off avenues of investigation, thus violating the canons of procedure articulated in chapter 6.

The philosopher interested in understanding the structures of reasoning and justification in the sciences must examine individual cases and their contextual features, which both fill out those structures and have the effect of localizing the epistemological judgments. For example, in a context, like industrial manufacture, in which the interest is in understanding the properties and processes of a system so as to construct a replica that functions in the same way, or has the same products (e.g., a cell system for producing human insulin), it may not be necessary to understand the unrepresentativeness of bacterial DNA. In a context, like riparian restoration or conservation, in which the interest is in under-

---

[46] Of course, the same individuals can be involved in these varying venues of discussion and controversy.

standing the properties and processes of a system so as to interact with it in its "natural" state, acknowledging the partiality based on one or a few models and consequent need for multiple approaches may be crucial to success. The monism or pluralism expressed in scientific judgments may be a function of the overall aims of research rather than a brute metaphysical commitment.

The pluralist philosopher must also say, I think, that it makes no sense to detach measurements and data descriptions from the contexts in which they are generated, or that, as soon as one does, one creates a new context relative to which they are to be assessed and understood. While contradictions within an approach require resolution, on the view I have set out here, there's no a priori requirement that either different approaches to studying the same general area yield compatible observation statements or measurements or only one of those different approaches can be correct. This account denies, that is, that there could be a single, comprehensive, and neutral observation language within which all observation can be registered. This would indeed require that contradictions in the language be eliminated, but observation reports cannot be detached from their theoretical contexts in that way.[47] On the other hand, they need not be symptoms of deep incommensurability. They may instead be signs that different approaches are producing different bodies of knowledge of the same complex system, each of which conforms to that system differently, as both Mercator and Peterson projections produce two-dimensional maps that conform, but differently, to the topography of the spherical planet Earth. It is, of course, possible that the contradiction will be eliminated by future developments, but a principled avoidance of metaphysical pluralism or monism must eschew requiring the disappearance or persistence of incompatibilities.

The only general requirements applicable across approaches would, instead, be hypothetical norms emerging from the contextualist analysis of evidence and evidential relations, such as "if you wish a claim to be rationally justified, then the claim and/or the approach within which it is advanced must be able to meet criticism." Incongruent, incompatible contents can pass such tests, but they must be appraised in the context of the local epistemologies by reference to which they are appraised. Not every way of assembling the elements of such local epistemologies will be successful. The test, however, is not conformity to some higher-level set of rules or principles but the ability of an epistemology to help a community achieve the understanding it seeks. If there is no complete view, then communities (and members of communities) must be freed up to pursue

---

[47] I am not denying the meaningfulness of the distinction between observational and nonobservational. The distinction is, however, as I (1990) suggested, context-relative.

their own cognitive-social interests in investigative approaches. If any community (whether local or the agglomeration of local communities) is to achieve the best understanding possible for it, then, at least until the end of science has been attained, pluralism, not monism, is required. The challenge posed by the plurality of contemporary science is not so much a metaphysical one but an educational one. How can the value of scientific research as a source of guidance for policy decisions be maintained in the face of the complexity of nature and the partiality and plurality of our knowledge of it? While I do not have an answer to the practical dimensions of this question, I believe that the social approach to knowledge provides some of the means to providing it.

CHAPTER NINE

Conclusion

IN THIS exploratory defense of the philosophical claim that knowledge, especially scientific knowledge, is social, I have drawn on the work of researchers in social and cultural studies of science and of researchers in philosophy of science and theory of knowledge. Both the sociological and philosophical researchers share an unspoken premise that structures their disagreements with each other—that cognitive rationality and sociality are mutually exclusive, or dichotomous. Put so baldly, it seems wrong: social practices can be cognitive practices and, conversely, rational, cognitive practices can also be social practices. Each party works with a caricature of the other's preferred explanatory factors. The sociological investigators, both the Strong Programme macrosociologists and the laboratory studies microsociologists, identify roles for social interests and social processes in the final content and in the minutiae of scientific research. They see these as incompatible with what they take to be a cognitive approach to understanding science because they take cognitive rationality to be rule-governed, algorithmic, calculation, insulated from psychological and social factors. The philosophical investigators, on the other hand, try to accommodate what they take to be the correct insights of the sociologists, while saving the rationality of science. The implication of their analyses is that scientists can sometimes be biased and that the accomplishments of any individual scientist are dependent on those of forerunners and colleagues. Nevertheless, defending the rationality of science involves, for them, showing that scientific activity can be conceptually sheared off from the social and historical context of particular scientific achievements. This is because they take social processes to be determined by social interests and power, and hence irrational.

The mutual caricatures—scientific inquiry is fully rule-governed calculation, or scientific inquiry is determined by social interests and power—are sustained by the rational-social dichotomy. This dichotomy is in turn sustained by a set of binaries that generate sharply contrasting conceptions of the content of knowledge, of the practices producing or warranting knowledge, and of the subject/agent of knowledge. I claim that these are three modalities of knowledge, each of which is differently understood by empirical researchers, on the one hand, and normative researchers, on the other. These differences make for dialectical gridlock.

I propose to break the gridlock by disassembling the dichotomy that generates them. The illusion that there are just two positions regarding scientific knowledge (rational and not social; social and not rational) is a product of a particular alignment of the dichotomized understandings of warrant, agency, and content. Realigning these makes evident multiple understandings of these dimensions. From these new possibilities a new set of interpretations involving interdependence of cognitive agency, plurality of content, and contextuality of productive practices or justification constitutes a positive alternative to the mutually exclusive understandings.

These interpretations permit drawing the normative distinctions important to philosophers within the empirical domain of human practices of inquiry rather than outside of it. They also require some rethinking of the elements that will go into the definitions that express those distinctions. In chapter 5, I argued that the three modalities of knowledge—knowledge-productive practices, knowing, and knowledge content—involve aspects invoked by the normative philosopher as well as aspects invoked by the empirical sociologist. Both conceptual analysis and empirical data from laboratory observation support the claim that the basic families of cognitive practice discussed by philosophers—observational-experimental practices and reasoning practices—have a social dimension. They get their warranting force in part from those social dimensions, which feature introduces contextual specificity to justification. Similarly, the relation of knowing gets a social twist. "S knows . . ." attributes a status to S on the basis of S's actual engagement in or presumed capacity to engage in certain discursive interactions. Cognitive agents are interdependent, and their knowing is a social status, not a kind of psychological state.

Finally, because scientific content is not adequately evaluated by use of simple true-false assessments, I propose a broader way of thinking about the relation of the content of knowledge to its object. Conformation is a semantic metacategory comprising iso- and homomorphism, similarity, and approximation, as well as truth. This introduces gradation into the evaluation of content, which can conform to its object in varying degrees and in different respects. These in turn involve a pluralist understanding of content because different representations can conform to the same object, by being more or less similar but still similar, or by picking out different features of the object to which they conform. The "getting it right or wrong" aspect of true-false evaluation is preserved. But what counts as enough and as the relevant respects is a function of the goals of inquiry, which are socially determined.

Chapter 5 stresses discursive interaction, especially criticism and the survival of criticism, as a key aspect of cognitive practices. This locates justification, or the production of knowledge, not just in the testing of hypotheses against data, but also in subjecting hypotheses, data, reasoning, and background assumptions to criticism from a variety of perspectives. Establishing what the data are, what the descriptive categories and their boundaries are, what counts as acceptable reasoning, which assumptions are legitimate and which not becomes a matter of social interactions as much as a matter of interaction with the material world. Because the assumptions that constitute the intellectual context of observation and reasoning are, by their nature, usually not explicit but tacit patterns of thought, the function of critical interaction is to make them visible as well as to examine their metaphysical, empirical, and normative implications. These discursive interactions are both constructive and justificatory. They can propel a group (whether lab group or subdisciplinary community) to the articulation of new accounts of a process it is trying to understand, and they are the processes by which a community persuades itself that an account is plausible, correct, worth adopting. Sociality does not come into play at the limit of or instead of the cognitive. Instead, these social processes *are* cognitive.

The social epistemological perspective adopted here stresses that cognition has social, as well as sensory and calculative, elements. The social dimensions are resources just as the more traditionally endorsed aspects of knowledge (sense perception and individual reason) are resources. Like these the social is vulnerable to problems such as innapropriate exercise of authority and shared biases invisible as such to a community otherwise critical. Such problems can, in particular instances, undermine the capacity of social cognitive processes to issue in knowledge. Thus, merely saying that there is a social dimension to cognitive processes is insufficient to show that *knowledge* is social. The social epistemologist must also show how the social dimensions of cognition have resources for the correction of those epistemically undermining possibilities. It is those resources that warrant the attribution of knowledge to cognitive practices, to cognitive agents, and to cognitive content.

I approach the task of identifying the resources for self-correction by drawing a parallel between an empirical and a logical aspect of scientific inquiry. Sociologists have stressed the contingency of inquiry, its openness to multiple outcomes of inquiry. This openness has a logical basis in the underdetermination of theory by evidence. This feature of evidential relations, a consequence of the gap between explanatory aspirations and evidential resources, stands in the way of any completely formal account of theory confirmation or acceptability. The empirical question is how belief, commitment, or theory and hypothesis acceptance are stabilized in the face of the openness of inquiry. The normative question is how they are stabilized in a nonarbitrary way that has probative value. The sociologists seize upon the contingency of inquiry as a basis for claiming that scientific judgment is in the end determined by, from a rational point of view, noncognitive social factors: interests, power, alliances. Philosophers, by contrast, either try to eliminate the gap of underdetermination or appeal to epistemic values as providing an impartial basis for identifying the epistemically superior from among a set of competing theories. Such efforts have been shown to be unsuccessful. The outcome of the resulting standoff is that any given scientific judgment is both overdetermined and underdetermined. If interests, power, and alliances are indifferent to evidential considerations, they (causally) overdetermine scientific judgment. And if strategies to eliminate underdetermination fail, evidential resources still (logically) underdetermine scientific judgment. The interaction of social and cognitive factors, both more richly understood than in the sociologists' and philosophers' accounts, makes possible more satisfactory explanations of particular scientific judgments. It also makes possible more complex assessments of scientific judgments.

From the vantage point of the social approach, underdetermination shows that judgments regarding evidential support for hypotheses are made against a background of substantive, methodological, and regulative assumptions. Such judgments are, thus, embedded in their intellectual contexts. The epistemological problem is not determining which of a set of alternatives is always the superior one, but rather specifying the conditions under which it is appropriate to rely on a given set of assumptions. The approach utilizes the social character of inquiry to address this problem. Those assumptions are epistemically acceptable which have survived critical scrutiny in a discursive context characterized by at least four conditions. These conditions are (1) the availability of venues for and (2) responsiveness to criticism, (3) public standards (themselves subject to critical interrogation), and (4) tempered equality of intellectual authority.

The social approach sees sociality (of critical discourse) as parallel with other human cognitive resources (of sense perception and reasoning) and the conditions as spelling out when it is appropriate to rely on the outcome of critical interactions. They are comparable, then, to conditions for relying on sense perception, such as, for example, possessing adequately functioning sense organs or being in the right conditions for the particular sensory modality: good light for vision, lack of acoustic interference for hearing, and the like. Equipped with the notions of epistemic acceptability and conformation, it becomes possible to provide definitions of "knowledge" in the three senses distinguished earlier. These definitions transfer, as promised, the normative distinctions investigated by the philosopher to the empirical situations investigated by the sociologist. Thus they constitute the basis for an epistemology for human subjects—cognitive agents characterized by sensory modalities attuned to their particular ranges of stimuli, reasoning capacities, and communicative abilities.

What are the consequences for *knowledge* on this account? Knowledge is partial. The contextual embeddness of inquiry and the locatedness of subjects impose limits on what is knowable from any given location or point of view. No set of knowledge-productive practices will exhaust the ways of acquiring knowledge about a phenomenon or process. Some practices will coevolve with increasing knowledge of a phenomenon, becoming more and more specific to their domain. Karin Knorr-Cetina's examples of very different practices characterizing high-energy physics and molecular biology illustrate this coevolution.[1] Any given knower will have knowledge limited by social, historical, and geographical location and point of view, and shaped by a particular set of knowledge productive practices.

Knowledge is plural. There may be multiple sets of practices, each capable of producing knowledge of the same processes or phenomenon. Different knowers differently situated and motivated by different cognitive goals may have different and nonreconcilable knowledge of the same phenomenon. There may be multiple epistemically acceptable correct (i.e., conforming) representations of a given phenomenon or process. Which among these counts as knowledge on which to act depends on the cognitive goals and particular cognitive resources of a given context.

Finally, knowledge is provisional. Sets of practices that produce knowledge in one context may be superseded by others as cognitive goals change or as more is learned about a phenomenon. Knowledge is attributed to cognitive agents relative to standards and criteria that are specific to contexts and that may change. And the content that constitutes the corpus of knowledge at any given time may be replaced by other content as goals and practices change and as the corpus itself grows, producing tensions with other parts or enabling new practices and the envisioning of new goals. Scientific activity itself changes the world we seek to know. Acting on our knowledge produces or makes salient objects and processes that outstrip the knowledge that made them possible.

Although plurality and provisionality characterize knowledge, at any given time, place, or context, there must be agreement about some matters—some observational, some regulative, perhaps some theoretical—in order that inquiry, including critical interaction, can proceed. The implication of provisionality is that these need not remain the same over time or across contexts. Undoubtedly, there is some constancy from one historically or geographically separated context to another, but it does not

---

[1] Knorr-Cetina 1999.

follow that what remains constant is the same for all contexts. And content that persists through changes may shift in centrality and function from one corpus to another. The examples of plurality in twentieth-century biology demonstrate the variety of generators of plurality—cognitive goals, methods of inquiry, substantive assumptions—and the mix of common and distinct elements that characterizes the relations between multiple approaches to the same phenomenon. Thus, the case for the social epistemological view advanced here rests on its integration of empirical sociological findings with normative conceptual analysis and on its ability to take theoretical plurality in stride.

I previously dubbed the kind of position I have defended in this book as "contextual empiricism." This is not quite right. A more accurate, if more cumbersome, label might be "critical contextual empiricism," which captures the social dimension I emphasize. This label expresses the central epistemological features of the view, but one of the consequences of the approach is to make salient the connections between cognitive practices and other human activity. This aspect is better captured by the locution "sociopragmatism." This makes the social dimension explicit and affirms the affinity of the overall orientation adopted here with views associated with American pragmatism. Knowledge is understood actively and dynamically. Knowledge is sought, not imprinted, and it is sought in order to achieve particular goals and is evaluated in relation to those goals. Knowledge produces the conditions of its own transformation. The growth of knowledge is not linear, but irregular, layered, and patchy.

LIMITATIONS OF THE ACCOUNT

Knowledge or Scientific Knowledge?

I have argued that knowledge is social. This argument has proceeded by taking scientific knowledge as the core model or notion of knowledge. Thus, implicitly, the knowledge that is claimed to be social is empirical knowledge. Two kinds of reservation about this strategy might be expressed. One has to do with the extension of claims about scientific knowledge to empirical knowledge in general. The other has to do with what might be thought of as paradigm cases of *non*social knowledge: first-person knowledge and a priori knowledge.

Does claiming that knowledge is social have the consequence of denying the status of knowledge to ordinary knowledge claims, such as that there is a cup of tea on the desk in front of me? These straightforward empirical judgments are surely paradigm cases of knowledge that do not need the cumbersome critical apparatus required for more arcane forms of scientific knowledge. I agree with the presupposition of this question: scientific inquiry is a distinctive human endeavor that consists in more intellectually demanding and creative activity than passively observing and recording resemblances. Nevertheless, what makes its outcome knowledge is not unique to science, but a feature of empirical knowledge generally.[2] In the more familiar situations of everyday empirical judgment we simply take for granted the assumptions (e.g., about the conditions in which our sensory organs are reliable) on which even the simplest of those judgments rest.[3] We presuppose a large body of critically screened background knowledge acquired as part of intellectual maturation, in our ordinary cognitive practice. And what warrants the attribution of knowledge (that a teacup is or is not on the desk) to me is my ability to respond to contextually appropriate criticism. "How do you know?" "I see a cuplike object." "Why *tea*cup?" "There's a tab hanging over the side." And so on. I can say or fail to say many things depending on the questions asked. My answers are used to determine whether it is appropriate to attribute knowledge to me. This response to the challenge to my analysis draws on the treatment of knowledge as a status attributed to cognitive agents on the basis of their ability to respond adequately to contextually appropriate challenges. There may well be a context in which it is useful to treat direct perceptual knowledge differently than other empirical knowledge. This, however, represents a path that has in the past led philosophers to problematic conclusions. As a pluralist, I do not need to universalize my account, or to claim that it will serve in all contexts of analysis. But I do claim that perceptual knowledge can be accommodated in the social approach.

The second reservation has to do with first-person knowledge. What can this account say about my claim to know, not that there is a cup on my desk, but that I am seated at my desk, or that I am having a visual sensation of green against a background of various shades of grey? Surely this does not depend on my relations with any of my communities. Several observations seem appropriate here. First, my understanding and correct usage of the terms I use to express what I know does depend on my relations with my communities. Second, it seems as unpromising to

---

[2] Thus, the strategy employed here differs from some naturalizing approaches in philosophy of science. I do not assume that science is knowledge-producing and attribute knowledge-productive capacity to its practices or the status of knowledge to their outcomes *tout court*. Instead, I ask what about scientific inquiry warrants our attribution and withholding of the status of knowledge to it.

[3] Amanda Vizedom reports that attempts to develop an artificial intelligence system capable of making the ordinary judgments expected of humans in various conditions requires equipping the system with thousands of items of "common knowledge" and the means to access them, without which it cannot function (Vizedom 2000).

try to define first-person knowledge on the basis of scientific knowledge as it is to define scientific knowledge on the basis of first-person knowledge. But the approach to knowledge developed here is not limited to scientific knowledge. More to the point, how we understand the content of first-person knowledge depends on the analysis of indexicals like "I," "here," "there," "my," "now." Does the use of such indexicals indicate a privileged mode of access to content otherwise expressible in third-person terms, such as "HL is seated at a desk," or does it indicate a particular kind of content expressible only via first-person indexicals? Is my first-person awareness of my awareness a content that can be epistemically evaluated? This is not the place to pursue such questions.[4] I will only note that neither of the definitions of "S knows that p" developed within the social framework would rule out the first-person awareness of proprioception as knowledge. One variant treats being justified in accepting some content as S's acceptance being the outcome of knowledge-productve practices in S's community C. As long as proprioception has the property of producing epistemically acceptable content that conforms to its object for C, it is a knowledge-productive practice for C. Presumably, there will be kinds of situation that are recognized as deceptive—attachment to virtual reality machines, perhaps—and standard ways of ruling out such possibilities in particular cases. The other variant focuses on response to criticism. Here, again, the standards adopted in C would presumably take account of the possibilities for error and moderate the expectation that error be ruled out or accounted for according to the stringency required by the context. As long as corrigibility is a feature of the knowable, the social account applies. If there is a category of the incorrigible, then we might have to treat that as a different kind of knowledge. My claim is that the social account of knowledge holds for empirical knowledge, of which scientific knowledge and (much) first-person knowledge are subspecies. I have made no claims about a priori knowledge and am prepared to remain similarly uncommitted about incorrigible first-person knowledge, if there is such a thing.[5] Once again,

---

[4] See Anscombe 1981; Evans 1982; Perry 1989; and of course, Wittgenstein 1953.

[5] Although formally uncommitted, I am inclined to think that a priori knowledge can be given a sociopragmatic account as well. It would require arguing that a priori knowledge is either substantive or analytic. If substantive, the sociopragmatic account holds, and if analytic, it reduces to the principle of noncontradiction. And the best justification for that principle is the one offered by Aristotle (1941) in *Metaphysics*, book IV, chap. 4: "The starting point for all such arguments [that things may not be both so and not-so] is not the demand that our opponent shall say that something either is or is not, . . . but that he shall say something which is *significant* both for himself and for another; for this is necessary, if he really is to say anything. . . . And again he who admits this has admitted that something is true apart from demonstration (so that not everything will be 'so and not-so')." This strikes me as sociopragmatism par excellence.

as a pluralist, I am under no obligation to universalize my account. Identifying some form of knowledge that is not social, or that can be understood in certain contexts as not social, has no implications for the central arguments offered here.

Forms of Plurality

The constrained elasticity of conformation and epistemic acceptability means that more than one account of a phenomenon can be correct, even though those accounts, if detached from their contexts, are irreconcilable. I illustrated this claim in chapter 8 with multiple examples from twentieth-century life science in Europe and North America. These are instances of plurality generated within the same overall cultural and civilizational context: industrial and postindustrial societies characterized by values shaped by a Judeo-Christian religious heritage (however much secularized in bourgeois democracies) and a history of expansion and attempted domination of other parts of the world. Thus, even within a roughly similar cultural, social, and intellectual context, multiple explanatory strategies merit being classified as knowledge or knowledge-producing. In addition to examples of this kind, however, are instances of epistemological variation produced by deliberately oppositional subcommunities, such as feminist communities, in the West. And there are systems of thought, value, and practice that have given rise to yet more different understandings of the natural world. Civilizations other than the European have produced sophisticated astronomical and medical systems. The history of science in China is documented in Joseph Needham's magisterial *Science and Civilization in China.*[6] South Asian scholars are beginning to untangle colonial from indigenous thought and religious from scientific thought in the precolonial period, and to identify a history of scientific thinking that predates the foundation of colonial scientific societies.[7]

The societies in which civilizationally distinct forms of scientific inquiry flourished in the past are also societies that currently support significant research efforts in the model of Western science and which stand in complicated relations to their own past. The efforts to identify indigenous scientific traditions and to link those with contemporary practices are fraught with controversy, both political and intellectual. The efforts to produce knowledge that can serve feminist and postcolonial emancipatory purposes are similarly fraught. They will undoubt-

---

[6] Needham 1954.
[7] See Prakash 1999; Habib and Raina 1999; Raina 1998.

edly issue in challenges to concepts of reason, science, and science's history that underlie much recent and current mainstream Western thinking about these matters. They will also provide opportunities for constructive interaction. This book is not about such possibilities. But it does offer an account of knowledge that is open to them.

NEW QUESTIONS

This approach invites philosophers to take a more expansive view of the history of science. Rather than seeing it as a field upon which to deploy zero-sum epistemologies, in which only one theory can be correct, we should be sensitive to the shifting relations of multiple research traditions and the complexity of the factors that succeed in producing provisionally stable representations of nature.[8] This shift brings certain empirical, philosophical, and social-institutional questions about the sciences to the fore. Empirically speaking, how in particular instances do institutional and organizational changes interact with (reflect, facilitate, direct, make visible, grow out of) intellectual change? Institutional and intellectual history are often pursued as independent streams. This epistemological approach encourages the view that scientific institutions and scientific content are interdependent but leaves uncharted the variety of forms of interdependency.

What strategies do partisan scientific communities employ to obtain a hearing? What strategies do they employ to acquire hegemony and under what circumstances? Partisanship may be intellectual or political or both. Rather than denying it a place in good science, this approach encourages investigating how it works, in what conditions it is successful and in what conditions not.[9]

What conditions prompt what kinds of unificationist strategies whether of integration or displacement? And what conditions permit the maintenance of plurality? How do institutional, political and economic factors interact with cultural and intellectual factors to sustain local epistemologies or to narrow the variety of approaches pursued?

From a philosophical viewpoint, who gets to set the different social goals for scientific inquiry? How should the criterion of tempered equality be interpreted and applied in the variety of circumstances and social settings in which scientific knowledge is assessed? What are the implica-

---

[8] I thank Susan Rensing for the zero-sum location.

[9] Latour's (1988) study of the mutual reinforcement of Pasteurians and French hygienists and his (1999) analysis of the linking of multiple social, intellectual, and material networks in the development of atomic physics research in France seem examples of this type of inquiry.

tions of incorporating cognitive goals into the apparatus of epistemic evaluation? Does thinking of knowledge as goal-oriented affect other philosophical concerns? How do different kinds of goal affect knowledge and practices?

From a social-institutional perspective, how might different modes of institutionalizing inquiry (university vs. field station; research institute vs. industrial laboratory) affect the content of knowledge? What are the implications for such institutions of the conditions of transformative criticism?

How can a society use science to address problems when scientifically relevant goals and community structures are not mutually aligned? What role could philosophy of science play in such situations?

These questions bring out the political dimensions of science and broaden our conception of what the philosophy of science can be about. I am not proposing that these replace, but that they be added to, traditional concerns about confirmation and explanation and about the metaphysical and ontological assumptions and commitments of particular scientific theories. As our future comes increasingly to rest on what we take the sciences to be telling us, it becomes increasingly important to subject their social and political aspects to philosophical investigation. How can scientific education help citizens acquire a tolerance for the provisionality, partiality, and plurality of knowledge? This requires that we come to share concepts of knowledge robust and flexible enough to survive the observation that socially and politically valenced views do play a role in the construction of knowledge, robust and flexible enough to survive the observation that there is more than one way to approach a question and often more than one correct answer. These observations ought not issue in a rejection of the concept of knowledge, but in a recognition of the complexity of the situations we seek to know and the uncertainty that accompanies our best efforts. What kinds of institutional changes are necessary to sustain the credibility, and hence value, of scientific inquiry while maintaining democratic decision making regarding the cognitive and practical choices the sciences make possible and necessary? The fate of knowledge rests in our answers.

References

Achinstein, Peter. 1968. *Concepts of Science*. Baltimore, Md.: Johns Hopkins University Press.

Amann, Klaus, and Knorr-Cetina, Karin. 1990. "The Fixation of (Visual) Evidence." In *Representation in Scientific Practice*, ed. Michael Lynch and Steve Woolgar, 85–122. Cambridge, Mass.: MIT Press.

Anderson, Elizabeth. 1995. "Knowledge, Human Interests, and Objectivity in Feminist Epistemology." *Philosophical Topics* 23: 59–94.

Annis, David. 1978. "A Contextualist Theory of Epistemic Justification." *American Philosophical Quarterly* 15, no. 3: 213–19.

Anscombe, Elizabeth. 1981. "The First Person." In *Collected Philosophical Papers*, vol. 2: *Metaphysics and the Philosophy of Mind*, ed. G.E.M. Anscombe, 21–36. Oxford: Blackwell.

Aristotle. 1941. *The Basic Works of Aristotle*. Ed. Richard McKeon. New York: Random House.

Barnes, Barry. 1977. *Interests and the Growth of Knowledge*. New York: Routledge.

———. 1983. "On the Conventional Character of Knowledge and Cognition." In *Science Observed: Perspectives on the Social Study of Science*, ed. Karin Knorr-Cetina and Michael Mulkay, 19–52. London: Sage.

Barnes, Barry, and David Bloor. 1982. "Relativism, Rationalism, and the Sociology of Knowledge." In *Rationality and Relativism*, ed. Martin Hollis and Steven Lukes, 21–47. Oxford: Blackwell.

Basu, S., Amita Chatterjee, and M. K. Chakraborty. N.d. "Graded Consequence: Its Location in Fuzzy Logics." Unpublished paper available from M. K. Chakraborty, Department of Pure Mathematics, Jadavpur University, Calcutta 700 032, India.

Beatty, John. 1981. "What's Wrong with the Received View of Evolutionary Theory?" In *PSA 1980 Proceedings of the 1980 Biennial Meeting of the Philosophy of Science Association*, vol. 2, ed. P. Asquith and R. Giere, 397–426. East Lansing, Mich.: Philosophy of Science Association.

———. 1985. "Pluralism and Panselectionism." In *PSA 1984: Proceedings of the 1984 Biennial Meeting of the Philosophy of Science Association*, vol. 2, ed. Peter Asquith and Philip Kitcher, 113–28. East Lansing, Mich.: Philosophy of Science Association.

———. 1987. "On Behalf of the Semantic View." *Biology and Philosophy* 2, no. 1: 17–23.

Beer, Gillian. 1983. *Darwin's Plots: Evolutionary Narrative in Darwin, George Eliot, and Nineteenth-Century Fiction*. London: Routledge and Kegan Paul.

———. 1986. "'The Face of Nature': Anthropomorphic Elements in the Language of the Origin of Species." In *Languages of Nature: Critical Essays on Science and Literature*, ed. L. J. Jordanova, 207–43. New Brunswick, N.J.: Rutgers University Press.

———. 1996. *Open Fields: Science in Cultural Encounter*. Oxford: Oxford University Press.

Beurton, Peter, Raphael Falk, and Hans-Georg Rheinberger, eds. 2000. *The Concept of the Gene in Development and Evolution*. Cambridge: Cambridge University Press.

Biagioli, Mario. 1993. *Galileo, Courtier*. Chicago: University of Chicago Press.

Bishop, Michael, and Steven Stich. 1998. "The Flight to Reference, or How Not to Make Progress in the Philosophy of Science." *Philosophy of Science* 65, no. 1: 33–49.

Bleier, Ruth. 1984. *Science and Gender*. Elmsford, N.Y.: Pergamon.

Bloor, David. 1982. "Durkheim and Mauss Revisited: Classification and the Sociology of Scientific Knowledge." *Studies in History and Philosophy of Science* 13: 267–97.

———. 1984. "The Strengths of the Strong Programme." *Scientific Rationality: The Sociological Turn*, ed. James Robert Brown, 75–94. Dordrecht: Reidel.

———. 1991. *Knowledge and Social Imagery*. 2d ed. Chicago: University of Chicago Press.

———. 1992. "Left and Right Wittgensteinians." In *Science as Practice and Culture*, ed. Andrew Pickering, 266–82. Chicago: University of Chicago Press.

Bolker, Jessica. 1995. "Model Systems in Developmental Biology." *BioEssays* 17, no. 5: 451–55.

Bronowski, Jacob. 1956. *Science and Human Values*. New York: J. Messner.

Brown, James, ed. 1984. *Scientific Rationality: The Sociological Turn*. Dordrecht: Reidel.

———. 1989. *The Rational and the Social*. London: Routledge.

———. 1994. *Smoke and Mirrors: How Science Reflects Reality*. New York: Routledge.

Cain, Joseph Allen. 1993. "Common Problems and Cooperative Solutions: Organizational Activity in Evolutionary Studies, 1936–1947." *Isis* 84: 1–25.

———. 1995. "Managing Synthesis: Community Infrastructure in the Synthesis Period of American Evolutionary Studies." Ph.D. dissertation, University of Minnesota.

———. 2000. "Woodger, Positivism, and the Evolutionary Synthesis." *Biology and Philosophy*, 15, no. 4: 535–51.

Carpenter, Stephen, Sallie Chisholm, and Charles Krebs. 1995. "Ecosystem Experiments." *Science* 269: 324–27.

Cartwright, Nancy. 1983. *How the Laws of Physics Lie*. Oxford: Oxford University Press.

———. 1991. "Replicability, Reproducibility, and Robustness: Comments on Harry Collins." *History of Political Economy* 23: 143–55.

———. 1995. "The Metaphysics of a Disunified World." In *PSA 1994: Proceedings of the 1994 Biennial Meeting of the Philosophy of Science Association*, ed. Richard Burian, Mickey Forbes, and David Hull, 357–64. East Lansing, Mich.: Philosophy of Science Association.

Chakraborty, M. K., and S. Basu. 1999. "Introducing Grade to Some Metalogical Notions." *Fuzzy Sets, Logics, and Reasoning about Knowledge*, ed. Didier Dubois, Henri Prade, and Eric Peter Klement, 85–99. Dordrecht: Kluwer Academic Publishers.

Churchland, Paul. 1985. "The Ontological Status of Observables: In Praise of the Superempirical Virtues." In *Images of Science*, ed. Paul Churchland and Clifford Hooks, 35–47. Chicago: University of Chicago Press.

Coady, C.A.J. 1992. *Testimony: A Philosophical Study*. Oxford: Oxford University Press.

Cohen, Stewart. 1987. "Knowledge, Context, and Social Standards." *Synthese* 73, no. 1: 3–26.

Collins, Harry. 1975. "The Seven Sexes." *Sociology* 9, no. 2: 205–24.

———. 1983. "An Empirical Relativist Programme in the Sociology of Scientific Knowledge." In *Science Observed: Perspectives on the Social Study of Science*, ed. Karin Knorr-Cetina and Michael Mulkay, 115–40. London: Sage.

———. 1985. *Changing Order*. London: Sage.

———. 1991. "The Meaning of Replication and the Science of Economics." *History of Political Economy* 23: 123–42.

Collins, Harry, and Trevor Pinch. 1993. *The Golem: What Everyone Should Know about Science*. Cambridge: Cambridge University Press.

Collins, Harry, and Steven Yearly. 1992a. "Epistemological Chicken." In *Science as Practice and Culture*, ed. Andrew Pickering, 301–26. Chicago: University of Chicago Press.

———. 1992b. "Journey into Space." In *Science as Practice and Culture*, ed. Andrew Pickering, 369–89. Chicago: University of Chicago Press.

Cox, James, and Alvin Goldman. 1994. "Accuracy in Journalism: An Economic Approach." In *The Social Dimensions of Knowledge*, ed. Frederick Schmitt. Lanham, Md.: Rowman and Littlefield.

Daston, Lorraine. 1992. "Objectivity and the Escape from Perspective." *Social Studies of Science* 22, no. 4: 567–618.

Downes, Stephen. 1993. "Socializing Naturalized Philosophy of Science." *Philosophy of Science* 60, no. 3: 452–68.

Duhem, Pierre Maurice Marie. 1954. *The Aim and Structure of Physical Theory*. Trans. Philip P. Wiener. Princeton, N.J.: Princeton University Press.

Dupré, John. 1993. *The Disorder of Things*. Cambridge, Mass.: Harvard University Press.

Ehrhardt, Anke, and Heino Meyer-Bahlberg. 1981. "Effects of Pre-Natal Sex Hormones on Gender-Related Behavior." *Science* 211: 1312–18.

Ereshevsky, Marc. 1992. "Eliminative Pluralism." *Philosophy of Science* 59, no. 4: 671–90.

———. 1998. "Species Pluralism and Anti-Realism." *Philosophy of Science* 65, no. 1: 103–20.

Evans, Gareth. 1982. *Varieties of Reference*. Oxford: Clarendon Press.

Fausto-Sterling, Anne. 1985. *Myths of Gender*. New York: Basic Books.

Fehr, Carla. 2000. "Pluralism and Sex: More than a Pragmatic Issue." Paper presented at the 2000 Biennial Meeting of the Philosophy of Science Association, Vancouver.

———. 2001. "The Evolution of Sex: Domains and Explanatory Pluralism." *Biology and Philosophy* 16, no. 2: 145–70.

Feyerabend, Paul K. 1962. "Explanation, Reduction, and Empiricism" In *Minnesota Studies in the Philosophy of Science*, vol. 3, ed. Herbert Feigl and Grover Maxwell, 28–97. Minneapolis: University of Minnesota Press.

Fine, Arthur. 1984. "The Natural Ontological Attitude." In *Scientific Realism*, ed. Jarrett Leplin, 83–107. Berkeley: University of California Press.

Foley, Richard. 1994. "Egoism in Epistemology." In *Socializing Epistemology: The Social Dimensions of Knowledge*. ed. Frederick Schmitt, 53–73. Lanham, Md.: Rowman and Littlefield.

Foucault, Michel. 1970. *The Order of Things: An Archaeology of the Human Sciences.* London: Tavistock.

———. 1972. *The Archaeology of Knowledge.* Trans. A. M. Sheridan Smith. New York: Pantheon Books.

Friedman, Michael. 1998. "On the Sociology of Scientific Knowledge and Its Philosophical Agenda." *Studies in the History and Philosophy of Science* 29a, no. 2: 239–71.

Fuller, Steve. 1988. *Social Epistemology.* Bloomington: Indiana University Press.

———. 1989. *Philosophy of Science and Its Discontents.* Boulder, Colo.: Westview Press.

Giere, Ronald. 1988. *Explaining Science: A Cognitive Approach.* Chicago: University of Chicago Press.

———. 1999. *Science without Laws.* Chicago: University of Chicago Press.

Gilbert, Margaret. 1987. "Modelling Collective Belief." *Synthese* 73, no. 1: 185–204.

Goldman, Alvin. 1979. "What Is Justified Belief?" In *Justification and Knowledge*, ed. G. S. Pappas, 1–23. Dordrecht: Reidel.

———. 1986. *Epistemology and Cognition.* Cambridge, Mass.: Harvard University Press.

———. 1987. "The Foundations of Social Epistemics." *Synthese*, 73, no. 1: 109–44.

———. 1995. "Psychological, Social and Epistemic Factors in the Theory of Science." In *PSA 1994: Proceedings of the 1994 Biennial Meeting of the Philosophy of Science Association*, ed. Richard Burian, Mickey Forbes, and David Hull, 277–86. East Lansing, Mich.: Philosophy of Science Association.

Gould, Steven J. 1981. *The Mismeasure of Man.* New York: W. W. Norton.

Grandy, Richard. 1987. "Information-Based Epistemology, Ecological Epistemology, and Epistemology Naturalized." *Synthese* 70, no. 1: 191–203.

———. 1992a. "Information, Observation, and Measurement from the Viewpoint of a Cognitive Philosophy of Science." In *Cognitive Models of Science: Minnesota Studies in the Philosophy of Science*, vol. 15, ed. Ronald Giere, 187–206. Minneapolis: University of Minnesota Press.

———. 1992b. "Theories of Theories: A View from Cognitive Science." In *Theories, Confirmation, and Other Distractions*, ed. John Earman, 75–94. Berkeley: University of California Press.

———. 2000. "On the Cognitive Analysis of Scientific Controversies." In *Scientific Controversies: Philosophical and Historical Perspectives*, ed. Peter Machamer, Marcello Pera, and Aristides Baltas, 67–77. New York: Oxford University Press.

Grasswick, Heidi. 1996. "Socialized Individuals in Epistemic Communities." Ph.D. dissertation, University of Minnesota.

Griesemer, James. 1991. "Material Models in Biology." In *PSA 1990: Proceedings of the 1990 Biennial Meeting of the Philosophy of Science Association*, vol. 2, ed. Arthur Fine, Micky Forbes, and Linda Wessels, 79–94. East Lansing, Mich.: Philosophy of Science Association.

Haack, Susan. 1993. *Evidence and Inquiry*. Cambridge, Mass.: Blackwell.

————. 1996. "Science as Social?—Yes and No." In *Feminism, Science, and the Philosophy of Science*, ed. Lynn Hankinson Nelson and Jack Nelson, 79–94. Dordrecht: Kluwer Academic Publishers.

Habib, S. Irfan, and Dhruv Raina, eds. 1999. *Situating the History of Science: Dialogues with Joseph Needham*. New Delhi: Oxford University Press.

Hacking, Ian. 1982. "Language, Truth and Reason." In *Rationality and Relativism*, ed. Martin Hollis and Steven Lukes, 48–66. Oxford: Blackwell.

————. 1992a. "On the Self-Vindication of the Laboratory Sciences." In *Science as Practice and Culture*, ed. Andrew Pickering, 29–64. Chicago: University of Chicago Press.

————. 1992b. "Statistical Language, Statistical Truth, and Statistical Reason: The Self-Authentication of a Style of Scientific Reasoning." In *Social Dimensions of Scientific Knowledge*, ed. Ernan McMullin, 130–57. Notre Dame, Ind.: University of Notre Dame Press.

————. 1995. "The Looping Effects of Human Kinds." In *Causal Cognition: A Multidisciplinary Approach*, ed. Dan Sperber, David Premack, and Ann J. Premack, 351–83. Oxford: Clarendon Press.

————. 1999. *The Social Construction of What*. Cambridge, Mass.: Harvard University Press.

Hamill, James F. 1990. *Ethno-Logic: The Anthropology of Human Reasoning*. Urbana: University of Illinois Press.

Hanson, Russell. 1958. *Patterns of Discovery: An Inquiry into the Conceptual Foundations of Science*. Cambridge: Cambridge University Press.

Haraway, Donna. 1989. *Primate Visions*. New York: Routledge.

————. 1991. *Simians, Cyborgs and Women*. New York: Routledge.

Harding, Sandra. 1991. *Whose Science? Whose Knowledge?: Thinking from Women's Lives*. Ithaca, N.Y.: Cornell University Press.

Hardwig, John. 1985. "Epistemic Dependence." *Journal of Philosophy* 82, no. 7: 335–49.

————. 1991. "The Role of Trust in Knowledge." *Journal of Philosophy* 88, no. 12: 693–708.

Harris, Marvin. 1974. *Cows, Pigs, Wars, and Witches: The Riddles of Culture*. New York: Random House.

Haslanger, Sally. 1993. "On Being Objective and Being Objectified." In *A Mind of One's Own: Feminist Essays on Reason and Objectivity*, ed. Louise Antony and Charlotte Witt, 85–126. Boulder, Colo.: Westview Press.

Hayles, N. Katherine. 1990. *Chaos Bound: Orderly Disorder in Contemporary Literature and Science*. Ithaca, N.Y.: Cornell University Press.

Hempel, Carl G. 1988. "Provisos: A Problem Concerning the Inferential Function of Scientific Laws." In *The Limits of Deductivism*, ed. Adolf Grünbaum and Wesley Salmon, 19–36. Berkeley: University of California Press.

Hess, David. 1995. *Science and Technology in a Multicultural World: The Cultural Politics of Facts and Artifacts*. New York: Columbia University Press.

Hesse, Mary. 1980. *Revolutions and Reconstructions in the Philosophy of Science.* Bloomington: Indiana University Press.

———. 1988. "Socializing Epistemology." In *Construction and Constraint: The Shaping of Scientific Rationality,* ed. Ernan McMullin, 97–122. Notre Dame, Ind.: University of Notre Dame Press.

Hubbard, Ruth. 1990. *The Politics of Women's Biology.* New Brunswick, N.J.: Rutgers University Press.

Hull, David. 1988. *Science as a Process: An Evolutionary Account of the Social and Conceptual Development of Science.* Chicago: University of Chicago Press.

Huxley, Julian. 1942. *Evolution: The Modern Synthesis.* New York: Harper Brothers.

Jordanova, Ludmilla. 1993. *Sexual Visions: Images of Gender in Science and Medicine between the Eighteenth and Twentieth Centuries.* Madison: University of Wisconsin Press.

Judson, Horace Freeland. 1979. *The Eighth Day of Creation: The Makers of the Revolution in Biology.* New York: Simon and Schuster.

Kaplan, Mark. 1994. "Epistemology Denatured." *Midwest Studies in Philosophy,* 19: 350–65.

Keller, Evelyn Fox. 1983. *A Feeling for the Organism: The Life and Work of Barbara McClintock.* San Francisco: W. H. Freeman.

———. 1985. *Reflections on Gender and Science.* New Haven, Conn.: Yale University Press.

———. 1992. *Secrets of Life, Secrets of Death: Essays on Language, Gender, and Science.* New York: Routledge.

———. 2000. *The Century of the Gene.* Cambridge, Mass.: Harvard University Press.

Kitcher, Phillip. 1991. "Socializing Knowledge." *Journal of Philosophy* 88, no. 11: 675–76.

———. 1992. "The Naturalists Return." *Philosophical Review* 101, no. 1: 53–114.

———. 1993. *The Advancement of Science: Science without Legend, Objectivity without Illusions.* Oxford: Oxford University Press.

Knorr-Cetina, Karin. 1981. *The Manufacture of Knowledge.* Oxford: Pergamon Press.

———. 1983. "The Ethnographic Study of Scientific Work." In *Science Observed: Perspectives on the Social Study of Science,* ed. Karin Knorr-Cetina and Michael Mulkay, 115–40. London: Sage.

———. 1999. *Epistemic Cultures: How the Sciences Make Knowledge.* Cambridge, Mass.: Harvard University Press.

Kornblith, Hilary. 1987. "Some Social Features of Cognition." *Synthese* 73, no. 1: 27–42.

———. 1994. "A Conservative Approach to Social Epistemology." In *Socializing Epistemology,* ed. Frederick Schmitt, 93–110. Lanham, Md.: Rowman and Littlefield.

Kuhn, Thomas. 1962. *The Structure of Scientific Revolutions.* Chicago: University of Chicago Press.

———. 1966. *The Copernican Revolution: Planetary Astronomy in the Development of Western Thought.* Cambridge, Mass.: Harvard University Press.

————. 1977. "Objectivity, Values, and Theory Choice." In *The Essential Tension: Selected Studies in Scientific Tradition and Change*, 320–39. Chicago: University of Chicago Press.

Latour, Bruno. 1983. "Give Me a Laboratory and I Will Move the World." In *Science Observed: Perspectives on the Social Study of Science*, ed. Karin Knorr-Cetina and Michael Mulkay, 141–70. London: Sage.

————. 1987. *Science in Action: How to Follow Scientists and Engineers through Society*. Cambridge, Mass.: Harvard University Press.

————. 1988. *The Pasteurization of France*. Cambridge, Mass.: Harvard University Press.

————. 1990. "Postmodern? No, Simply Amodern." *Studies in History and Philosophy of Science* 21: 145–71.

————. 1992. "One More Turn after the Social Turn." In *Social Dimensions of Science*, ed. Ernan McMullin, 272–94. Notre Dame, Ind.: University of Notre Dame Press.

————. 1993. *We Have Never Been Modern*. Trans. Catherine Porter. New York: Harvester Wheatsheaf.

————. 1999. *Pandora's Hope: Essays on the Reality of Science Studies*. Cambridge, Mass.: Harvard University Press.

Latour, Bruno, and Steven Woolgar. 1986. *Laboratory Life: The Construction of Scientific Facts*. 2d ed. Princeton, N.J.: Princeton University Press.

Lattery, Kevin. 1999. "The Epistemology of Experimental Systems in Biological Research." Ph.D. dissertation, University of Minnesota.

Laudan, Larry. 1984a. "The Pseudo-Science of Science?" In *Scientific Rationality: The Sociological Turn*, ed. James Brown, 41–74. Dordrecht: Reidel.

————. 1984b. *Science and Values*. Berkeley: University of California Press.

Lawton, John. 1995. "Ecological Experiments with Model Systems." *Science* 269: 328–31.

Levins, Richard, and Richard Lewontin. 1985. *The Dialectical Biologist*. Cambridge, Mass.: Harvard University Press.

Lewontin, Richard, Steven Rose, and Leon Kamin. 1984. *Not in Our Genes*. New York: Pantheon.

Lloyd, Elisabeth. 1994. *The Structure and Confirmation of Evolutionary Theory*. Princeton, N.J.: Princeton University Press.

————. 1995a. "Feminism as Method: What Scientists Get That Philosophers Don't." *Philosophical Topics* 23, no. 2: 189–220.

————. 1995b. "Objectivity and the Double Standard for Feminist Epistemologies." *Synthese*, 104, no. 3: 351–81.

Longino, Helen. 1990. *Science as Social Knowledge: Values and Objectivity in Scientific Inquiry*. Princeton, N.J.: Princeton University Press.

————. 1993. "Subjects, Power, and Knowledge: Description and Prescription in Feminist Philosophies of Science." In *Feminist Epistemologies*, ed. Linda Alcoff and Elizabeth Potter, 101–20. New York: Routledge.

————. 1994. "The Fate of Knowledge in Social Theories of Science." In *Socializing Epistemology: The Social Dimensions of Knowledge*, ed. Frederick Schmitt, 135–57. Lanham, Md.: Rowman and Littlefield.

————. 1996. "Cognitive and Non-Cognitive Values in Science: Rethinking the

Dichotomy." In *Feminism, Science, and the Philosophy of Science*, ed. Lynn Hankinson Nelson and Jack Nelson, 39–58. Dordrecht: Kluwer Academic Publishers.

———. 1997. "Feminist Epistemology as Local Epistemology." *Aristotelian Society, Proceedings,* suppl. 71: 19–35.

Lynch, Michael. 1985. *Art and Artifact in Laboratory Science: A Study of Shop Work and Shop Talk in a Research Laboratory.* London: Routledge.

———. 1992. "Extending Wittgenstein: The Pivotal Move from Epistemology to the Sociology of Science." In *Science as Practice and Culture*, ed. Andrew Pickering, 215–65. Chicago: University of Chicago Press.

Lynch, Michael, and Samuel Edgerton. 1988. "Aesthetics and Digital Image Processing: Representational Craft in Contemporary Astronomy." *Sociological Review Monograph* 35: 184–220.

Magnus, David. 2000a. "Down the Primrose Path: Competing Epistemologies in Early Twentieth Century Biology." In *Biology and Epistemology*, ed. Richard Creath and Jane Maienschein, 91–121. Cambridge: Cambridge University Press.

———. 2000b. "Conceptual Ambiguities in the Concept of a Gene." Paper presented at the 2000 Biennial Meeting of the Philosophy of Science Association, Vancouver.

Maienschein, Jane. 2000. "Competing Epistemologies and Developmental Biology." In *Biology and Epistemology*, ed. Richard Creath and Jane Maienschein, 122–37. Cambridge: Cambridge University Press.

Mayo, Deborah. 1991. "Sociological versus Metascientific Views of Risk Assessment." In *Acceptable Evidence: Science and Values in Risk Management*, ed. Deborah Mayo and Rachelle Hollander, 249–79. Oxford: Oxford University Press.

McMullin, Ernan. 1983. "Values in Science." In *PSA 1982: Proceedings of the 1994 Biennial Meeting of the Philosophy of Science Association*, vol. 2, ed. P. Asquith and T. Nickles, 3–28. East Lansing, Mich.: Philosophy of Science Association.

Mill, John Stuart. 1859. *On Liberty*. London: John W. Parker and Son. Reprint, ed. Gertrude Himmelfarb, Harmondsworth: Penguin, 1974, 1982.

Mirowski, Philip, and Esther-Mirjam Sent. forthcoming. *Science Bought and Sold*. Chicago: University of Chicago Press.

Mitchell, Sandra. 1995. "Complexity and Pluralism." Lecture given at the University of Minnesota Center for Philosophy of Science.

Monod, Jacques. 1971. *Chance and Necessity*. New York: Knopf.

Nader, Laura, ed. 1996. *Naked Science: Anthropological Inquiry into Boundaries, Power, and Knowledge*. New York: Routledge.

Needham, Joseph. 1954. *Science and Civilization in China*. Cambridge: Cambridge University Press.

Nelson, Lynn Hankinson. 1993. "Epistemological Communities." In *Feminist Epistemologies*, ed. Linda Alcoff and Elizabeth Potter, 121–60. New York: Routledge.

Olby, Robert. 1974. *The Path to the Double Helix*. Seattle: University of Washington Press.

Paul, Diane. 1995. *Controlling Human Heredity*. New York: Humanities Press.

Peirce, Charles S. 1868. "Some Consequences of Four Incapacities." *Journal of Speculative Philosophy* 2: 140–57. Reprinted in Charles S. Peirce, *Selected Writings*, ed. Philip Wiener, 39–72. (New York: Dover Publications, 1958.)

————. 1877. "The Fixation of Belief." *Popular Science Monthly* 12: 1–15. Reprinted in Charles S. Peirce, *Selected Writings*, ed. Philip Wiener, 92–112. (New York: Dover Publications, 1958.)

————. 1878. "How to Make Our Ideas Clear." *Popular Science Monthly* 12: 286–302. Reprinted in Charles S. Peirce, *Selected Writings*, ed. Philip Wiener, 114–36. (New York: Dover Publications, 1958.)

————. 1905. "Issues of Pragmaticism." *Monist* 15: 481–99. Reprinted in Charles S. Peirce, *Selected Writings*, ed. Philip Wiener, 204–23. (New York: Dover Publications, 1958.)

————. 1958. *Selected Writings*. Ed. Philip Wiener. New York: Dover Publications.

Perry, John. 1989. "The Essential Indexical." *Nous* 13: 3–21.

Pickering, Andrew. 1984. *Constructing Quarks: A Sociological History of Particle Physics*. Edinburgh: Edinburgh University Press.

Pollock, John. 1984. "Reliability and Justified Belief." *Canadian Journal of Philosophy* 14, no. 1: 103–14.

Popper, Karl. 1968. *Conjectures and Refutations*. 2d ed. New York: Harper and Row.

————. 1972. *Objective Knowledge*. Oxford: Oxford University Press.

Potter, Elizabeth. 1996. "Underdetermination Undeterred." In *Feminism, Science, and the Philosophy of Science*, ed. Lynn H. Nelson and Jack Nelson, 121–38. Dordrecht: Kluwer Academic Publishers.

Proctor, Robert. 1988. *Racial Hygiene: Medicine under the Nazis*. Cambridge, Mass.: Harvard University Press.

Provine, William. 1992. "Progress in Evolution and Meaning in Life." In *Julian Huxley: Biologist and Statesman of Science*, ed. C. Kenneth Waters and Albert Van Helden, 165–80. Houston, Tex.: Rice University Press.

Quine, W. V., and J. S. Ullian. 1970. *The Web of Belief*. New York: Random House.

Raina, Dhruv. 1996. "Evolving Perspectives on Society and History: A Chronicle of Modern India's Scientific Enchantment and Disenchantment." *Social Epistemology* 11, no. 1: 3–24.

————. 1998. "Beyond the Diffusionist History of Colonial Science." *Social Epistemology* 12, no. 2: 203–13.

Rasmussen, Nicolas. 1995. "Mitochondrial Structure and the Practice of Cell Biology in the 1950s." *Journal of the History of Biology* 28: 381–429.

Ravetz, Jerome. 1971. *Scientific Knowledge and Its Social Problems*. Oxford: Oxford University Press.

Rediehs, Laura. 1998. "Relational Realism." Ph.D. dissertation, University of Minnesota.

Rorty, Richard. 1982. *Consequences of Pragmatism: Essays, 1972–1980*. Minneapolis: University of Minnesota Press.

Rosenberg, Alexander. 1994. *Instrumental Biology or the Disunity of Science*. Chicago: University of Chicago Press.

Rouse, Joseph. 1987. *Knowledge and Power: Toward a Political Philosophy of Science*. Ithaca, N.Y.: Cornell University Press.

————. 1996. *Engaging Science*. Ithaca, N.Y.: Cornell University Press.

Roush, Wade. 1995. "When Rigor Meets Reality." *Science* 269: 313–15.

Ruse, Michael. 1991. "Are Pictures Really Necessary? The Case of Sewall Wright's Adaptive Landscapes." In *PSA 1990: Proceedings of the 1990 Biennial Meeting of the Philosophy of Science Association*, vol. 2, ed. Arthur Fine, Micky Forbes, and Linda Wessels, 63–78. East Lansing, Mich.: Philosophy of Science Association.

Ryle, Gilbert. 1946. "Knowing How and Knowing That: The Presidential Address." *Aristotelian Society, Proceedings* 46: 1–16.

Sapp, Jan. 1987. *Beyond the Gene*. Oxford: Oxford University Press.

Schmaus, Warren, Ullica Segerstrale, and Douglas Jesseph. 1992. "Symposium on the 'Hard Program' in Sociology of Scientific Knowledge." *Social Epistemology* 6, no. 3: 241–320.

Schmitt, Frederick. 1988. "On the Road to Social Epistemic Interdependence." *Social Epistemology* 2: 297–307.

Shapin, Steven. 1982. "The History of Science and Its Sociological Reconstruction." *History of Science* 20: 157–211.

————. 1988. *Review of Science in Action: How to Follow Scientists and Engineers through Society*, by Bruno Latour. *Social Studies of Science* 18, no. 3: 533–50.

Shapin, Steven, and Simon Schaffer. 1985. *Leviathan and the Air Pump*. Princeton, N.J.: Princeton University Press.

Simpson, George Gaylord. 1944. *Tempo and Mode in Evolution*. New York: Columbia University Press.

Smocovitis, Vassiliki B. 1992. "Unifying Biology: The Evolutionary Synthesis and Evolutionary Biology." *Journal of the History of Biology*, 25, no. 1: 1–65.

————. 2000. "Serious Matters: On Woodger, Positivism, and the Evolutionary Synthesis." *Biology and Philosophy*, 15, no. 4: 553–58.

Solomon, Miriam. 1992. "Scientific Rationality and Human Reasoning." *Philosophy of Science* 59, no. 3: 439–55.

————. 1994a. "Social Empiricism." *Nous* 28, no. 3: 323–43.

————. 1994b. "A More Social Epistemology." In *Socializing Epistemology: The Social Dimensions of Knowledge*, ed. Frederick Schmitt, 217–233. Lanham, Md.: Rowman and Littlefield.

————. 1995. "Multivariate Models of Scientific Change." In *PSA 1994: Proceedings of the 1994 Biennial Meeting of the Philosophy of Science Association*, ed. Richard Burian, Mickey Forbes, and David Hull, 287–97. East Lansing, Mich.: Philosophy of Science Association.

————. Forthcoming. *Social Empiricism*. Cambridge, Mass.: MIT Press.

Squier, Susan M. 1994. *Babies in Bottles: Twentieth-Century Visions of Reproductive Technology*. New Brunswick, N.J.: Rutgers University Press.

Suppe, Frederick. 1977. *The Structure of Scientific Theories*. 2d ed. Urbana: University of Illinois Press.

Suppes, Patrick. 1984. *Probabilistic Metaphysics*. Oxford: Blackwell.

Thagard, Paul. 1978. "Why Astrology Is a Pseudoscience." In *Proceedings of the 1978 Biennial Meeting of the Philosophy of Science Association*, ed. Peter Asquith and Ian Hacking, vol. 1: 223–34. East Lansing, Mich.: Philosophy of Science Association.

Traweek, Sharon. 1988. *Beamtimes and Lifetimes: The World of High Energy Physicists.* Cambridge, Mass.: Harvard University Press.

———. 1992. "Border Crossings." In *Science as Practice and Culture,* ed. Andrew Pickering, 429–65. Chicago: University of Chicago Press.

van Fraassen, Bas. 1989. *Laws and Symmetry.* Oxford: Oxford University Press.

———. 1980. *The Scientific Image.* Oxford: Oxford University Press.

Vizedom, Amanda. 2000. "Philosophical Knowledge as Social Knowledge: A Case Study in Social Epistemology." Ph.D. dissertation, University of Minnesota.

Waters, C. Kenneth. 1991. "Tempered Realism about the Force of Selection." *Philosophy of Science* 58, no. 4: 533–73.

———. 1992. "Introduction: Revising Our Picture of Julian Huxley." In *Julian Huxley: Biologist and Statesman of Science,* ed. C. Kenneth Waters and Albert Van Helden, 1–27. Houston, Tex.: Rice University Press.

———. 2000. "The Gene-Centered Point of View." Paper presented at the 2000 Biennial Meeting of the Philosophy of Science Association, Vancouver.

Watson, James. 1968. *The Double Helix.* New York, N.Y.: Atheneum.

Welbourne, Michael. 1981. "The Community of Knowledge." *Philosophical Quarterly* 31, no. 125: 302–14.

Wimsatt, William. 1991. "Taming the Dimensions—Visualizations in Science." In *PSA 1990: Proceedings of the 1990 Biennial Meeting of the Philosophy of Science Association,* vol. 2, ed. Arthur Fine, Micky Forbes, and Linda Wessels, 111–35. East Lansing, Mich.: Philosophy of Science Association.

Wittgenstein, Ludwig. 1953. *Philosophical Investigations.* Trans. G.E.M. Anscombe. Oxford: Blackwell.

Woolgar, Steve. 1983. "Irony in the Social Study of Science." In *Science Observed: Perspectives on the Social Study of Science,* ed. Karin Knorr-Cetina and Michael Mulkay, 239–66. London: Sage.

———. 1992. "Some Remarks about Positionism: A Reply to Collins and Yearly." In *Science as Practice and Culture,* ed. Andrew Pickering, 327–42. Chicago: University of Chicago Press.

Index

acceptance vs. warrant, 49–50. *See also* cognitive vs. noncognitive factors; normative vs. empirical studies of science; reasons vs. causes
Achinstein, Peter, 118n
actor-network theory, 28, 33–35, 36
aims of inquiry. *See* goals of inquiry
Amann, Klaus, 99–100
ambiguity, 143. *See also* knowledge, multiple senses of
Annis, David, 104–06
antifoundationalism, 21, 40–41
antirealism, 54–56, 121
approach in science, differences of, 188–89, 195–96. *See also* plurality
a priori knowledge, 210n
Aristotle, 210n
artificial intelligence, 2–3n, 209n
assumptions. *See* background assumptions
Austin, John, 21
authority. *See* cognitive authority; intellectual authority
autonomy, individual. *See* individuals

background assumptions, 125–28, 176–77, 205; and local epistemologies, 184–89, 197; publicity of, 104. *See also* public standards; underdetermination
background knowledge, 209
Barnes, Barry, 11n, 15–18, 20–22
basic beliefs, 17–18
Basu, S., 162n
Beatty, John, 113, 190–91
behavioral biology, explanation in, 180, 183, 199–200
belief, causes of, 15–17, 79, 82. *See also* justification; knowledge-productive practices; reasons vs. causes
bias, 46, 65, 166, 167–68
Bishop, Michael, 55n
Bloor, David, 11n, 15–18, 20–22, 40–41, 62, 85
Bolker, Jessica, 180–82, 198
Boyd, Richard, 141
Boyle, Robert, 18–20

Bronowski, Jacob, 19–20
Brown, James, 8, 42

Cain, Joe, 191–93, 196n
Callon, Michel, 28, 34
Carnegie Foundation, 196
Carroll, Lewis, 17
Cartwright, Nancy, 101n, 110, 112–13, 175
case studies, probative role of, 13–15, 37–38
causality, 199n
Central Dogma (of molecular biology), 194–96
Chakraborty, Mihal, 162n
Chatterjee, Amita, 162n
Churchill, Frederick, 191
classification, 41–42, as social, 100
closure. *See* controversy, closure of; disagreement, resolution of
cognitive agency, interdependence of, 89–93, 91–92, 107–08, 204–05
cognitive agent: ideal vs. empirical, 160; purity vs. impurity of, 71–73, 74–75. *See also* subject
cognitive authority, 19–20, 45–46, 71–73, 79, 156, 168–72; of science, 22; vs. intellectual authority, 133
cognitive communities: constitution of, 133, 145–46, 176; diversity of, 154–55. *See also* communities, scientific; epistemology, local; individuals, and community
cognitive interdependence, 107–08, 122–23, 156. *See also* cognitive agency
cognitive labor, division of, 74–75
cognitive practices, sociality of, 8–9, 97–123, 204
cognitive progress, 52–54, 60–62, 65. *See also* goals of inquiry
cognitive science, 43
cognitive vs. noncognitive factors, 12, 44–50, 57–59. *See also* belief, causes of; interests; justification; normative vs. empirical studies of science; reasons vs. causes

Cohen, Stewart, 104–06
coherence conditions, 40–41
coherentism, 81
Collins, Harry, 22–25, 101–02
common knowledge, 209n
Commoner, Barry, 194
common sense, 3, 56
communicative impasse. *See* normative vs.
empirical investigators
communities, scientific, 37, 72–76. *See also*
cognitive communities; epistemologies,
local; public standards
completeness. *See* science, completeness of
conformation, 8–9, 115–21, 136–40, 143–
44, 168, 211; and goals of inquiry, 119;
sociality of, 119–20; and truth, 117–18,
120–21
constructivism, 25, 29, 54, 56–59, 91, 119–
20. *See also* normative vs. empirical
studies of science; social construction;
social constructivism; social studies of
science
content: complexity of, 118–19; propositional vs. nonpropositional, 113–15;
success of, 108–21; true vs. accepted,
82–85. *See also* knowledge, as content
context: erasure of, 28–29; of inquiry, 51,
177; laboratory vs. social, 33–34, 200;
and rationality, 30; and scientific judgment, 26–27, 200–01
context dependence, 150–51; of measurement, 201; of scientific knowledge, 143–
44; of scientific practice, 37
contextual empiricism, 208
contextualism, 92–93, 105. *See also* background assumptions; underdetermination
controversy, 17, 176–83; closure of, 24,
60–61, 64. *See also* disagreement, resolution of; negotiation
conventionality, 41, 85, 116
convergence, of beliefs, 53
counterinduction, 160
creationism, 156–59
credibility, 32; 172
credit, as scientific value, 32, 71, 74, 76
Crick, Francis, 193–94
critical interaction, 3, 104, 161, 153, 204–
05; and justification, 189; norms of,
129–35, 138. *See also* epistemic
acceptability
cross-cultural communication, 130n

cultural studies of science, 7–8, 12–13, 25.
See also laboratory studies; social studies
of science
Cycorp, 2–3n

Darwinism, 57–58
Daston, Lorraine, 3n
data, flexibility of, 30, 100, 102
decision-theoretic approach. *See* scientific
judgment, decision theoretic approach to
defeasibility, of knowledge claims, 105–06.
See also critical interaction
Descartes, René, 150
developmental biology, model organisms
in, 180–82
DeVries, Hugo, 178
dichotomizers' way, 90–92
disagreement, resolution of, 23, 74–75
disambiguation, 78, 85
discovery vs. justification, 14
discursive interaction. *See* critical
interaction
disunity of reason, 30. *See also* pluralism;
plurality
division of cognitive labor, 74–75
DNA, disagreements about, 193–97
Douglas, Mary, 40
Downes, Steven, 106n, 150n
Duhem, Pierre, 62, 126, 139n
Dupré, John, 175
Durkheim, Emile, 40

ecology, debates in, 177–78, 184, 197
economic approach: in epistemology, 30,
171; to science, 32, 33n, 70–76
Edgerton, Samuel, 99
Edinburgh school, 7
education, scientific, 213
electron microscopy, 186; debates in, 179–
80; standards in, 198
eliminationism, 90–92
empirical adequacy, 185–86
empirical knowledge. *See* knowledge
empirical relativism. *See* relativism,
empirical
empirical success. *See* success, empirical
empirical vs. normative approaches. *See*
normative vs. empirical approaches; normative vs. empirical investigators;
normative vs. empirical studies of
science

environmentalism, 174, 185
epistemes. *See* Foucault, Michel
epistemic acceptability, 9, 135, 136–40, 143–44, 211; and false content, 158–159; and pluralism, 188
epistemic cultures. *See* Knorr-Cetina, Karin
epistemic virtues, 184–85
epistemic vs. social-political factors in scientific judgment, 45–6. *See also* acceptance vs. warrant; cognitive vs. noncognitive factors; normative vs. empirical studies of science; reasons vs. causes
epistemology: for empirical subjects, 97; and idealization, 37–38, 95, 106–07, 160; internalism vs. externalism in, 81n, 88n; local, 177, 184–89; local vs. general, 173–74, 201–02; and metaphysics, 12, 67; modesty in, 95, 140; naturalized vs. analytic, 106; normative, 71, 87n, 173–74. *See also* cognitive agent; knowledge; naturalism; normative vs.empirical studies of science; social epistemology
error, 123, 205
ethnography of science, 25, 26–33
ethnomethodology, 99
evidence, 50, 104, 126–28, 206. *See also* experiment; justification; observation; reasons vs. causes; underdetermination
evidentiary standards, 66. *See also* methods; public standards
evolution: as model for epistemology, 53–54; as model of science, 62n, 65–66. *See also* evolutionary theory; selection theory in social sciences
evolutionary synthesis, 190–93
evolutionary theory, 57–58, 178–79, 190–93
experiment, 18–20, 22–25; and cognitive interdependence, 152–3; in ecology, 177–78, 184, 197; repeatability of, 22–23, 27, 101–02; social dimensions of, 99–100
explanatory model, 114
externalism. *See* epistemology, internalism vs. externalism in
external standard. *See* Kitcher, Philip

Fehr, Carla, 193
feminism, 75, 174, 185, 211
Feyerabend, Paul, 94n, 125

Fine, Arthur, 56n
Foley, Richard, 156
Foucault, Michel, 86–87, 120n, 147
foundationalism, 21, 81–82
Franklin, Rosalind, 194
Friedman, Michael, 21n
Fuller, Steve, 9, 42, 73n, 165, 170–72

geological revolution, 102, 166
Giere, Ronald, 42, 113, 116n, 166
Gilbert, Margaret, 131n
goals of inquiry, 53, 69–70, 124, 142, 157–58, 176, 186, 212–13; and public standards, 160–62
Goldman, Alvin, 8, 42–43, 44–49, 70–71, 163–164
Gould, Stephen J., 190
Grandy, Richard, 78n, 100–01, 166n
Grasswick, Heidi, 147
gravity waves, 22–25

Haack, Susan, 42–43, 49–51
Hacking, Ian, 86, 102n, 110–13, 196n
Hamill, James, 162n
Hanson, Russell, 125
Harding, Sandra, 164–65
Hardwig, John 152–53
Harris, Marvin, 161
Hempel, Carl, 128n
Hesse, Mary, 11n, 40, 42, 104n
history of science, 41; internalist, 13, 21–22, 33; philosophy of science and, 212; sociological, 13, 16
Hobbes, Thomas, 18–20
Hollis, Martin, 17
homomorphism, 114
Hull, David, 42–43, 46n, 53n, 70–71
Huxley, Julian, 191

idealization: in epistemology, 37–38, 95, 106, 160; in the sciences, 110, 112–13
individualism, 44–49, 54, 56, 89–93, 147, 151; vs. individuality, 147
individuals: and community, 75–76, 145–56; in social account of knowledge, 122–23, 154–56
inquiry: as dynamic, 187–88; institutions of, 213; questions in, 197. *See also* goals of inquiry; knowledge-productive practices; success
inscriptions, traffic in 32

intellectual authority: vs. cognitive authority, 133; equality of, 131–34, 212–13.
See also critical interaction, norms of
interactionism, methodological, 27, 31
interdependence. *See* cognitive agency;
cognitive interdependence; cognitive
practices; individuals; knowledge-productive practices
interests, 11, 13; fusion of, 28; vs. reasons,
46–49; translation of, 33–34. *See also*
cognitive vs. noncognitive factors; reasons vs. causes
interest thesis, 17–18
internalism. *See* epistemology, internalism
vs. externalism in; history of science,
internalist; social studies of science
intersubjectivity, 101–02; methodological,
30. *See also* cognitive interdependence
isomorphism, 114, 118

Jesseph, Douglas, 22n
Jordan, David Starr, 178
justification, 34, 78–80, 81–82, 87–88,
127; vs. discovery, 14; and rational-social
dichotomy, 89–93. *See also* evidence;
knowledge-productive practices; reasons
vs. causes

Kant, Immanuel, 147
Kaplan, Mark, 106, 150n, 173
Keller, Evelyn Fox, 195
Kitcher, Philip, 8, 42–43, 51–67, 69–76,
92n, 109, 166
Knorr-Cetina, Karin, 7–8, 25–31, 32, 33n,
99–100, 204
knowing: vs. knowledge production, 148–
49, 153; and response to criticism, 152.
See also "S knows that *p*"
knowledge: a priori, 208; as attribute, 80–
82, 138; vs. belief, 153, 155–56; as content, 82–85, 87, 89–93, 108–21, 136;
dissemination of, 150–52; as dynamic,
134–35, 208; empirical, 208, 210; first-
person, 209–11; as knowledge productive practices; 78–80; multiple senses of,
77–93, 88–89, 135–40, 203–04; ordinary vs. scientific, 2–3, 124, 208–09;
partiality of, 9, 143–44, 198, 207–08;
plurality of, 1, 9, 93–95, 207–08; practical, 110; provisionality of, 9, 135, 143–
44, 174, 207–08; as relation, 80–82, 138;

social account of, 128–144; sociality of,
1, 9; as status, 10, 204, 209; tacit, 104n
knowledge-productive practices, 78–80,
87–88, 97–107, 137
knowledge and social organization, 19–20
Kornblith, Hilary, 2n
Kuhn, Thomas, 125, 149, 188n

laboratories. *See* experiment; methods
laboratory studies, 7–8, 11, 25–37.
Lakatos, Imre, 21
Latour, Bruno, 7–8, 24–25, 31–37, 42–49,
57–59, 103n, 119–20, 189, 212n
Lattery, Kevin, 181
Laudan, Larry, 8, 11n, 42–43, 54–55, 85,
185
laws, scientific, 110, 112–13
Leplin, Jarret, 141
Levins, Richard, 32n
Lewontin, Richard, 32n
Lloyd, Elisabeth, 79n
Locke, John, 150
logical empiricism, 52, 125
Lukes, Steven, 17
Lynch, Michael, 25, 99

Magnus, David, 178–79, 195n
Manichaeanism, cognitive, 75
maps, 116–18, 201
Mauss, Marcel, 40
Mayo, Deborah, 164–65
McClintock, Barbara, 194–95
measurement, 94, 111–13, 143; context
dependence of, 201; in ecology, 177–78
Merriam, John, 196
methods, 184–87, 197; in ecology, 177–78,
197; in evolutionary theory, 178–79,
190–91. *See also* experiment; knowledge-
productive practices; public standards;
reasoning, styles of
microcognitive acts, 36
microsociological approach, 42. *See also*
Knorr-Cetina, Karin; laboratory studies;
Latour, Bruno
Mill, John Stuart, 3–4
Mitchell, Sandra, 180, 199
model organisms, 180–81, 198
models, theories as. *See* theories, as models
monism, 44, 5, 65, 67, 94–95, 140, 175,
189, 197, 199; vs. nonmonism, 89–93
moralism in science studies, 76